Do-It-Yourse

HARMONICA

BY KONSTANTIN REINFELD

To access audio and video, visit:
www.halleonard.com/mylibrary
Enter Code
5359-2762-3863-4752

Front cover photo by Giorgio-adconfact
Back cover photo by Stephan Pick

ISBN 978-1-70514-375-9

Visit Hal Leonard Online at
www.halleonard.com

World headquarters, contact:
Hal Leonard
7777 West Bluemound Road
Milwaukee, WI 53213
Email: info@halleonard.com

In Europe, contact:
Hal Leonard Europe Limited
Dettingen Way
Bury St Edmunds, Suffolk, IP33 3YB
Email: info@halleonardeurope.com

In Australia, contact:
Hal Leonard Australia Pty. Ltd.
4 Lentara Court
Cheltenham, Victoria, 3192 Australia
Email: info@halleonard.com.au

CONTENTS

Song Index with Harmonica Positions

About the Audio and Video

Throughout the book, you will find audio and video symbols like the ones shown above. These are references to the audio and video recordings that come with this book. Featured on them are demonstrations of the techniques, methods, examples, and songs you will be learning. You can even play along with them.

On page 1 of the book, you will find a URL and a code number. This is your personal access to these files. Use your web browser to open the Hal Leonard My Library website (**www.halleonard.com/mylibrary**). Enter your code, and you will have full access to listen to, view, and download the files.

My Library also includes the multi-functioned audio player PLAYBACK+, which allows you to slow down the audio tracks for this book without changing pitch *and* set loop points for difficult passages you want to isolate for practice. This is a very useful tool for learning harmonica!

INTRODUCTION

Welcome to the realm of the diatonic harmonica, also referred to as (blues) harp. I assume that if you've gone as far as making the decision to learn the harmonica, you've already developed an interest, if not a love, for the music—and something about the harmonica in particular has "lit the fire." If you want to become a good harmonica player and a good musician, immerse yourself in the music. Listen to the old masters, the contemporary players—everything you can get your hands on.

Ultimately, this music is meant to be played, not read. By this, I mean it's important to use your ear and depend on it as much as, if not more than, the written music. For the purposes of this book, the harmonica tablature is necessary, but the skills you learn here will give you the foundation to be able to put melodies together based on what you hear. This is not to say that you should expect to hear everything. Even advanced players still find themselves referring to tablature; but for the most part, you should start to identify melodies purely by hearing them.

You'll find 125 songs and myriad topics covered over 27 lessons. With styles ranging from classical to jazz and rock to folk, there is plenty of material for every taste. The chord symbols enable you to play the songs together with other musicians. In addition to lessons and songs, you can find more information on the music and notes throughout. Finally, you can dive deeper into the world of the diatonic harmonica by checking out the "Harmonica Talk" section at the end of the book.

As you work on the early exercises in this book, you will essentially be forming muscle memory—also known as "habits." For example, you need to play a breathing pattern hundreds, maybe thousands, of times before you can do it without thinking. That's muscle memory. For this reason, it's important to be very careful when first learning any particular concept. If you learn it incorrectly and form the incorrect habit, it can be quite a chore to change or relearn it.

You might skip a day here and there, but try to never miss more than one or two days in a row, especially in the early stages. When you first learn something, repetition is a good way to remember it. When it's new to you, skipping several days in a row can cause you to lose or forget most of what you learned, and this is a setback.

The title *Do-It-Yourself Harmonica* means you're giving yourself lessons, and a lesson should be only as much as you can process at one time. Learning—and mastering—the material in this book could be a project that takes a few years. There's definitely a lot of work to be done, but there's no reason to make it painful, right?

It is worth noting that once you learn the diatonic harmonica, you will have the basic skill and understanding to easily study any other member of the harmonica family, including chromatic, bass, or chord harmonicas. Learning to play the harmonica can be a fulfilling hobby or a serious pursuit. Either way, it is a highly rewarding experience. Whatever your goals, we hope you enjoy the journey and discover the fun of playing the harmonica.

Different Harmonicas

Factors of Good Playing

One of the exciting things about music is the rhythm and speed with which it is sometimes played. This can also be a source of frustration for the beginner. Every student I've ever had (including myself) wanted to play groovy and fast, just like the records. There are several factors involved before you can speed things up. In order, they are:

1. **Accuracy.** This is most important. It is critical that you play as accurately as possible. If this means you need to stop and think before you hit the next note, that's fine. Just make sure to keep the air flowing when practicing. This is the only available "eyesight" when playing harmonica and tells you where you are on the instrument.
2. **Smoothness.** After you play a pattern or song (or part of a song) enough to start forming muscle memory, you'll find that you don't have to think too hard about the notes anymore. Here's where smoothness enters the picture. By smoothness, I mean an equal amount of time given to all notes. (Of course, this refers to when you are playing patterns made up of the same type of notes, like quarter notes or eighth notes; we'll get more into this later.) It still doesn't have to be very fast—just smooth. Don't play (anything) faster than you can play (it) smoothly. Playing the easy parts quickly and then slowing down for the harder parts is not a good habit to get into.
3. **Speed.** Finally, after you have achieved accuracy and smoothness, you can begin to speed up the tune. As mentioned above, avoid the temptation to play the easy or familiar parts faster and the hard parts slower. Don't play any faster than the hardest part of the tune—you can't play any faster than your brain will let you. When those tricky parts get learned, you'll be able to play them faster. Then, you can speed everything up along with them. With systematic practice, you'll be playing faster—sooner.

At the same time, I find that playing along with recordings is a great exercise because they won't stop and wait for you. You have little choice but to try to keep up. If you make a mistake, ignore it and just keep going, solely focusing on the rhythm this time. As you learn more phrases, new songs will get up to speed sooner.

A Few More Words Before Getting Started

The invention and development of the diatonic harmonica is rooted in folk music. It comes in various forms. The one we focus on here is the 10-hole version, which was first produced by harmonica maker Joseph Richter from Haida, Bohemia, in the mid-19th century. Surprisingly, this type became the perfect blues instrument. Since then, the harmonica has shown its potential as a big, all-around talent. Regardless of whether it's jazz, classical, or pop ... the possibilities of this small instrument are endless! Even though this is an instruction book for beginners, I would like to explore all these different territories with you.

The harmonica enables you to express your deepest feelings. At the same time, it is hard to understand how its sounds are being produced. Viewers and listeners can barely make out the harmonica in the musician's hands, and even as a player, it takes some time to comprehend the hidden physics of the instrument and to master the countless possibilities of expression. Playing harmonica is a feeling, and that's the beauty of the instrument. Here, after all, there are no fingers flying over a keyboard, contorted grips on the neck of a violin, or drumsticks racing across timpani and cymbals. Everything happening between your diaphragm, your lips, and your hands remains invisible. Besides singing, the harmonica is one of the most personal instruments out there, and in the course of time, you will gradually develop a strong and intimate relationship with it. From the very beginning, the sounds you produce on the instrument can be rewarding and contribute to a long-term enthusiasm for the harmonica. Playing the harmonica just feels good!

In this book, I would like to teach you about the unlimited possibilities the harmonica offers and show you the best techniques to achieve results most efficiently. Again, the songs in this book include blues, jazz, Indian/Middle Eastern/Eastern European, folk/Irish/bluegrass, Latin/Brazilian, rock/pop, and classical music styles.

Thanks to Herbert Quelle (author of the harmonica novels *Monika's Blues: On the Trail of the German Harmonica*, *African-American Blues Culture*, and *Kein falscher Zungenschlag: Black Music Matters*) for proofreading the manuscript. Also, thanks to Hanno Busch, who played guitar on the recordings for this method, and to Klaus Geske Stiftung for providing the video location.

LESSON 1:
Parts of the Harmonica

Let's look at the 10-hole diatonic harmonica and its parts.

1: Comb

2: Upper Reed Plate (Blow Reeds)

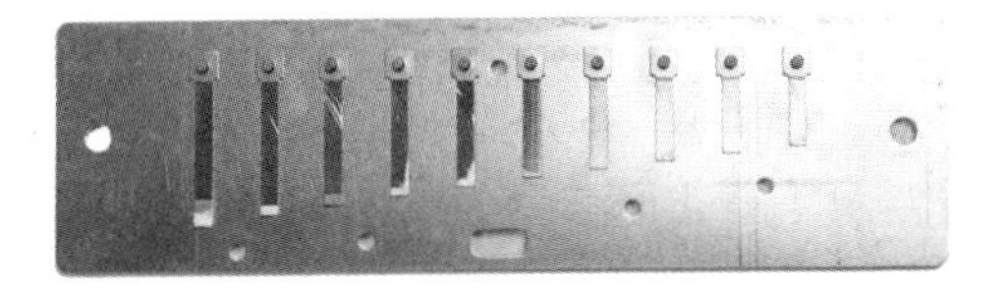

3: Lower Reed Plate (Draw Reeds)

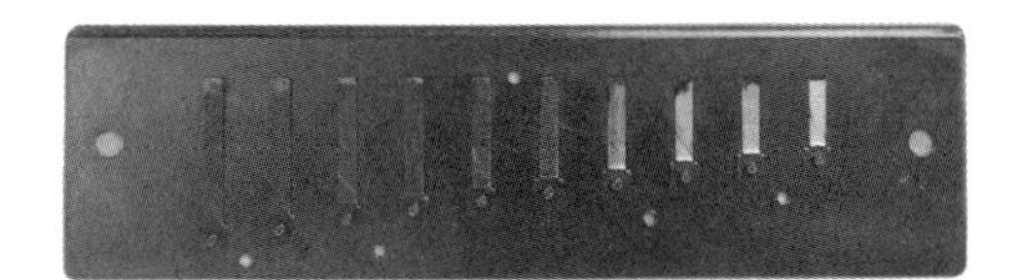

4: Upper Cover Plate

5: Lower Cover Plate

The harmonica is usually an assembly of five basic parts:

1: The comb is located in the middle of the instrument, sandwiched between reed plates. Over the years, many plastic and metallic combs were used to provide an alternative to the traditional wooden combs. As you can see, its name is derived from the 10 channels cut into the slab, which give its dividers the appearance of the teeth of a comb. The channels guide the air from your mouth to the reeds attached to the reed plates.

2, 3: The reeds themselves are traditionally made of brass or bronze alloys, stainless steel being a newer alternative, and they pave the way for air passage. When you blow or draw through the instrument, the reed alternately blocks and unblocks its airways and vibrates to produce sound. Each note you hear is a reed vibrating in response to your breath. A long and heavy reed vibrates slowly and plays a low note. A short reed vibrates quickly and plays a high note.

Typically, **reed plates** are made from brass, with steel being a more recent option. The reeds themselves are generally riveted or welded onto the reed plate, and the reed plates are nailed or screwed onto the comb.

4, 5: The cover plates shield the reed plates and help project the harp's sound to the listener. The covers also allow you to hold the harp without interfering with the reeds, basically providing you with a mouthpiece. Cover plates are usually made of metal.

TOOLBOX

A Quick Note Concerning Instrument Maintenance

You can tap the harmonica against your hand or your thigh with the holes facing down to the ground to minimize moisture from accumulating and damaging the instrument.

LESSON 2:
Holding the Instrument

There are many possible ways to hold the harmonica. However, considering its size, you always want to make sure to enhance the resonant cavity of the instrument.

Independent of your preference, your left hand should be the one leading. Hold the cover plates between your thumb and index finger. Already, you could try to form a little cavern behind the instrument with your left-hand fingers. Make sure to get the harmonica facing the right way with the low notes to the left of your mouth.

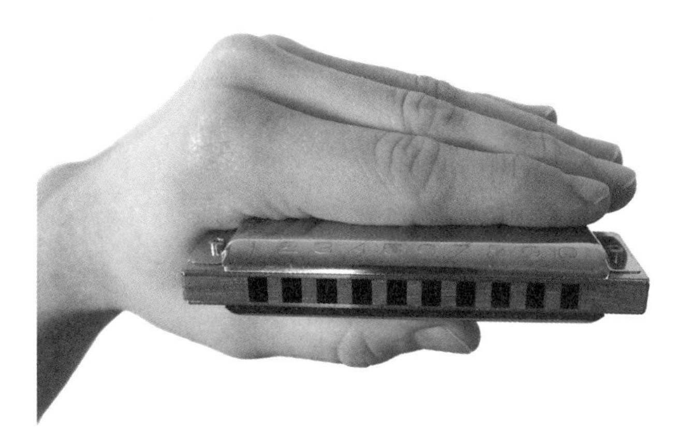

In order to create a big tone, you should leave enough space for your lips on both cover plates. This way you can take the harmonica farther into your mouth, creating a warm sound and making harsh overtones less audible. For now, your right hand focuses the tone behind the instrument, while giving you more control over its movement.

Nowadays, I'm using my hands more and more to dampen unpleasing overtones even more, especially on higher-pitched harmonicas. The cupping technique will be explained in greater detail later on.

The lowest-keyed regular harmonica is a G instrument, while the highest is an F# instrument. That being said, the C harmonica is located approximately in the middle of the spectrum, giving us the best of both worlds. Every instrument covers the range of three octaves, consisting of 37 notes. On the C harmonica, that's C4 to C7. In comparison, the vocal range of a soprano spans C4 to C6, and possibly higher.

As a consequence, the diatonic harmonica is not only one instrument but rather 12. Even though some advanced harmonica players can play one single harmonica in all 12 keys, they will still carry harmonicas in several keys with them. Every harmonica key sounds different in relation to the key the music is in, and playing the same song on different-key harmonicas always offers new possibilities, which is absolutely beautiful!

LESSON 3:
Breathing Technique

Besides other free-reed mouth organs, the harmonica is one of the very few wind instruments that offers the possibility of playing notes by both blowing and drawing. You are literally breathing through the instrument, which makes playing melodies feel very natural.

To make use of the resonance chamber of your body, breathe into your belly instead of your chest. Remind yourself of this as soon as you catch yourself raising your shoulders while drawing through the instrument.

Your tone will not always benefit from using a lot of air. Rather, form your mouth cavity as though you were going to articulate big vowel sounds, and don't move too much air. Practicing with little air will not only please your neighbors but also yourself. The progress of developing a warm tone will be much faster.

Open your mouth wide and leave your lips relaxed before placing the harmonica between your lips. The front of the harmonica should touch the right and left corners of your mouth, where your upper and lower lips meet.

Now you can let your mouth drop onto the harp using the moist part of your lips. This cushion will make it possible for you to smoothly slide between different parts of the harmonica. Try to stay relaxed while forming an airtight seal with the harp.

With your lips on the harp, inhale and exhale slowly, having holes 1–3 in your mouth. (**Note:** This example is shown in standard notation and tablature. We will look at both in the next lesson.)

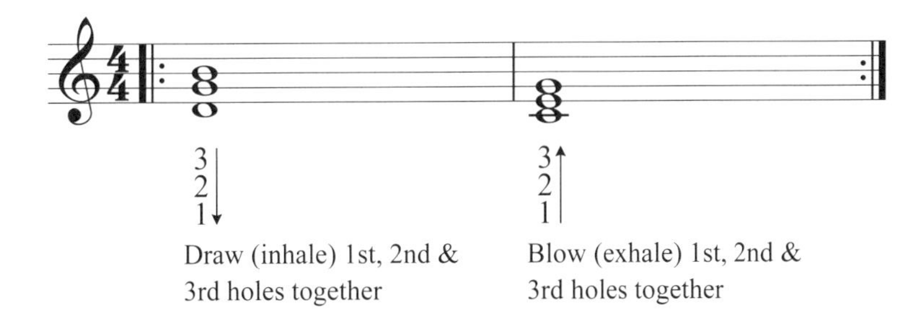

LESSON 4:
Notation

Harmonica music can be notated two different ways: on a musical staff and in tablature.

The musical staff shows pitches and rhythms, while the bar lines divide it into measures. The pitches are named after the first seven letters of the alphabet.

Tablature represents harmonica music graphically. You will find harmonica tabs below the music notation on all the lead sheets and examples in this book. They will tell you which hole(s) to play and which technique(s) to use in order to produce the corresponding note(s). **In the tab, numbers followed by an upward arrow are blow notes, and numbers followed by a downward arrow are draw notes.**

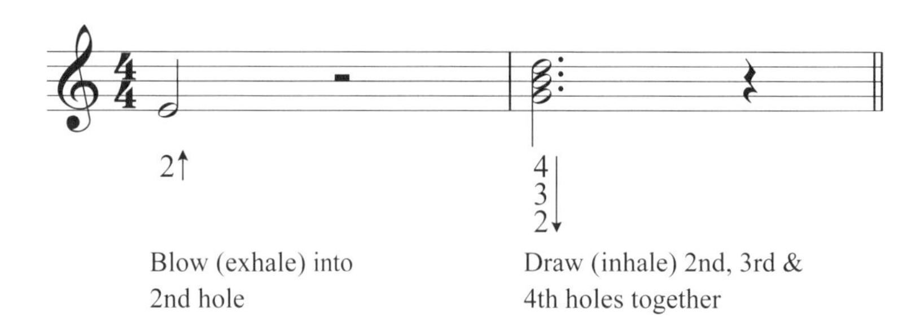

Bent notes are represented by downward and upward arrows with hash marks to indicate half-step increments.

Blow Bends

- 1/2 step
- 1 step

Draw Bends

- 1/2 step
- 1 step
- 1 1/2 steps

Overbends (*overblows* and *overdraws*) are advanced techniques that include arrows as well, but with an "o" added to the arrowhead.

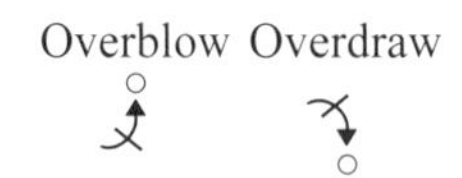

Let's get an overview of reading music. Music is a language that you can read and write. It has its own symbols and structure that you might not be familiar with. However, if you surround yourself with it regularly, you will get more and more fluent.

The Staff

Music is organized on a staff of five horizontal lines. It is capable of displaying many different parameters, but most importantly, it shows how music moves over time (*rhythm*) and how high or low notes are (*pitch*).

While rhythm is organized horizontally along the staff, pitch is organized vertically using the lines and spaces.

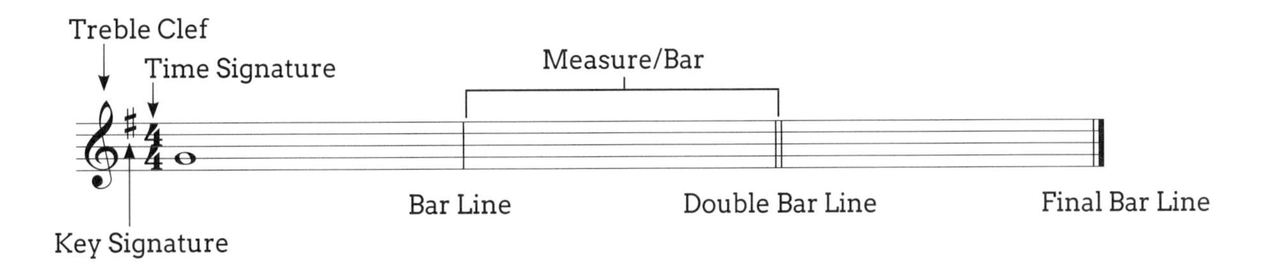

Treble Clef

The *treble clef* introduces the second line as the note G. Actually, the symbol itself represents an ornate G, and it is also known as *G clef*. Notice that it curls around the second line to establish G.

Bar Lines

Bar lines divide the staff into measures. A *double bar line* is used to indicate the end of a short example or section within a piece. The *final bar line* marks the end of a song.

Measures

A *measure* is the space between bar lines. It's also called a *bar*. The rhythm is established from left to right through this space.

Key Signature

The *key signature* appears at the beginning of each line of music and assigns either sharps or flats for particular notes for the duration of a song.

Spaces

Notes in the spaces in ascending order happen to spell the word FACE.

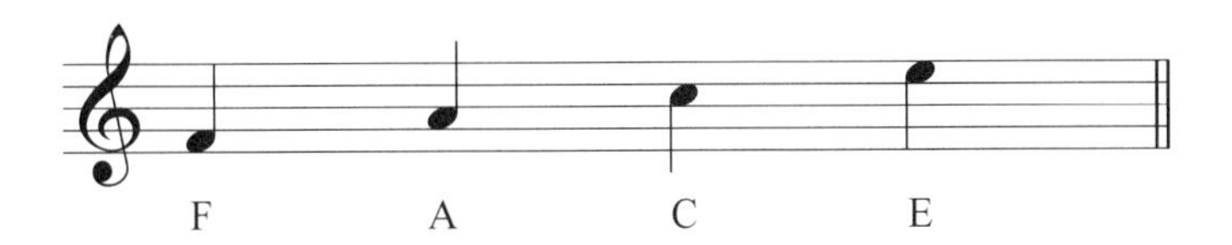

Lines

An acronym commonly used to remember notes on the lines in ascending order is Every Good Boy Does Fine.

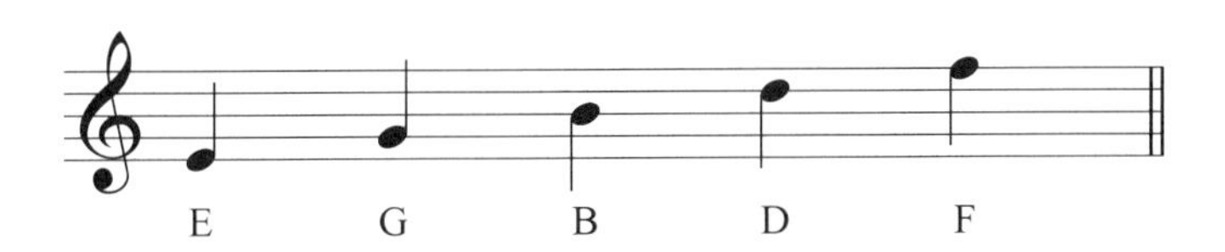

Music Alphabet

When the spaces and lines are combined, you'll see that music ascends alphabetically from A to G and then starts over again. You may find it helpful to memorize and locate A as you learn.

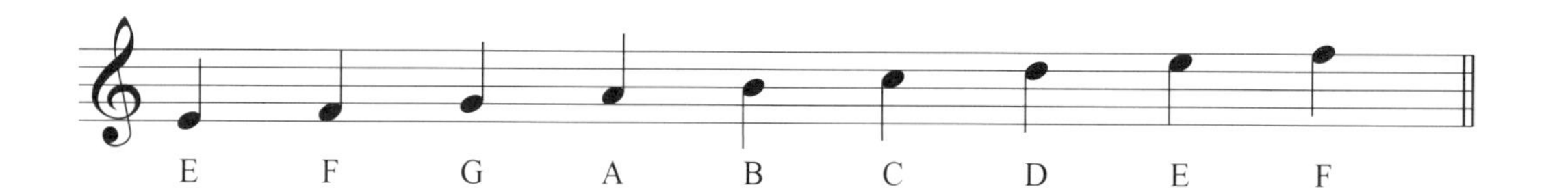

Ledger Lines

The staff can be thought of as an infinite number of lines; five of them are visible and the rest are invisible. When a note is needed above or below the staff, small lengths of line, called *ledger lines*, become visible. For instance, high B is in the space above the first ledger line. Low C is on the first ledger line below the staff. Notice that this is a continuation of the music alphabet.

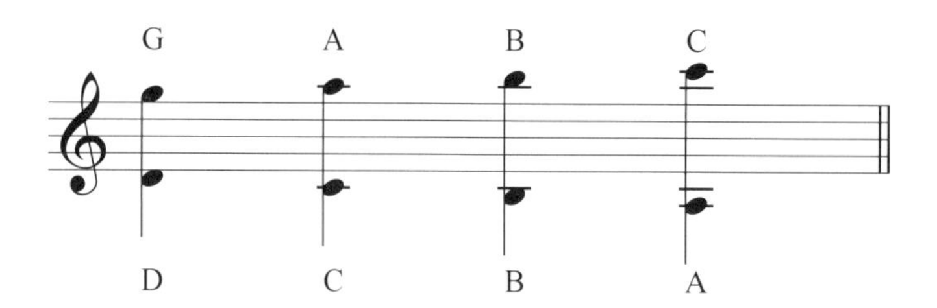

Accidentals

A *half step* is the smallest *interval*, or distance between two notes. A note is altered by one half step in the following three ways:

♭ A *flat* lowers a note by one half step.

♯ A *sharp* raises a note by one half step.

♮ A *natural* cancels a sharp or flat.

These are known as *accidentals*. An accidental applies to a note for one measure. In the following example, the last note does not require a natural to cancel the flat; this is accomplished by the *key signature*.

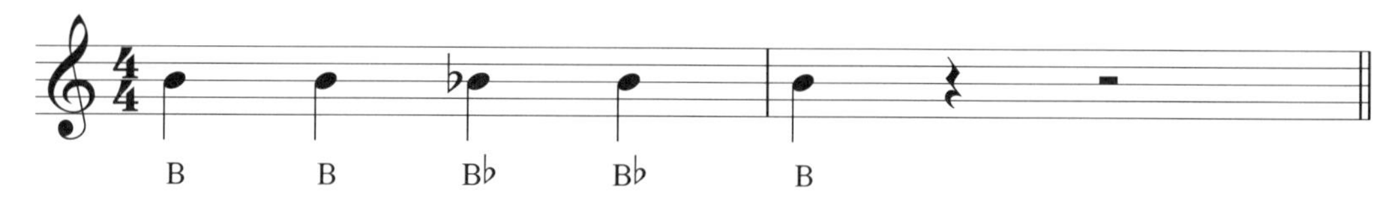

Sometimes (as in this book), you'll see *courtesy accidentals* as reminders. The next example will sound the same as the previous example.

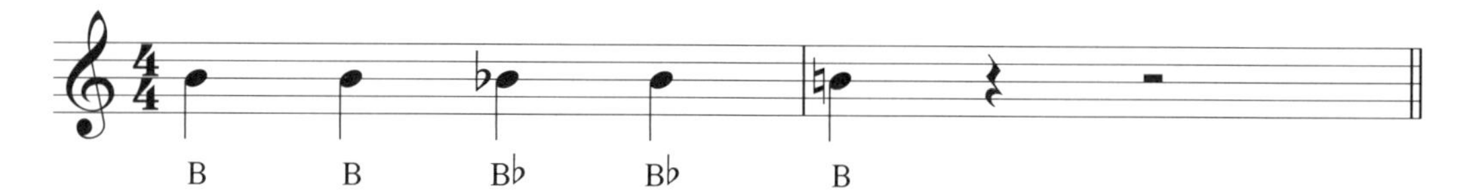

Here are two examples of accidentals in the context of a key signature, which assigns sharps to all F and C notes. The natural symbol cancels each one until the next measure. (Notice there is a courtesy reminder in the second measure of each.)

Rhythm

Time Signatures

The *time signature* is positioned on the left side of the staff after the treble clef and specifies how many beats are contained in each measure (the top number) and which note value is equivalent to a beat (the bottom number). The most common time signature is 4/4. The bottom number in 4/4 determines the following durations—or *values*—indicating both sound (notes) and silence (rests):

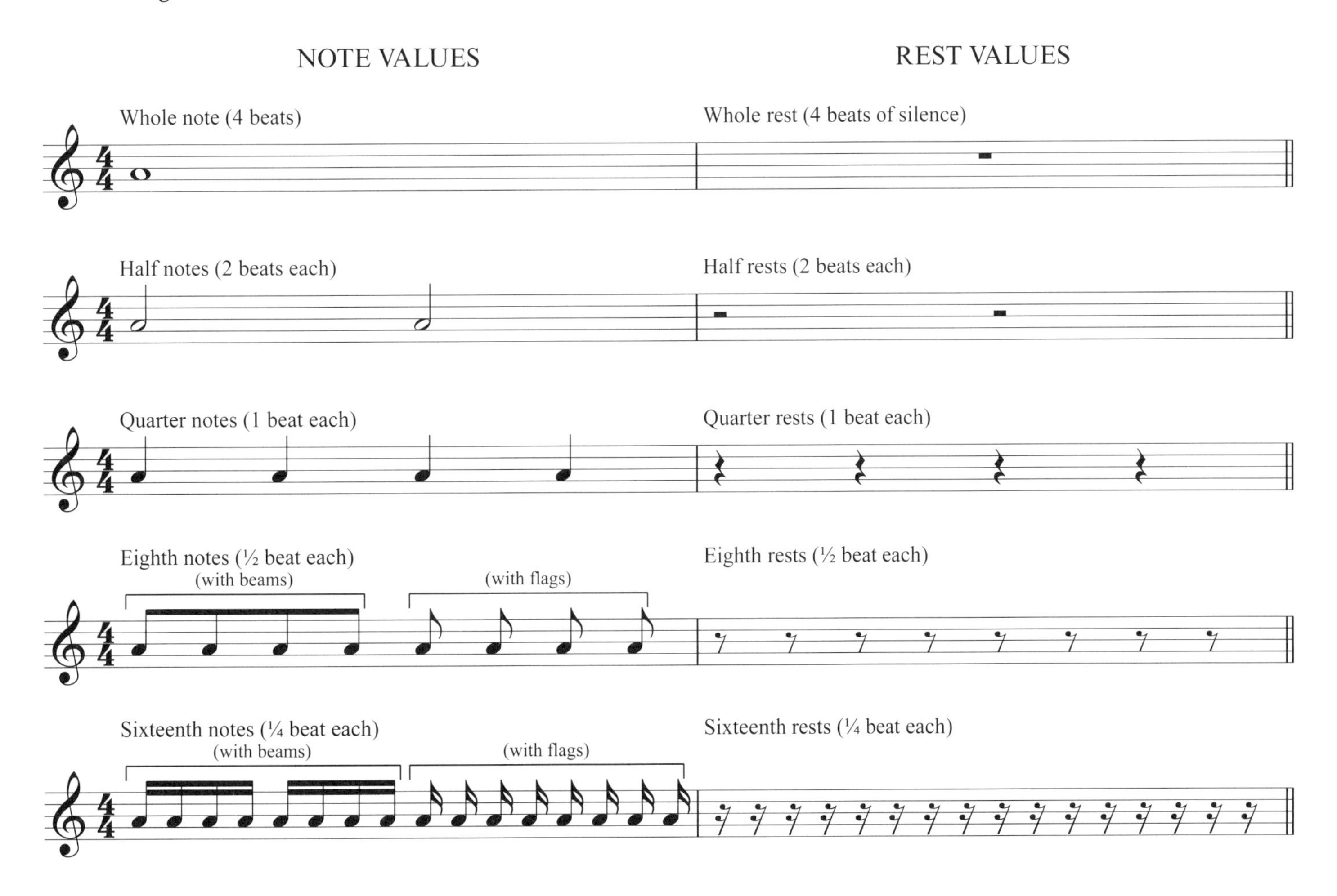

Counting Method

In this book, we will count rhythm using the method shown in the chart below. Note durations from the previous section have been placed into a table with 16 columns. This table is always theoretically present in a musician's thinking when playing in 4/4 time. It represents the ways in which notes and beats can be divided into smaller parts.

Subdividing

Subdivide notes in order to keep your place and play with rhythmic accuracy. This is done by thinking internally, tapping a foot, or using a metronome. You can do this right now: whistle, hum, or simply exhale while tapping your foot and counting in your head (stop on 5). You just performed a whole note.

Here's another example of subdividing you can do right now. Clap four quarter notes while counting eighth notes: "1-&-2-&-3-&-4-&" (& = and). You'll say a number on each clap with &'s between the claps. We call the numbers *downbeats* and the &'s *upbeats*.

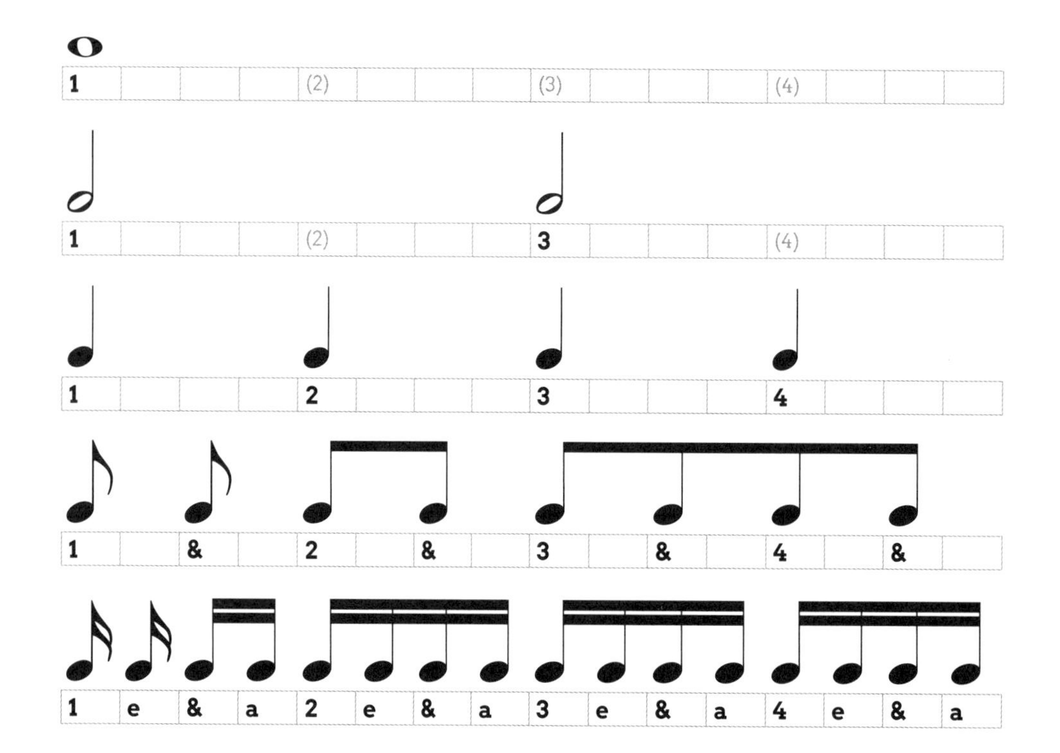

Rests

Rests are counted and subdivided just like notes, but they are silent. Some rests are added in the next chart, with the counting italicized in parentheses. For the half note in the second line, clap on all the downbeats and say a long "one," stopping on the third beat.

Ties

A *tie* is a curved line that joins together two notes of the same pitch. If two quarter notes are tied, they become a single note worth two beats; you can see this on beats 3 and 4 of the quarter-note line in the following chart.

Addition

As you saw with the ties, rhythm involves a little math. Notice beat 4 of the sixteenth-note line (bottom right of chart). There is an eighth rest instead of two sixteenth rests because it is more efficient and easier to read: 1/16 (𝄿) + 1/16 (𝄿) = 2/16 or 1/8 (𝄾).

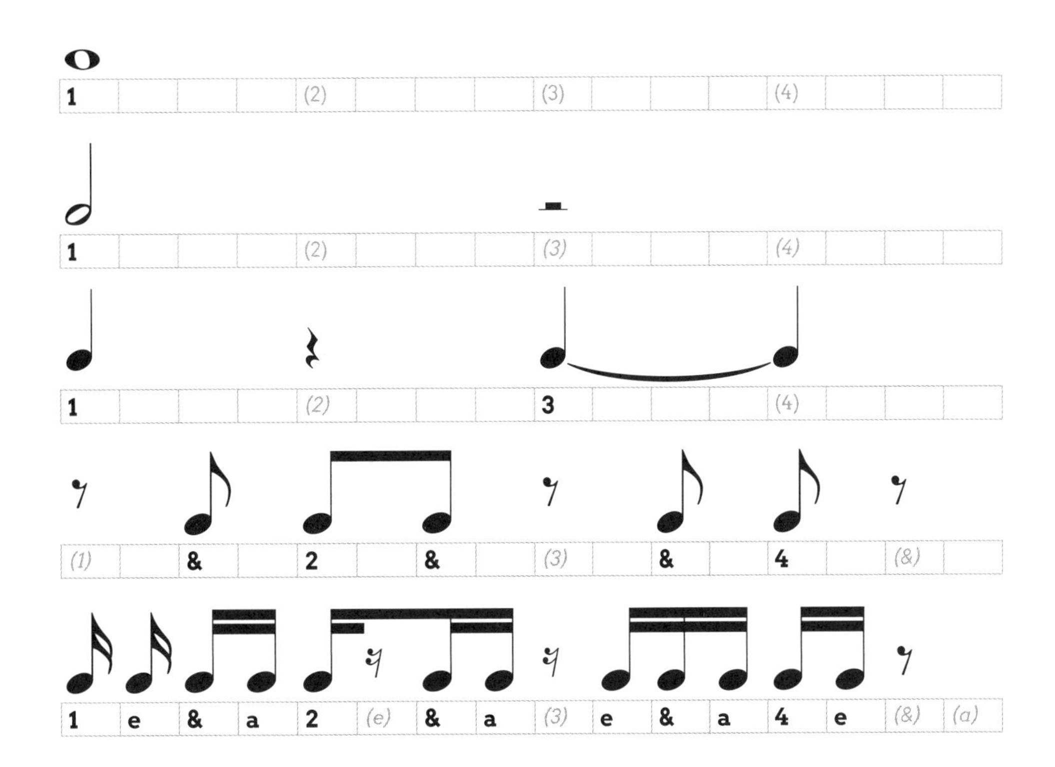

Another bit of math we do involves dotted rhythms. A *dot* adds half of a note's value to itself. A second dot adds half the value of the previous dot.

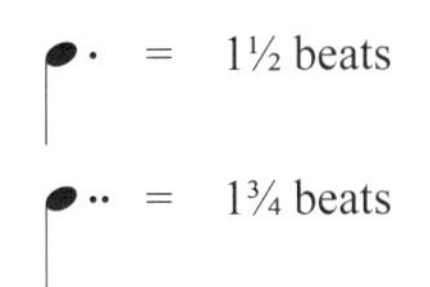

LESSON 5:

Rhythmic Playing and Chugging

The most beautiful feature about the harmonica is that it can play melodies, *chords* (three or more notes played at the same time), and rhythms. With the G and C chords being your point of departure, you can now start to talk through the instrument and rhythmize the breathing exercise. In this lesson, you will get to know five different chugging rhythms.

Don't be afraid to articulate the syllables very clearly and start out very slowly. It is helpful to practice these without the instrument at first. This will help you to build up speed later on and make your rhythmic statement much clearer. Of course, you can work with a metronome to keep time; however, I would also suggest that you feel the rhythm in your body and free yourself by moving along to the music in any way that feels natural to you. You could also walk along in quarter notes.

> **TOOLBOX**
>
> **Repeat Bars**
>
> *Repeat bars* are the vertical bar lines with two dots shown at the start and end of the following example. These tell you to repeat the measures between them. So, when you reach the repeat bar at the end, return to the first repeat bar (without stopping) and play those measures again.

Hah-Kuh Tah-Kuh

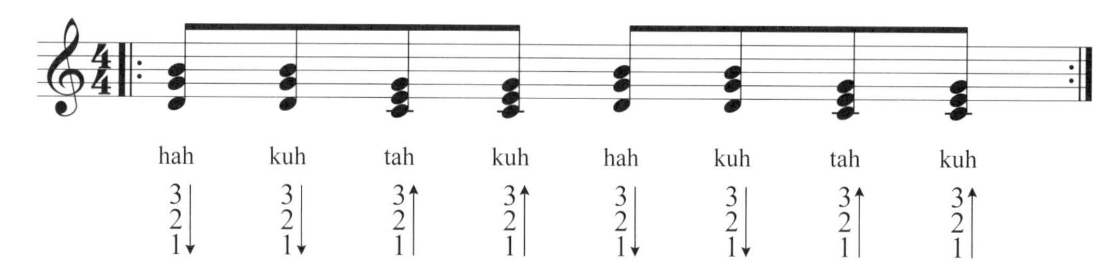

This first chugging rhythm might remind you of a train imitation already—a discipline that was very popular in the 1920s and 1930s, with DeFord Bailey being one of the harmonica masters during that time period. It was very common to imitate sounds of your surroundings. Both the so-called "fox chase" and the train imitation are still alive in the harmonica world and a must-have in every harmonica player's repertoire. The American blues harmonica player and maker of customized harmonicas, Joe Filisko from Chicago is probably the world's foremost authority interpreting this style of playing.

In order to play a basic train imitation, you only have to think about three syllables. Blow through the instrument using the vowel "hah" and say "tah-kuh" through the draw chord. The "hah" is as long as the "tah-kuh." Highlighting the two draw chords will give your imitation more texture.

Hah Tah-Kuh (Train Imitation)

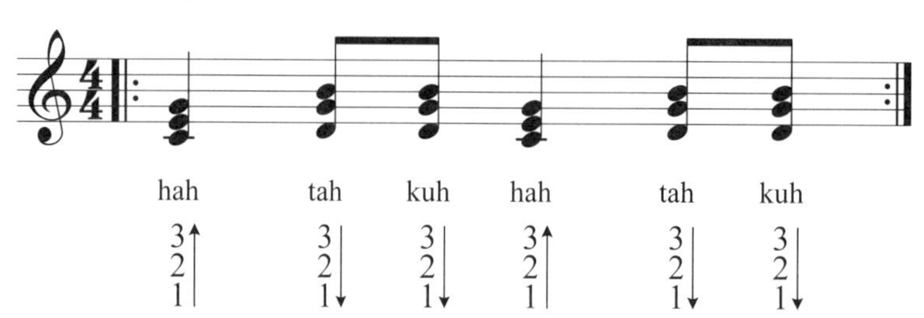

TOOLBOX

Triplets

A *triplet* is a three-note pattern that fills the duration of a typical two-note pattern. For instance, an eighth-note triplet is made of three equal eighth notes played over the time of two regular eighth notes (one beat).

You can keep using the same syllables, but start to think in triplets now. In this case, you divide the quarter note into three equally long parts. The first syllable takes up two of them, while the second claims only one. The "hah" is twice as long as the "kuh," and the "tah" is twice as long as the second "kuh." This variation will already start to feel like a good bluesy accompaniment, often called a *shuffle* rhythm.

Hah-Kuh Tah-Kuh Shuffle

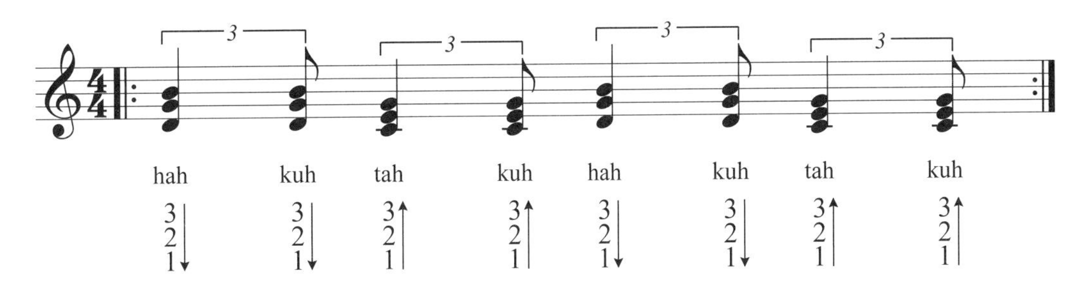

These chugging rhythms are already giving you the feeling of playing in the key of the draw chord, which is G major. Probably 95% of the blues harmonica songs you know are played in the key of the draw chord, also called *2nd position*. You can try to support the rhythm with your hands by opening your right hand on the longer syllable of the two.

After thinking in triplets for your first bluesy "hah-kuh tah-kuh" chugging rhythm, you can even pronounce the three-note groupings using new syllables. This time, the articulation is a little smoother, using the plosive "d" instead of "t."

Hidle-Dah Hodle-Dah

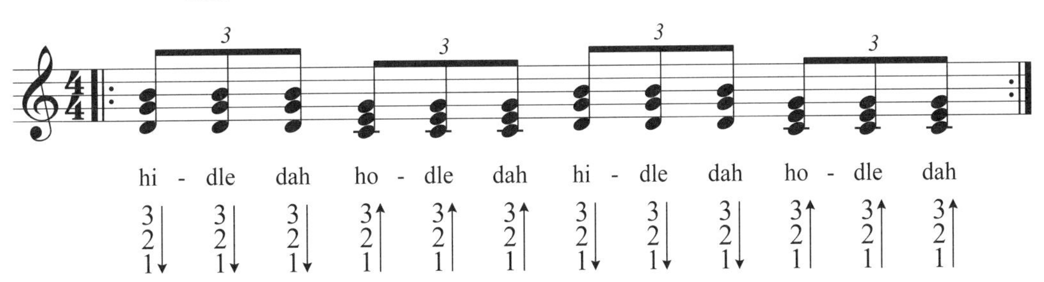

You'll probably realize that the blow-draw pattern for this final chugging rhythm is a little imbalanced, which is not uncommon at all. As a harmonica player, you usually play more draw notes than blow notes. There are 22 draw notes available, while you can only produce 18 notes on the blow.

Take a close look at the faster change of breathing directions in the second half of the bar, thinking "blow-draw blow" while saying "kah-kee koh."

Vee Kee-Kee Kah-Kee Koh

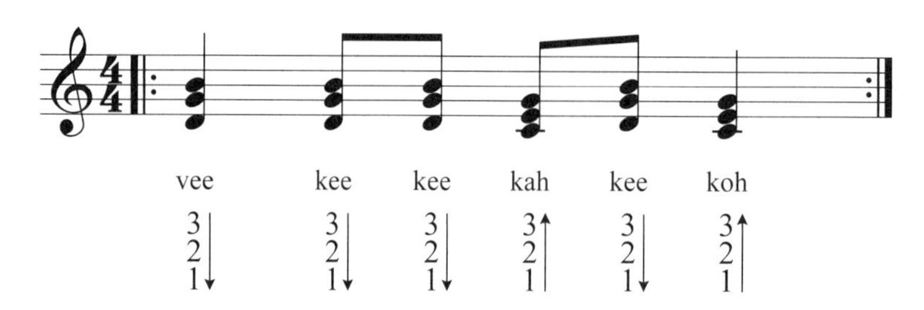

> Sometimes the syllables of these chugging rhythms can start to transform a little when playing them at faster tempos. This is normal and is to be expected.

LESSON 6:

Note Names and Harmonica Layout

Before moving on to single notes, it makes sense to check out the layout of the instrument and discover the locations of the notes hidden inside the harmonica.

The notes on almost all other common instruments—especially the piano—are much more visible than on the harmonica. In this lesson, you will slowly start to visualize the harmonica layout.

Following are the notes that are naturally built inside the C diatonic harmonica. The blow notes provide you with a C major *triad* (three-note chord) spread over three octaves (for more on octaves, see Lesson 8).

Blow Notes

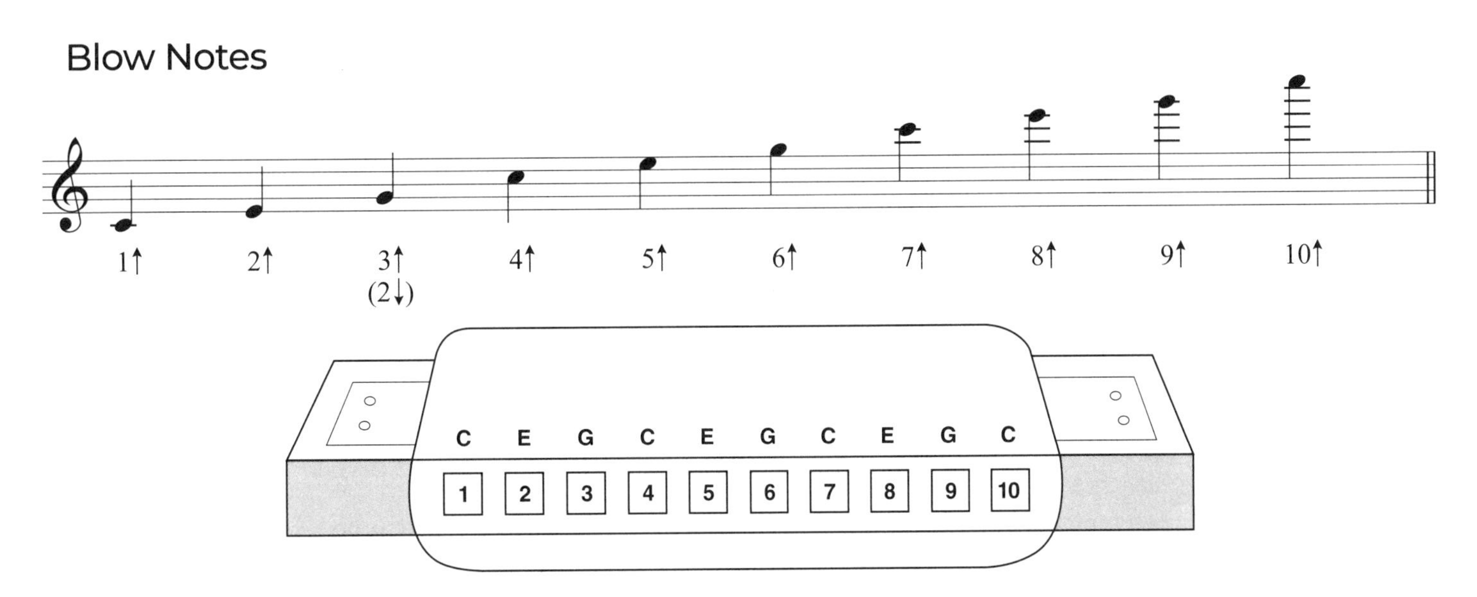

The structure of the draw notes is not as symmetrical. You have already put the G major triad (D-G-B) in the lower octave of the instrument to good use. Now you can find a D minor triad (D-F-A) in the middle and upper octaves. Including the B note on the 7-hole draw, only the middle octave provides us with all the notes required to play the C major scale (see Lesson 8). In the lower octave, both an F and an A are missing. In the upper octave, a B is missing.

Draw Notes

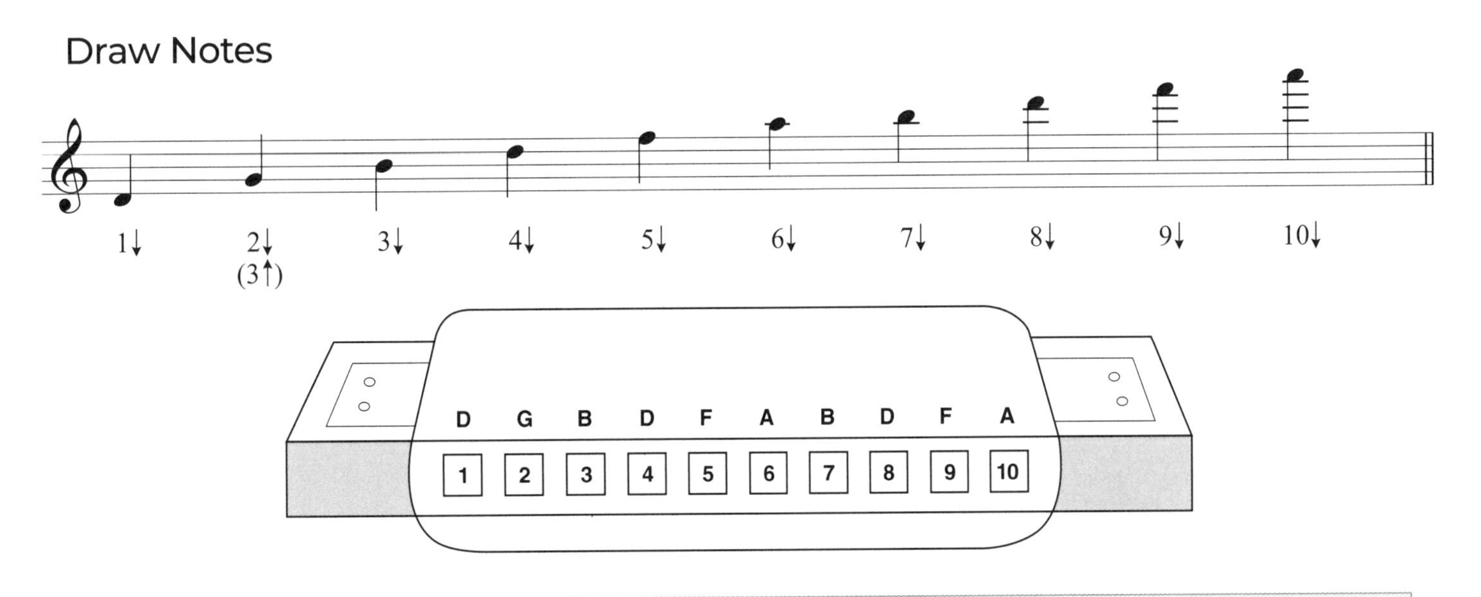

The breathing pattern changes between holes 6 and 7! On holes 1–6, the blow notes are lower than the draw notes; on holes 7–10, the draw notes are lower than the blow notes.

LESSON 7: Single-Note Playing

There are two popular ways to play a single note on the harmonica: lip pursing (puckering) and tongue blocking.

TOOLBOX

Embouchure
Embouchure is the way in which a musician applies the lips and mouth to an instrument to produce a musical tone.

Lip Pursing/Puckering

The pucker embouchure is very straightforward. Return to Lesson 3 and play a chord. Let the harp slide forward as if it is slowly slipping out of your mouth, while gently pressing the corners of your mouth inward to maintain the seal between your lips and the instrument.

Your mouth position could make you feel like you are pouting as the corners of your mouth get closer together. With the smaller opening, there will be fewer notes sounding. Push your lips forward as much as you need to in order to isolate a single note. Try to keep your lips as relaxed as possible while maintaining an airtight seal.

With time and practice, you will be able to have the harp farther inside your mouth and still coax a single note out of your instrument. Your upper lip could even cover two-thirds of the cover plate.

You could also begin by practicing this technique on hole 1, where there is no lower note that can be sounded. At the same time, you want to keep thinking about big vowels enlarging your mouth cavity. Despite working on playing single notes, you should stay in touch with the instrument using the moist part of your lips.

If you are still struggling to focus your airstream, try slightly tilting the harmonica as shown below.

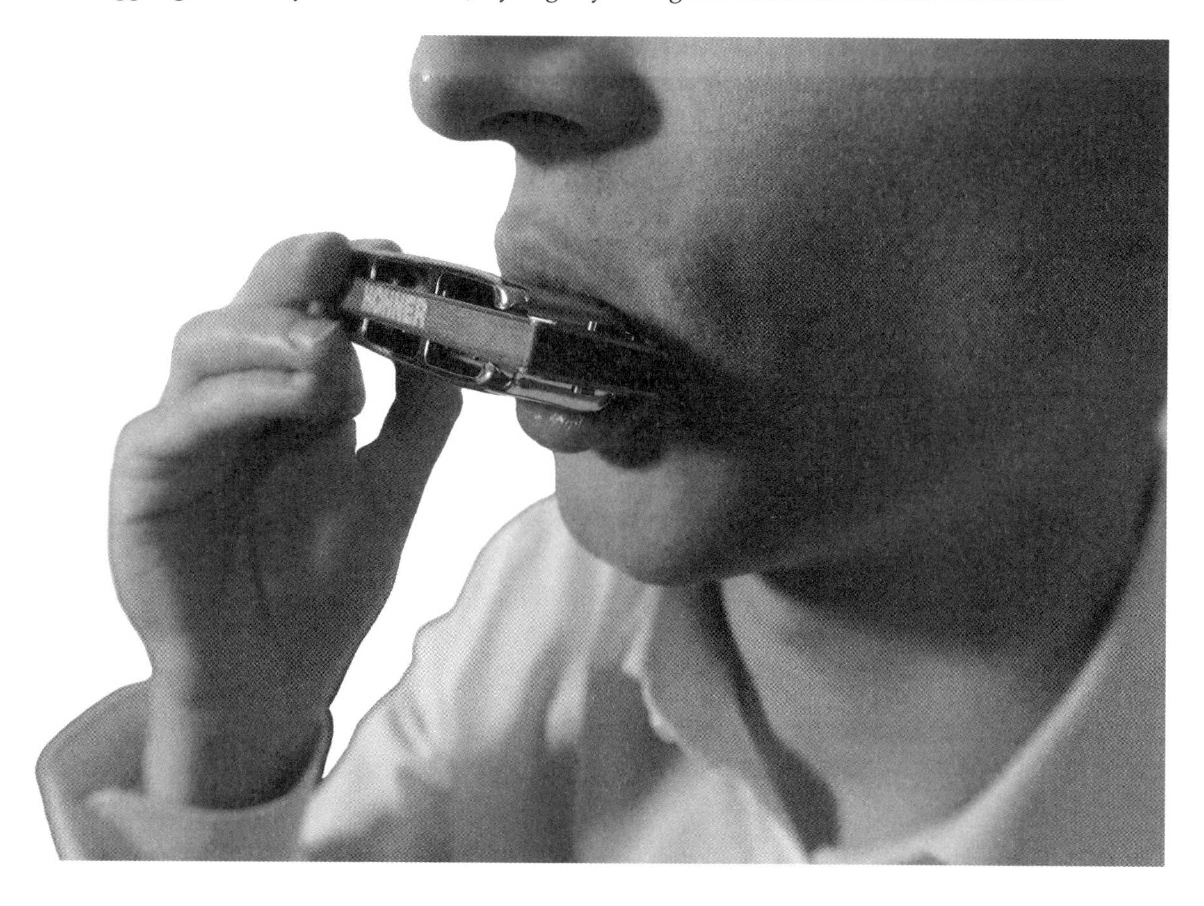

Try again to follow the breathing exercise from Lesson 3, but this time, play hole 1 only.

Lip Pursing

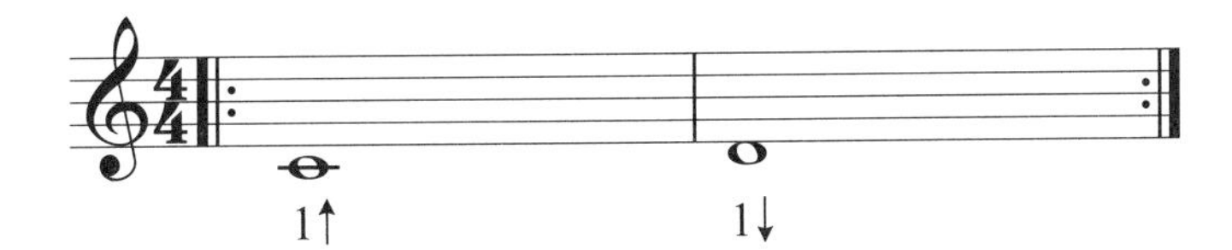

Lip pursing is the technique that I used when first learning the harmonica, and I still use it 90% of the time. It really provides a lot of flexibility—both for your lower jaw and your tongue—keeping articulation in mind. At the same time, you can still produce a big tone.

However, you should also check out this next essential embouchure.

Tongue Blocking

Chordal and rhythmic accompaniment, tongue slapping, octaving, fluttering, and many other great effects all become available once you crack this technique.

Return to Lesson 3 again and play the C major chord on holes 1–3. Now, close down holes 1 and 2 using the top of your tongue, creating a broad surface that glides against the harmonica. Touch the left edge of your tongue against the left corner of your lips, leaving an opening between the right edge of your tongue and the right corner of your lips until you can hear only the note G on hole 3.

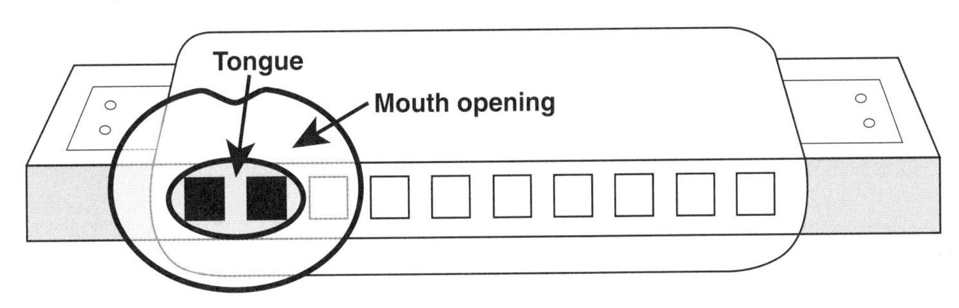

Practice tongue blocking on the rhythmic accompaniments in the following exercises.

Tongue Blocking

I used the tongue-blocking technique exclusively for a while, inspired by the American electric blues harmonicist Dennis Gruenling. Now, I am happy to be able to switch between the two embouchures seamlessly.

I suggest that you start out working on your single-note playing using the lip-pursing technique. Then, check out the tongue-blocking technique as soon as you want to expand your sound palette. However, if the tongue blocking embouchure feels more natural to you after playing the previous exercises, then you should stick to it.

LESSON 8:
The C Major Scale

TOOLBOX

Steps, Octaves, and Scales

- A *half step* is the distance of two adjacent notes on the piano, and a whole step is the distance of two consecutive half steps.
- An *octave* is the distance from one note to the nearest note with the same name 12 half steps higher or lower.
- A *scale* is an arrangement of notes in a specific order of whole steps and half steps.

Let's focus on playing the C major scale in the middle octave. In this octave, or area of the harmonica, all the *natural notes* are available without using any advanced playing techniques. (Natural notes are the white keys on a piano; they are neither sharped nor flatted.) The *tonic* is the first note of the scale. It is the note on which the scale is built and from which it gets its name. The tonic of the C major scale is C.

The notes of the C major scale are C–D–E–F–G–A–B–C. It can be very helpful to think about the change of breathing directions first: blow draw, blow draw, blow draw, draw blow. Remember about the change of breathing directions between holes 6 and 7. Keep drawing between A and B. Even if you cannot play a single note yet, this is very important to remember. As long as you follow the breathing pattern, the major scale is identifiable.

C Major Scale

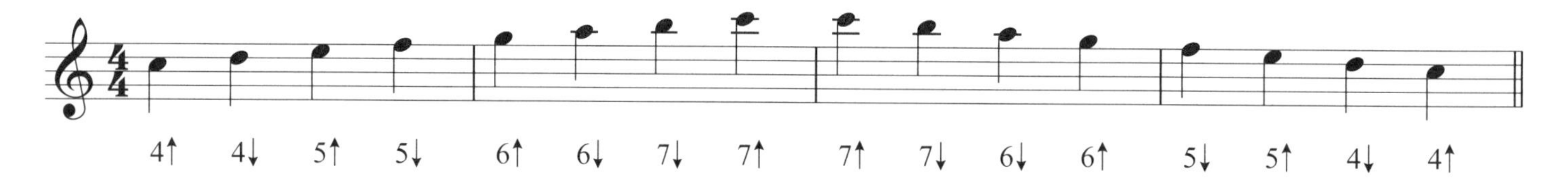

This might be your first time moving around on the instrument, and for now, all holes are still adjacent. You still want to think about your preferred way of moving between two notes. Make sure that the harp glides easily in your mouth. As long as the inner surfaces of your lips stay in touch with the cover plates, there should be no friction to cause your lips to drag along while jumping from one hole to another.

It is relatively easy to change breathing directions on one hole, but to play the C major scale, you need to jump to adjacent holes while changing the breathing directions.

As you can imagine, jumping from one hole to another gets harder the farther apart the two notes are, and as soon as advanced playing techniques are involved, this can get quite challenging. Depending on the context, you can cover the distances by moving your head, the harmonica, or your lower jaw. Combining two options or moving them in opposite directions can help you in certain situations. Just experiment with it while keeping your embouchure and especially your upper lip stable.

There are many beautiful patterns that can help you to play the C major scale by heart very soon. The following exercise uses three-note groupings, starting with the first three notes of the scale (C–D–E) and ascending in *2nds* (**D**–E–F, **E**–F–G, etc.). A 2nd is the distance of two consecutive scale tones, like C to D, D to E, and so on.

C Major Pattern 1

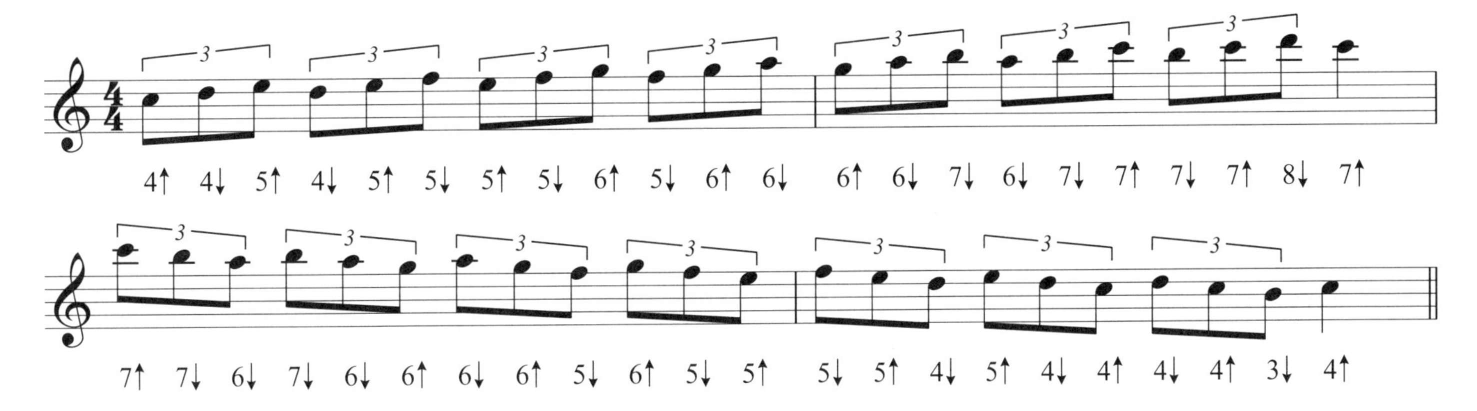

It is great to work with patterns that are fully notated, but you will benefit even more from figuring out patterns yourself. Obviously, it will take a little more time to do the math, but being forced to visualize the structure of the harmonica helps you to feel freer using the C major scale and gets you one step further toward improvising with it at some point. This is what UK-based blues harmonica player Lee Sankey calls "Brainstrument," and you will benefit from this practice enormously. Lee Sankey's theory is that musicians don't play their actual physical instrument, but rather a visual representation of it. Mapping out the structure and the layout of the harmonica in your mind could even enable you to practice in your head.

Try to start out playing new scales and patterns very consciously and slowly. Move on to the next hole when you are a hundred percent sure that you are going to hit the right note. Otherwise, just stay where you are and keep breathing through the instrument. Don't stop the airflow!

This practice will help you to play more precisely, distinctly, and articulately as soon as you speed up your playing. Focus on connecting the notes, and make the patterns sound as beautiful as possible. It can also help to move your body along to the music and imagine yourself being a classical musician performing in a concert hall with great acoustics. Do whatever feels natural to you.

Also, you can start to *accent* the first note of each three-note grouping by playing it louder using a little more air or supporting it by opening your hands.

3rds

The leapfrog exercise is one of the most popular patterns, breaking down the scale into *3rds* (or every *other* scale tone, like C to E, D to F, etc.). Most of the time, you just stay on the same breathing direction while moving to an adjacent hole. Again, the transition between holes 6 and 7 is an exception, and it is worthwhile to isolate this section and practice by looping the four notes ascending (G–B–A–C) and descending (C–A–B–G).

Leapfrog in C Major

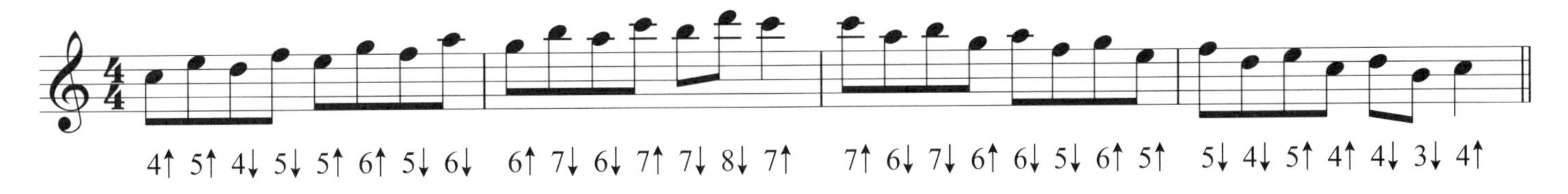

TOOLBOX

Make the Patterns More Interesting

As soon as you get bored playing these patterns, try to add rhythm to them. Make up your own rhythmic motif or play to a drum/percussion track online.

Triads

The triads in C major take the leapfrog exercise to another level by adding another note to the pattern. Playing this exercise, you will be introduced to the major and minor triads hidden inside the C major scale, which is another important step before diving deeper into music theory.

Start out by playing the 1st, 3rd, and 5th notes of the scale, *arpeggiating* the C major triad. (To arpeggiate means to play the notes of a chord one by one rather than simultaneously.) The 2nd, 4th, and 6th notes of the scale make up a D minor triad, etc.

C–E–G = C major
D–F–A = D minor
E–G–B = E minor
F–A–C = F major
G–B–D = G major
A–C–E = A minor
B–D–F = B diminished

In total, the major scale contains seven triads. Three of them are major, three of them are minor, and the last one is diminished. In the following exercise, we will arpeggiate all these triads.

Triads in C Major: Exercise 1

To take this even further, you could alternate directions on each arpeggio. In other words, ascend the C major triad, descend the D minor triad, ascend the E minor triad, descend the F major triad, and so on.

Triads in C Major: Exercise 2

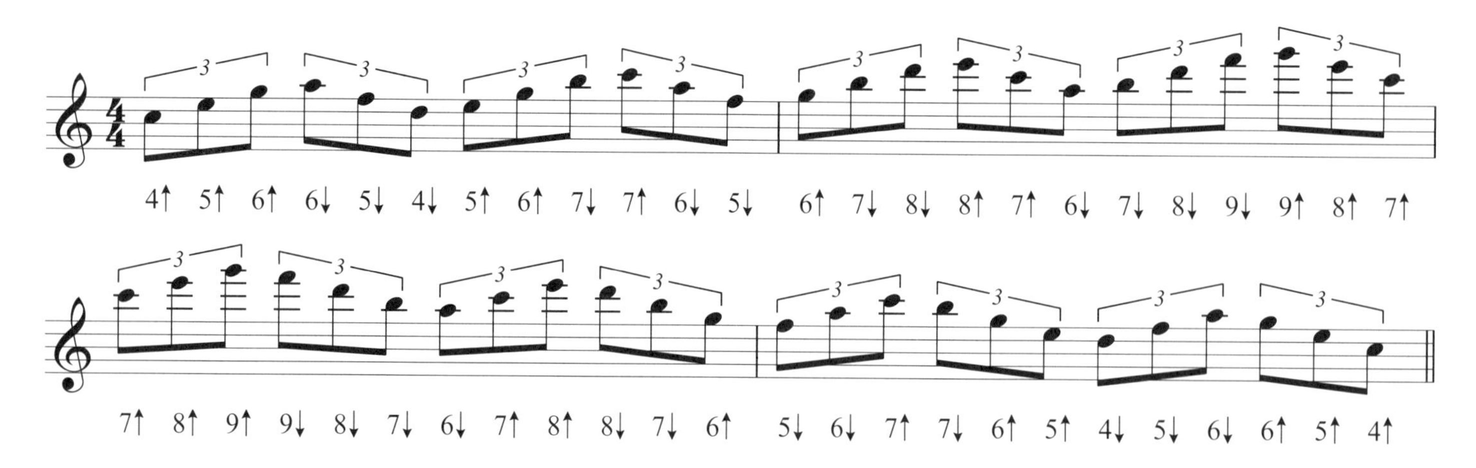

Articulation

As soon as you start playing melodies on the harmonica, you will run into situations that require you to repeat a single note twice or even more. This is the time to think about *articulation*, or the way in which notes are performed. Just think of the softer syllables you already used to play some of the chugging rhythms.

Now, imagine hitting a key on the piano repeatedly. It's very easy to do, and the instrument itself will articulate the note for you. As harmonica players, we have to get active ourselves. Of course, you could just blow or draw through a hole twice, but that won't sound very natural, and the separation of the notes will be too unclear. For that reason, you want to reactivate your tongue, touching it to the palate and saying "dah" through the instrument.

You can practice this by using the C major scale again, but this time while articulating every single note multiple times. A general rule could be the following: The first time you play any natural note on the harmonica, you don't have to articulate. The instrument itself does it for you. However, the second time, you have to get active with your tongue and talk through the instrument.

Play the first line by saying "hah-dah" on every pitch. Continue with "hah-dah-dah" in lines 2 and 3 before using "hah-dah-dah-dah" in lines 4 and 5.

Accent the first note of the groupings to speed up the exercise effortlessly.

Articulation in C Major

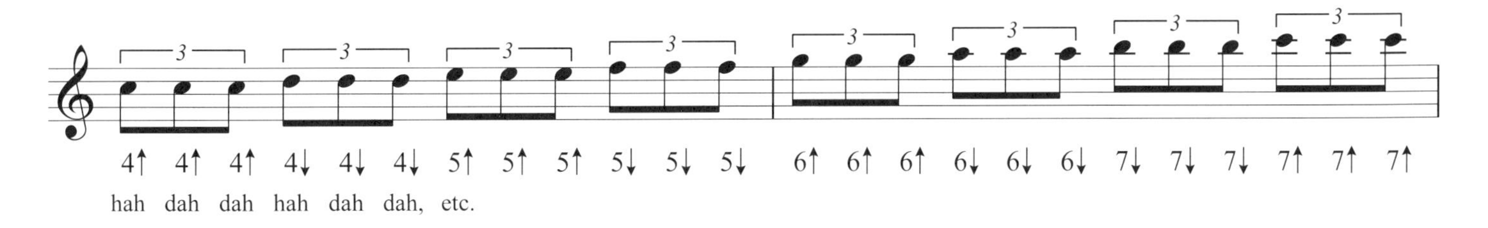

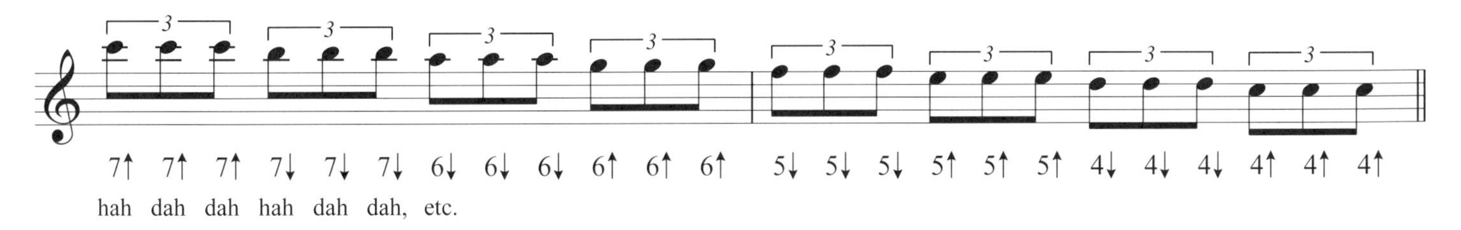

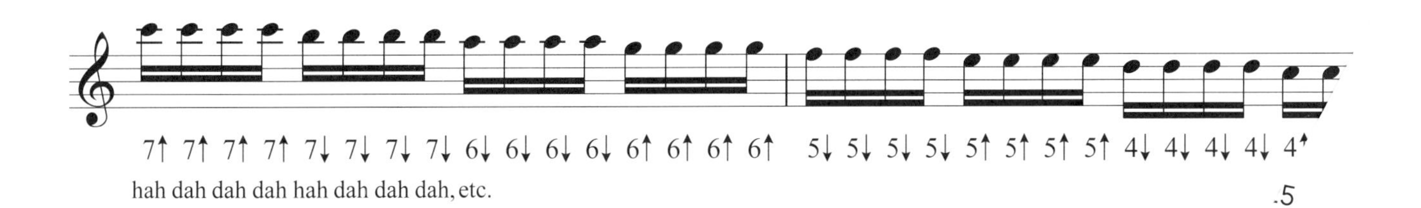

Droning

The following "drone" exercise is the last C major pattern and consists of two-note groupings. (**Note:** This can also be thought of as a *pedal-tone* exercise. A pedal tone is a sustained or continually repeated note with changing melody notes above or below it.) The first note of each grouping stays on the tonic, while the other notes outline the scale. This exercise will help you to hear every single note of the scale in relation to the tonic, basically turning this into an ear-training exercise for intervals. (You could also play the regular scale along to a drone in C, included in the audio material, for this purpose. In this case, the drone is a traditional long, sustained note.) As you progress through this exercise, the distance between the holes increases; this will help you get used to the dimensions of the instrument.

Imagine brushing your teeth. Do you move your head or your toothbrush? Do you even move both at the same time? For now, I would suggest that you do what feels most comfortable while holding the harmonica in your hands. Using both movements in opposite directions at the same time can be very useful, because it minimizes the general distance of the movement. You could also experiment with including some lower jaw movement in your playing.

In this case, tilting the harmonica horizontally using your wrist can also help you to master the exercise and minimize the general movement even more.

Drone Exercise in C Major

LESSON 9:

Playing in D Minor

Let's take a quick side trip and explore playing in the key of the harmonica's third chord, which is located in the middle and upper octaves. This is what harmonica players refer to as playing in 3rd position, which means our root note is D.

Combining the root note on 1-hole draw with the actual triad drawing in at the middle octave offers you many possibilities in terms of accompaniment. Just alternate between D minor and C major to perform a quite authentic reggae rhythm.

> **TOOLBOX**
>
> **Swing Eighths**
> *Swing eighths* are one way in which the shuffle, or swing feel, can be notated. Swing eighth notes are written as regular eighth notes, but they are played in a triplet rhythm in which the first eighth note is twice as long as the second one. Swing rhythm is indicated at the beginning of a piece of music with the symbol:

Reggae 

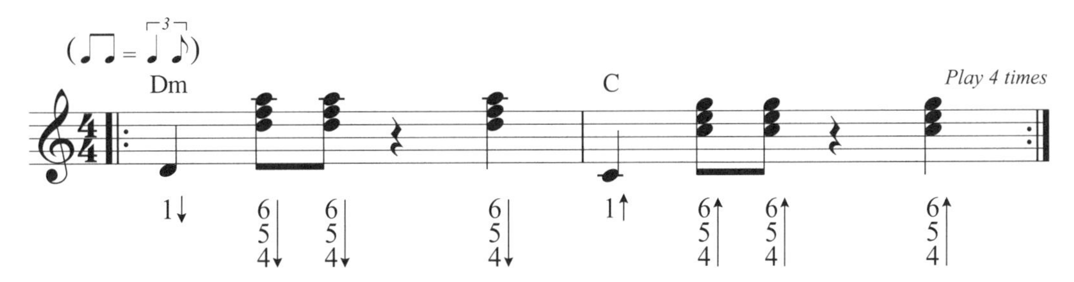

You can also use the two chords to play a Latin accompaniment displaying an Andalusian cadence, which is a type of Flamenco progression with four descending chords.

Latin Groove 

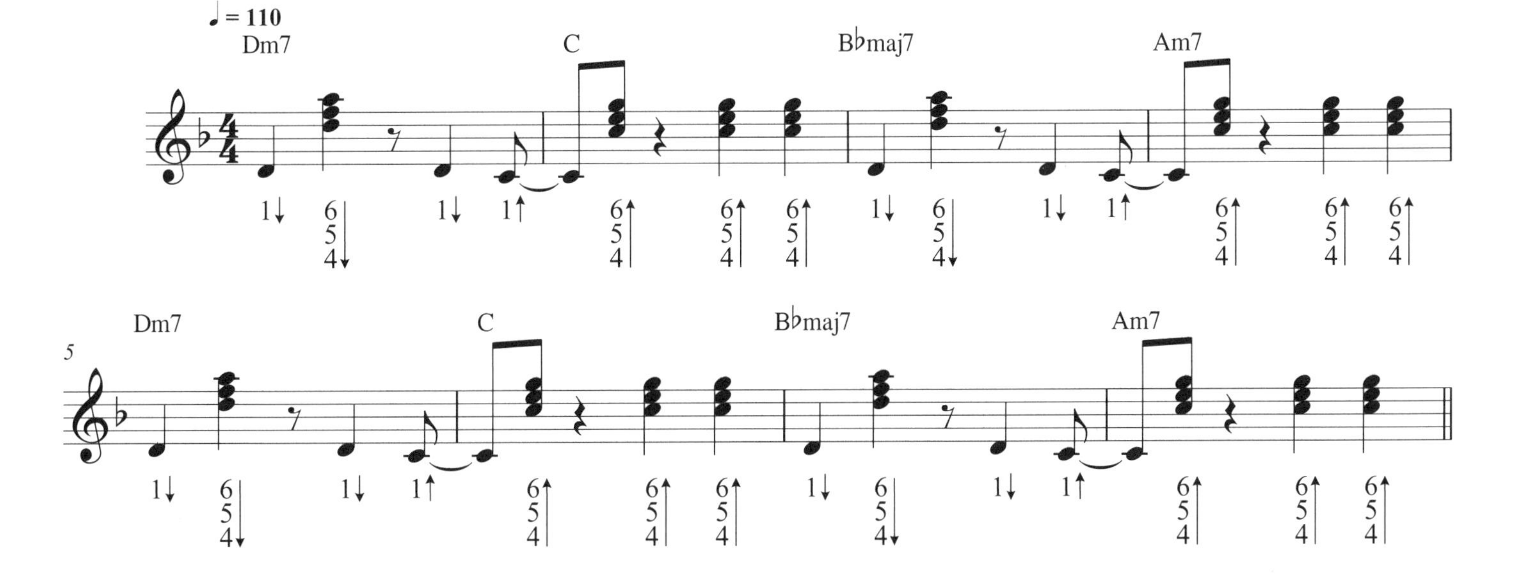

LESSON 10:

Easy Songs in 1st Position

This is a collection of beautiful melodies playable in the key of the harmonica itself (1st position). **You don't need any advanced techniques to play the following songs, and you could play them all on a C harmonica by just reading the tab. However, the standard notation is in the original key, and the harmonica for that key is given below the song titles.** Either approach is fine, but keep in mind that the accompanying audio tracks won't always match your pitch if you play everything with a C harmonica.

> **TOOLBOX**
>
> **Metronome Markings**
> A *metronome* is a time-keeping device. Metronome markings tell you the *tempo* (speed) of a piece of music in *beats per minute* (BPM). For example, the metronome marking for "Hallelujah" tells you that the tempo is 64 dotted-quarter-note beats per minute. The tempo for "Oh! Susanna" is 110 quarter-note beats per minute.

"Hallelujah" is a song by Canadian singer Leonard Cohen. The song found greater popular acclaim through recordings by John Cale and Jeff Buckley. The original version is written in 12/8 time (12 beats per measure with the eighth note receiving the beat), which evokes both early rock 'n' roll and gospel music. Written in the key of C major, the chord progression matches lyrics from the song: "goes like this, the fourth, the fifth, the minor fall, the major lift" (C–F–G–Am–F).

You can find countless harmonica recordings of this piece online, and just like the other melodies included here, "Hallelujah" is a great exercise for articulation. The melody, with its many repeated notes, requires you to talk through the instrument more than usual. I would suggest that you apply a soft syllable like "dah." The melody sounds one octave higher than written, and this is indicated in the music with the symbol *8va*.

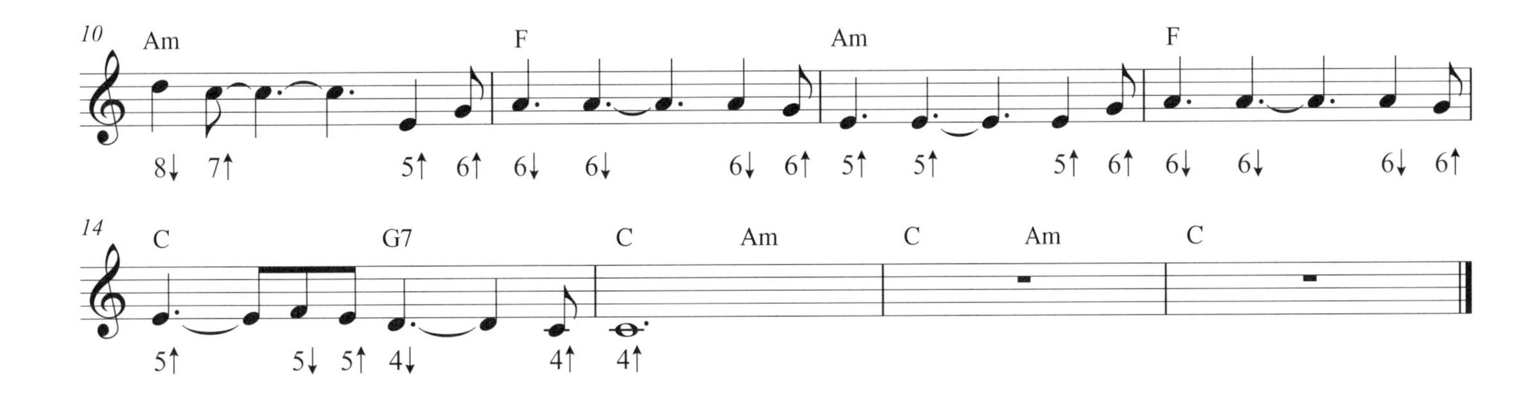

"Oh! Susanna" might be one of the most popular melodies to play on the harmonica. The folk song was written by Stephen Foster and published in 1848. The first two phrases of the melody are based on the major pentatonic scale, which you will learn about in Lesson 19. Focus on the breathing rhythm to make the notation sound good immediately. When playing this melody, you never have to skip a hole between two consecutive notes.

OH! SUSANNA

Words and Music by Stephen C. Foster

C Harmonica

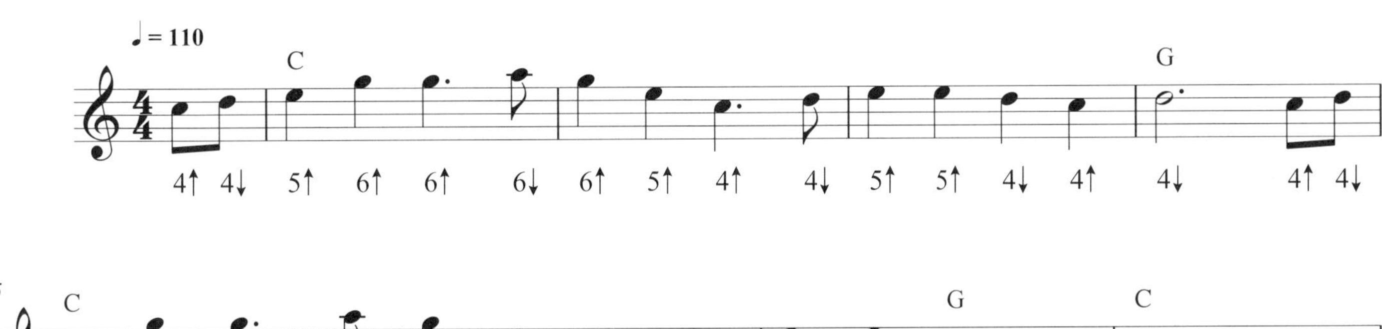

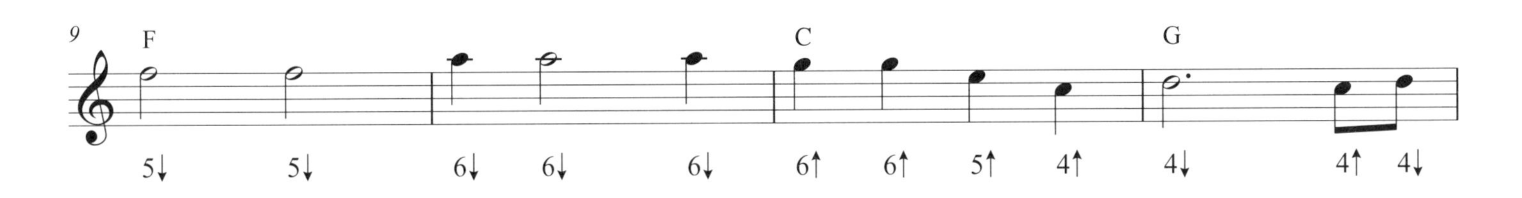

"Sete Anéis" is a wonderful composition by Brazilian composer and multi-instrumentalist Egberto Gismonti. The chromatic harmonica virtuoso Gabriel Grossi plays the song beautifully on his album *Arapuca* (2007). The melody sounds one octave higher than written.

SETE ANÉIS

By Amim Egberto Gismonti

F♯ Harmonica

"Break My Stride" by Matthew Wilder is the last example of extreme articulation in this lesson. It was released in 1983, and a cover version by the German project Blue Lagoon came to my attention in 2004.

Try to be careful playing the 7-hole draw here. Using too much air or articulating the note too intensely can potentially block the draw reed. Remember to use a big oral cavity, thinking about big vowels. The melody sounds one octave higher than written.

BREAK MY STRIDE

Words and Music by Greg Prestopino and Matthew Wilder

F Harmonica

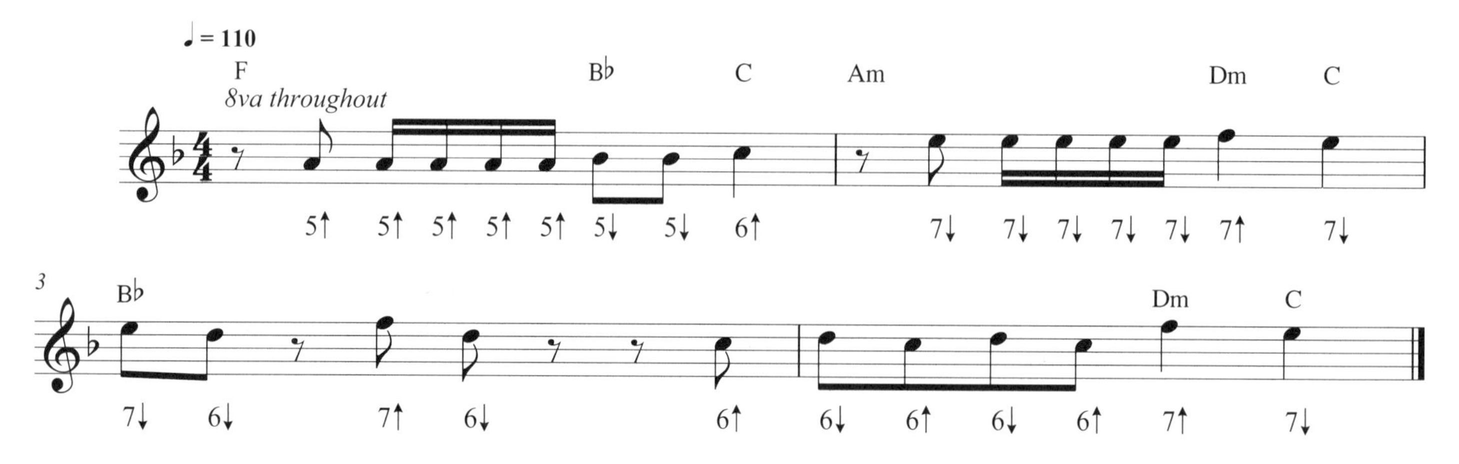

Songs Featuring the Harmonica

There are quite a few popular songs that feature the harmonica on the original recordings. The following three songs are well-known for their harmonica melodies.

"Hey! Baby" by Bruce Channel (1961) features Delbert McClinton playing an A harmonica in 1st position. However, you can also find a few performances online in which the song is played on a D harmonica. Playing a D instrument in 2nd position could make the melody sound a little more bluesy. The movie *Dirty Dancing* popularized the song worldwide in 1987.

HEY! BABY

Words and Music by Bruce Channel and Margaret Cobb

A Harmonica

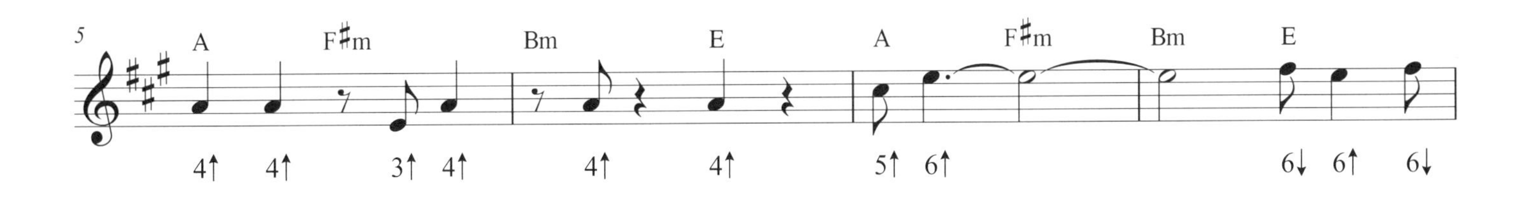

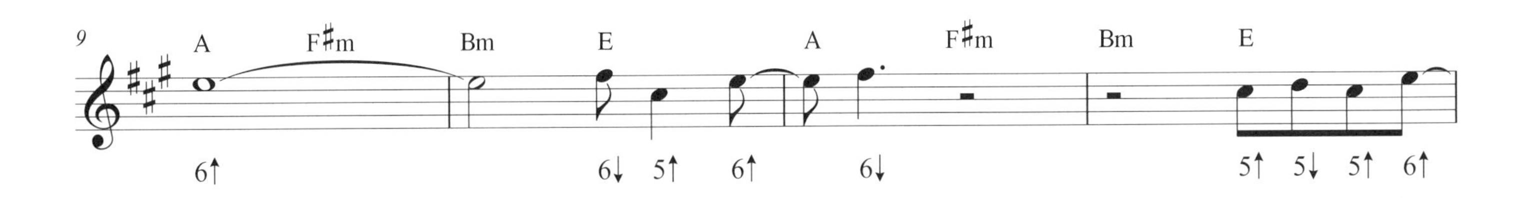

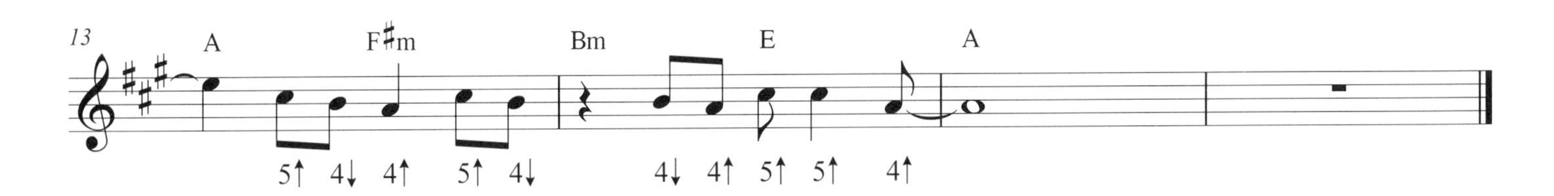

The introduction to "Piano Man" might be one of the best-known harmonica parts ever. Billy Joel's first hit and signature song was released in 1973. He recorded it in the key of C, which makes it a great song for you to learn on the harmonica and play along to. It has a 3/4 "waltz" time signature (three beats per measure with the quarter note receiving the beat) and begins with a jazzy piano solo before moving into its piano and harmonica introduction.

PIANO MAN

Words and Music by Billy Joel

C Harmonica

"Dirty Old Town" by the Pogues also features a harmonica intro. If you listen closely, you might notice that drummer and harmonica player Andrew Ranken plays a 3-hole blow instead of the 2-hole draw to smooth the transition to the 4-hole blow. The song was written by Ewan MacColl in 1949 and was made popular by the Dubliners.

DIRTY OLD TOWN

Words and Music by Ewan MacColl

D Harmonica

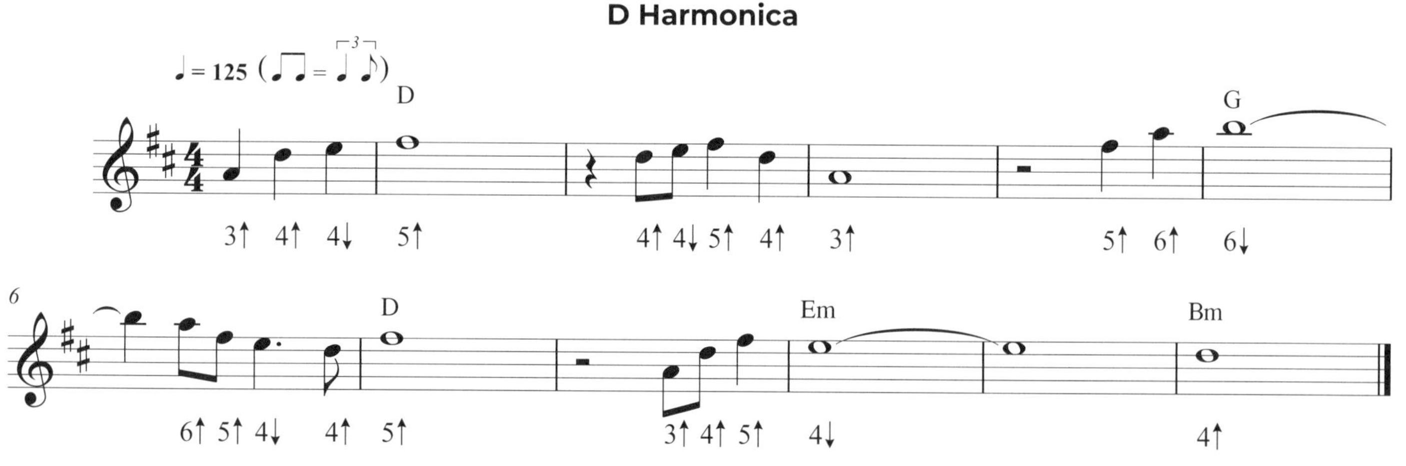

Many other popular melodies are playable without any bends. "Stand by Me" (1961) is an all-time classic written by Ben E. King and should be part of every harmonica player's repertoire. The original recording is in A major and uses a version of the common chord progression now called "the '50s progression." The notation is in C major, as is the accompanying audio.

TOOLBOX

Quarter-Note Triplet

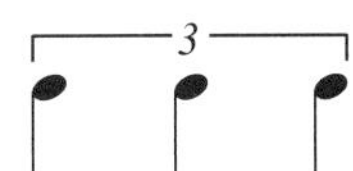

A *quarter-note triplet* is three quarter notes over the same amount of time as two quarter notes or a single half note.

STAND BY ME

Words and Music by Jerry Leiber, Mike Stoller and Ben E. King

C Harmonica

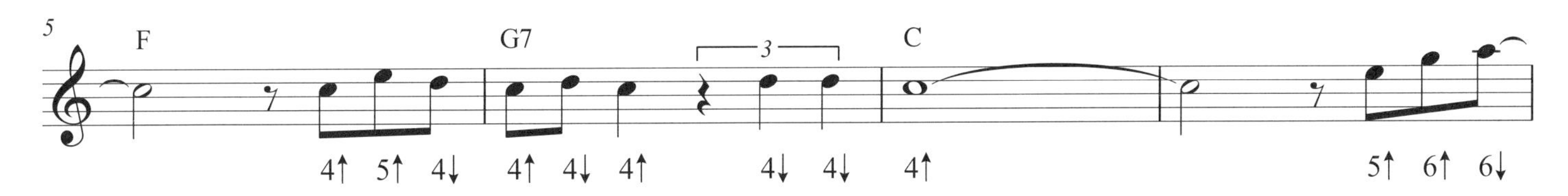

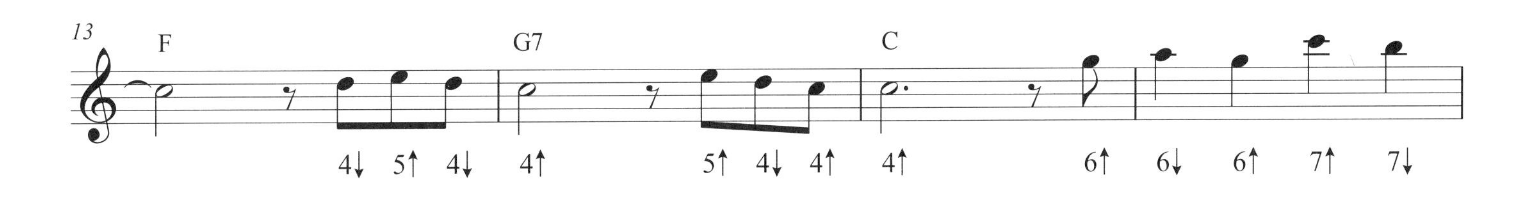

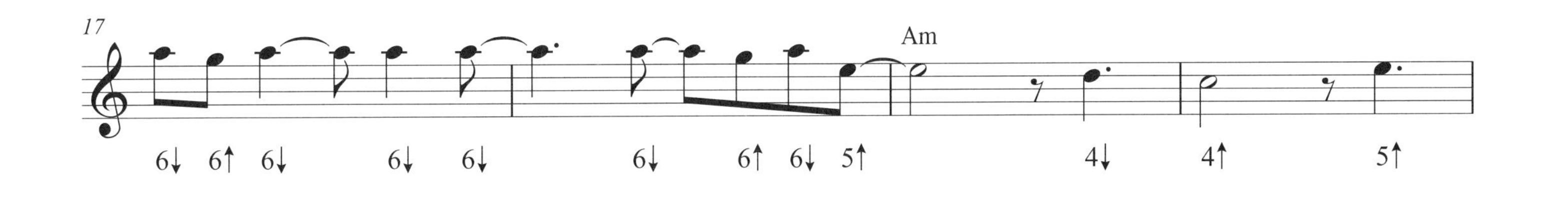

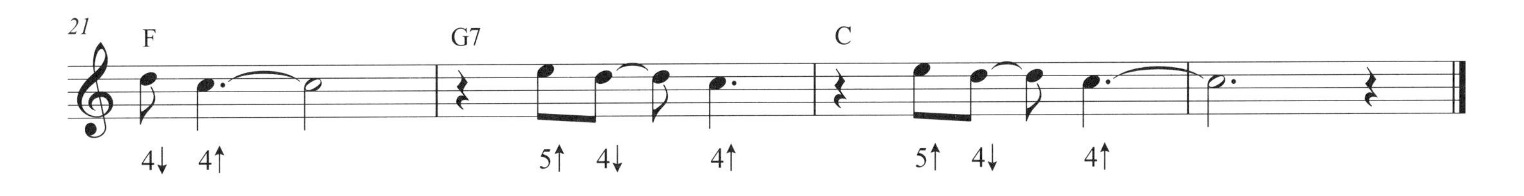

Let's move on to two more recent songs. "Just the Way You Are" is a pop, R&B, and soft rock ballad. Its instrumentation features piano and a hip-hop breakbeat. The debut solo single by American singer-songwriter Bruno Mars was the best-selling digital single of 2011, selling more than 12.5 million copies. You can find a beautiful harmonica recording of the song online by the Malaysian duo Aiden N Evelyn.

JUST THE WAY YOU ARE

Words and Music by Bruno Mars, Ari Levine, Khari Cain, Philip Lawrence and Khalil Walton

F Harmonica

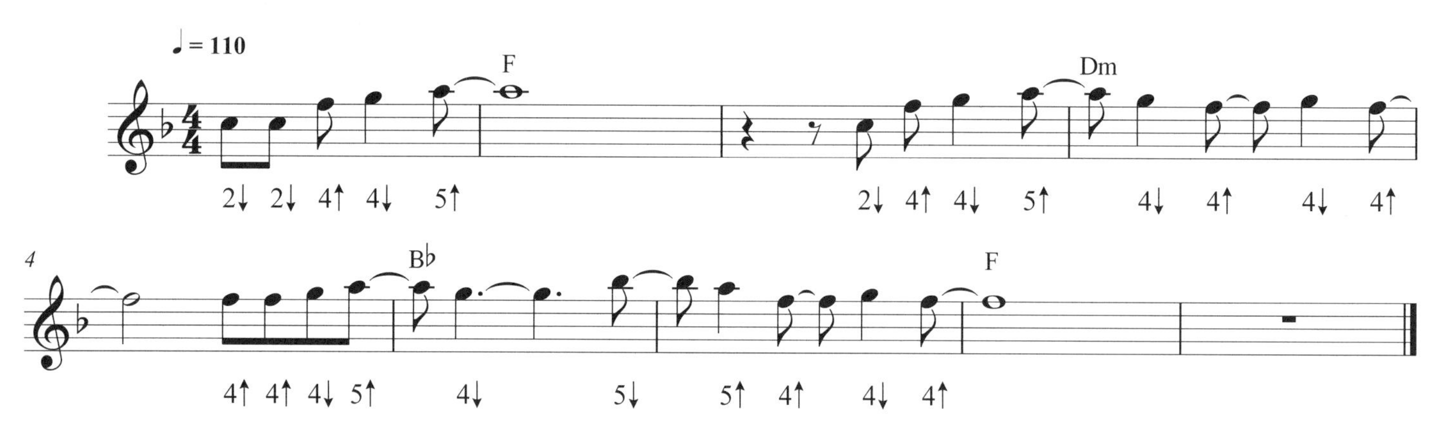

"Stay With Me" is a song by English singer Sam Smith. The song has become Smith's most successful single to date. The chord progression is persistent throughout the entire song, and it is accompanied by a contemporary drumbeat and a refrain sung in a gospel style.

STAY WITH ME

Words and Music by Sam Smith, James Napier, William Edward Phillips, Tom Petty and Jeff Lynne

C Harmonica

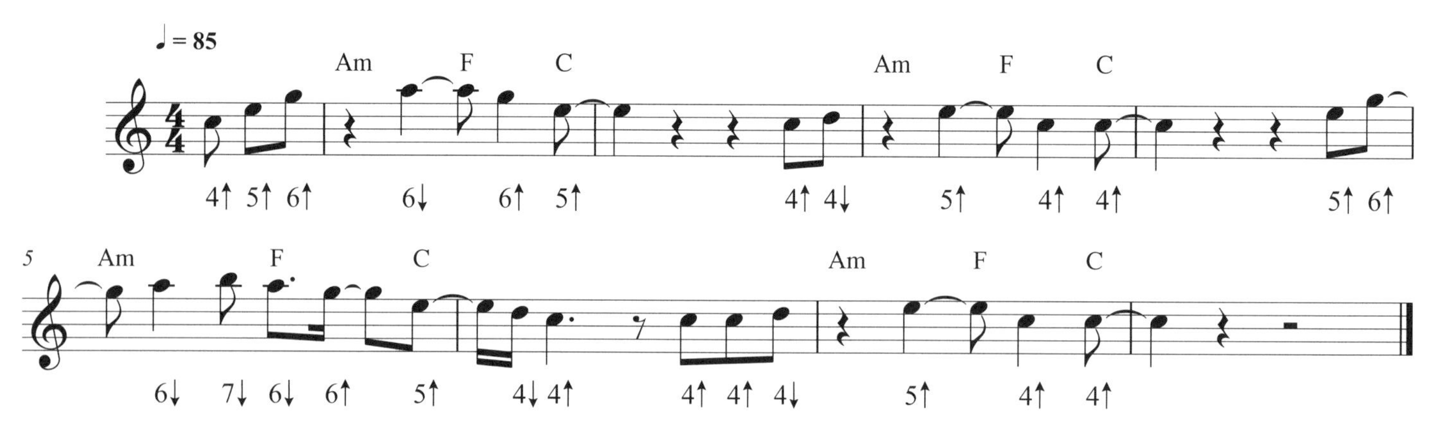

"Narcotic" (1998) by Liquido was popularized again only recently. YouNotUs released a remix of the song in 2019. The original synthesizer melody was played on a Roland D70, and it feels rather unusual to play on the harmonica. Even though the notes and the rhythm feel very repetitive, the emphasis of the offbeats is the driving force behind the melody.

NARCOTIC

Words and Music by Wolfgang Schroedl

D♭ Harmonica

The theme from the TV show *ALF* was composed, coincidentally, by a man named Alf Clausen. Hearing the original instrumental, it might not surprise you to learn that he played bass as a teenager. Notice the quarter-note triplets in bars 1, 5, 8, and 10.

THEME FROM "ALF"

from the Television Series

Words and Music by Alf Clausen

C Harmonica

"The Way You Look Tonight" is an easy-to-play jazz standard written by Jerome Kern. Try to play along with Frank Sinatra's recording in the key of E♭ and replicate his phrasing of the melody. It is common for the rhythms in jazz standards to be simplified in the notation in order to give musicians more freedom for their own interpretation. The melody sounds one octave higher than written.

THE WAY YOU LOOK TONIGHT

Words by Dorothy Fields
Music by Jerome Kern
E♭ Harmonica

"Take Me Home, Country Roads" is a song about West Virginia. The single was performed by John Denver in 1971 and was a success on its initial release. In March 2014, it became one of the four official state anthems of West Virginia.

The melody is well-known worldwide, and I'm sure you also know it by heart. However, just refer to the chapter on rhythm to get more comfortable performing sixteenth notes.

TAKE ME HOME, COUNTRY ROADS

Words and Music by John Denver, Bill Danoff and Taffy Nivert
A Harmonica

"Tennessee Waltz" is a popular country music song written in 1946, and it became a multimillion seller after the release of Patti Page's recording in 1950. As of 1974, it was the biggest-selling song ever in Japan.

TENNESSEE WALTZ

Words and Music by Redd Stewart and Pee Wee King

G Harmonica

"Cherry Pink and Apple Blossom White" is our next popular song, with music by Louiguy written in 1950. Pérez Prado's popular recording of the song features trumpeter Billy Regis, whose trumpet sound would slide down and up before the melody would resume. In 1961, Jerry Murad's Harmonicats released an album featuring the song. **Note:** This arrangement includes some bent notes at the end. Don't worry about playing those for now; you can simply hold out the final C note. Come back later after you've learned how to bend and try it out!

TOOLBOX

1st and 2nd Endings

The next song includes *1st and 2nd endings*, which are another way to repeat portions of notation. When you reach the end of the measure with the bracketed "1" above it—the 1st ending—the repeat bar here tells you to return back to the earlier repeat near the start of the song. After playing through those measures again, skip over the 1st ending this time and go straight to the 2nd ending (bracketed "2") and continue on from there.

CHERRY PINK AND APPLE BLOSSOM WHITE

from UNDERWATER

French Words by Jacques Larue
English Words by Mack David
Music by Marcel Louiguy

C Harmonica

The "Minuet in G Major" is part of a pair of movements from a suite for harpsichord by Christian Petzold. Due to its publication in the 1725 *Notebook for Anna Magdalena Bach*, it used to be attributed to J.S. Bach. The melody is among the best-known pieces of music literature and your first step into classical music. Try to connect the melody more than usual; cause the notes to swell in volume to bring them to life. If you look for live recordings of American harmonica player and singer Jason Ricci, you might catch him playing the melody during one of his cadenzas.

MINUET IN G MAJOR

from NOTEBOOK FOR ANNA MAGDALENA BACH

By Christian Petzold

G Harmonica

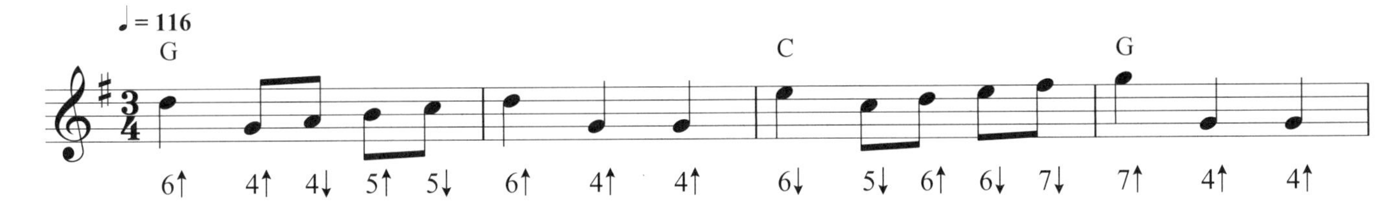

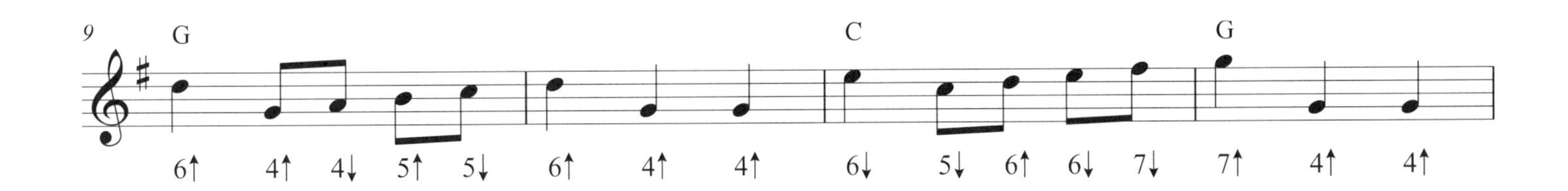

"Hey Jude" is a song by the English rock band the Beatles and was released as a non-album single in August 1968. It was written by Paul McCartney and credited to the Lennon-McCartney partnership. **Note:** There are overblows in bar 23 that can be neglected for now; they are usually just included in this bridge section. After you've learned about the overblow technique later in the method, come back to this song and try them out.

TOOLBOX

D.S. al Coda

This tells you to go back and play from the dal segno sign 𝄋 and play to the "To Coda" indication, then skip down to the Coda 𝄌 .

HEY JUDE

Words and Music by John Lennon and Paul McCartney

G Harmonica

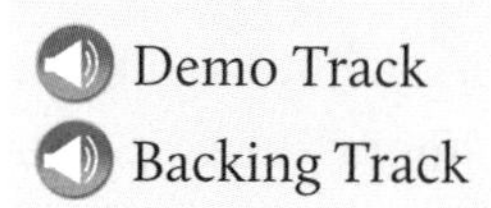

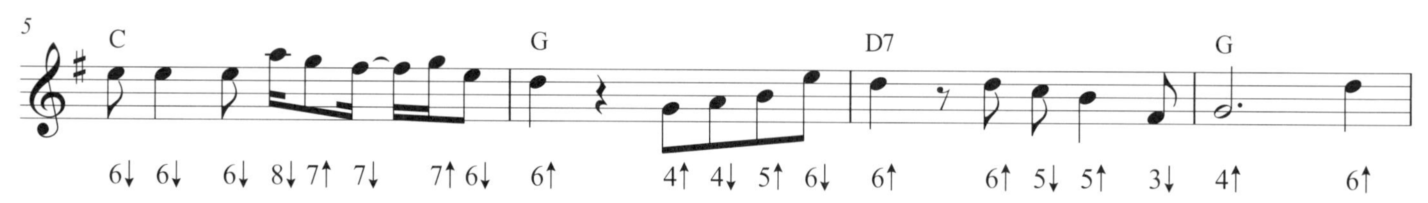

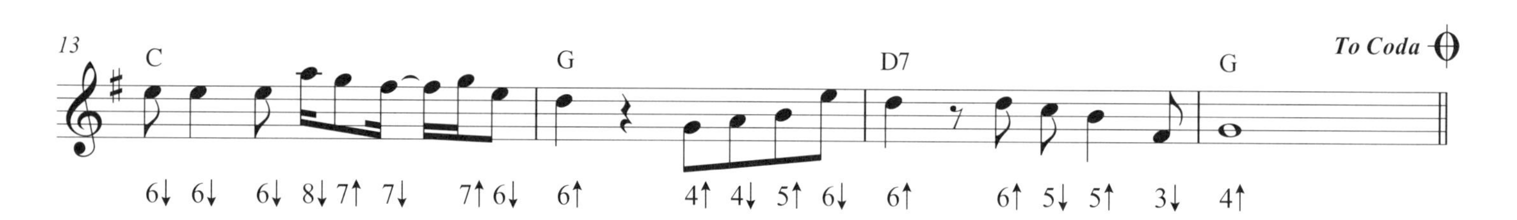

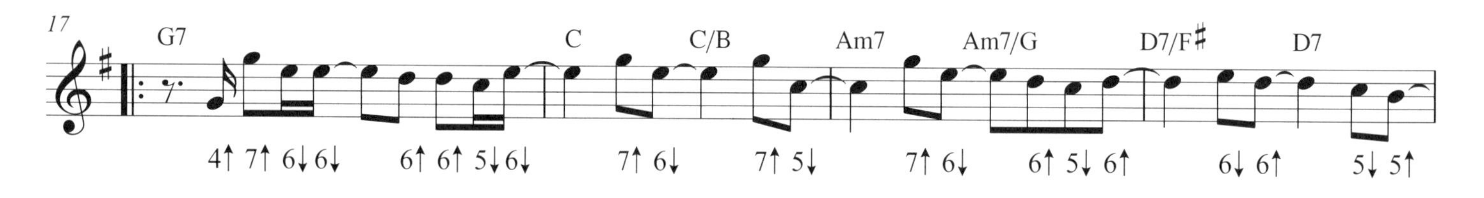

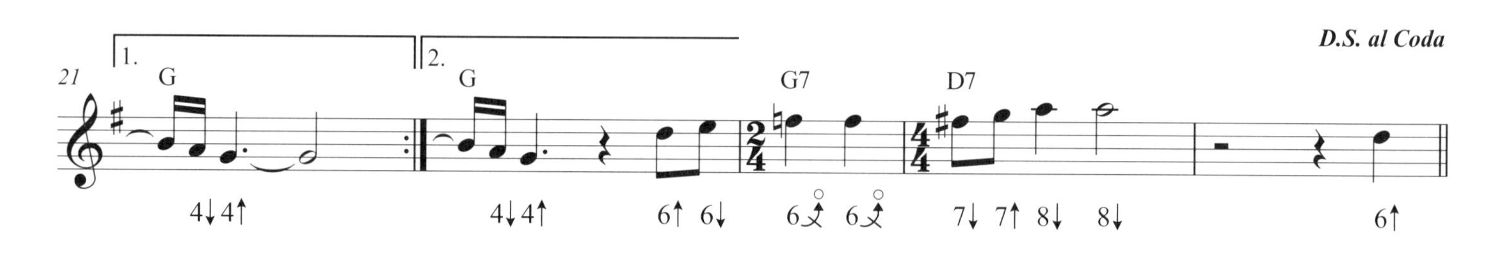

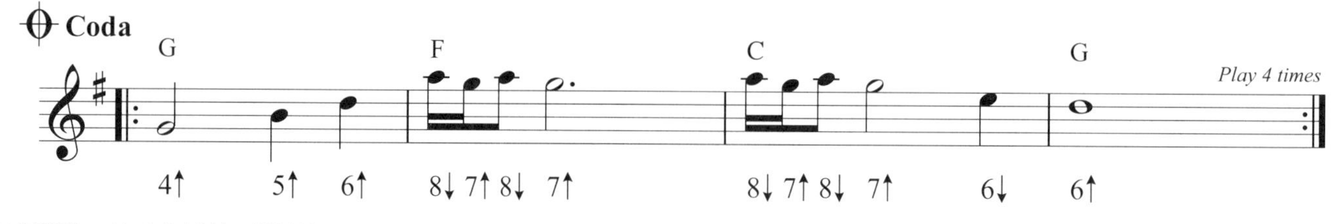

Written by Sting, “Every Breath You Take” is a song by the English rock band the Police. As their signature song, it generated between a quarter and a third of Sting’s music publishing income in 2010, and it was recognized as being the most played song in radio history in 2019.

EVERY BREATH YOU TAKE

Words and Music by Sting

A♭ Harmonica

The harmonica really lends itself to surprising other people with a little serenade. It might be one of your goals to play "Happy Birthday to You" at the next birthday celebration you are invited to. The following version features the melody both in 3/4 and 4/4 time signatures. **Note:** This recording includes a fancy ending with one overblow. For now, you can skip that and just play a final G note instead. Come back later after you've learned to overblow and try it out!

> **TOOLBOX**
>
> **Fermata**
>
> A *fermata* is indicated with the symbol 𝄐. It tells you to hold the note or chord for longer than its written value.

HAPPY BIRTHDAY TO YOU

Words and Music by Mildred J. Hill and Patty S. Hill

G Harmonica

Demo Track

Backing Track

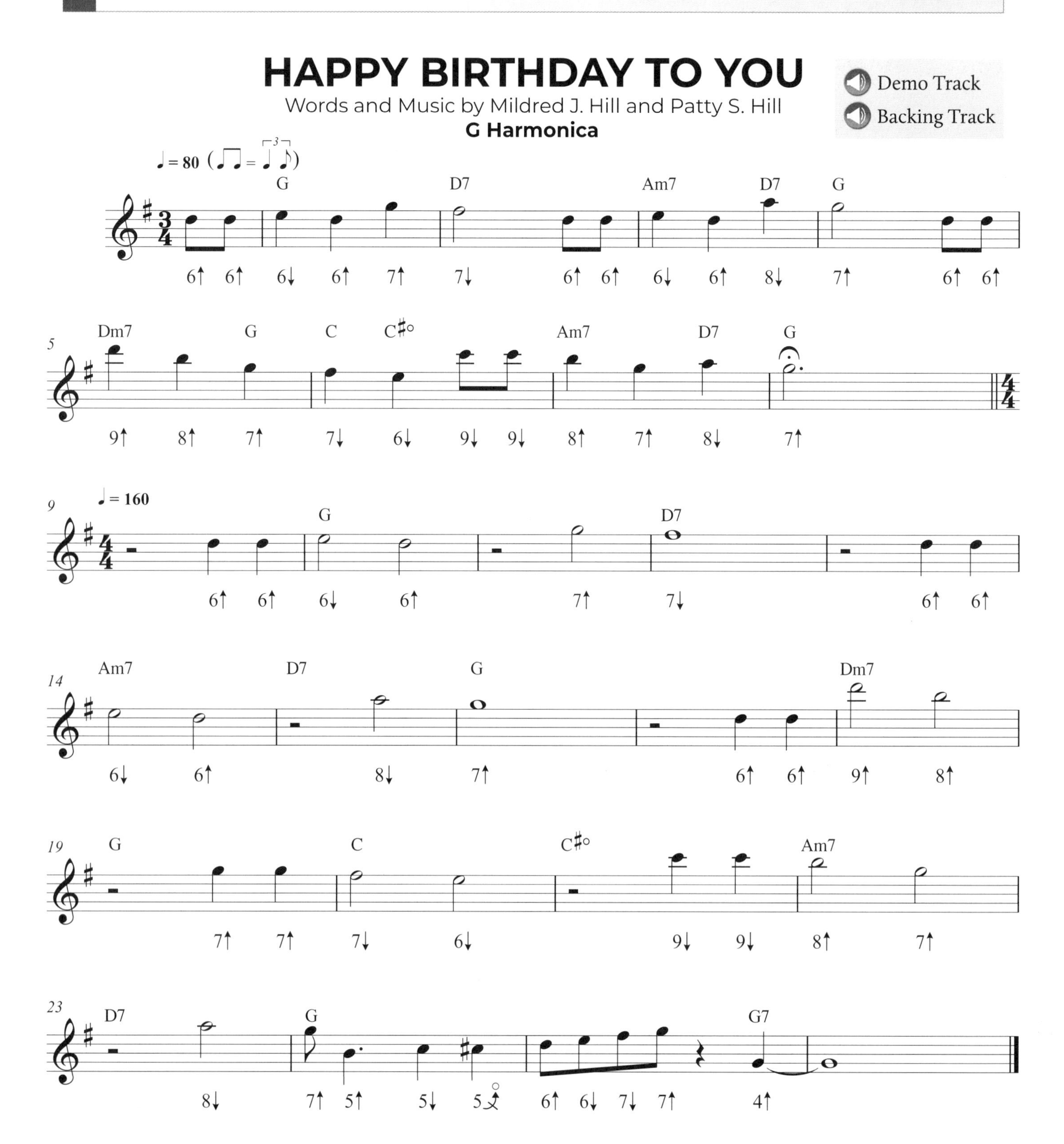

LESSON 11:
Cupping and Tremolo

It's time to spice up the melodies and add some movement to longer notes.

Tremolo is a rhythmic change of volume and/or tone color. The most common technique for creating the tremolo effect is by *cupping* with your right hand. I demonstrate this technique in the accompanying video, and you can see that I prefer to use the heel of my hand to create an intense effect. In order to do that, you should position both of your thumbs in parallel on the lower cover plate:

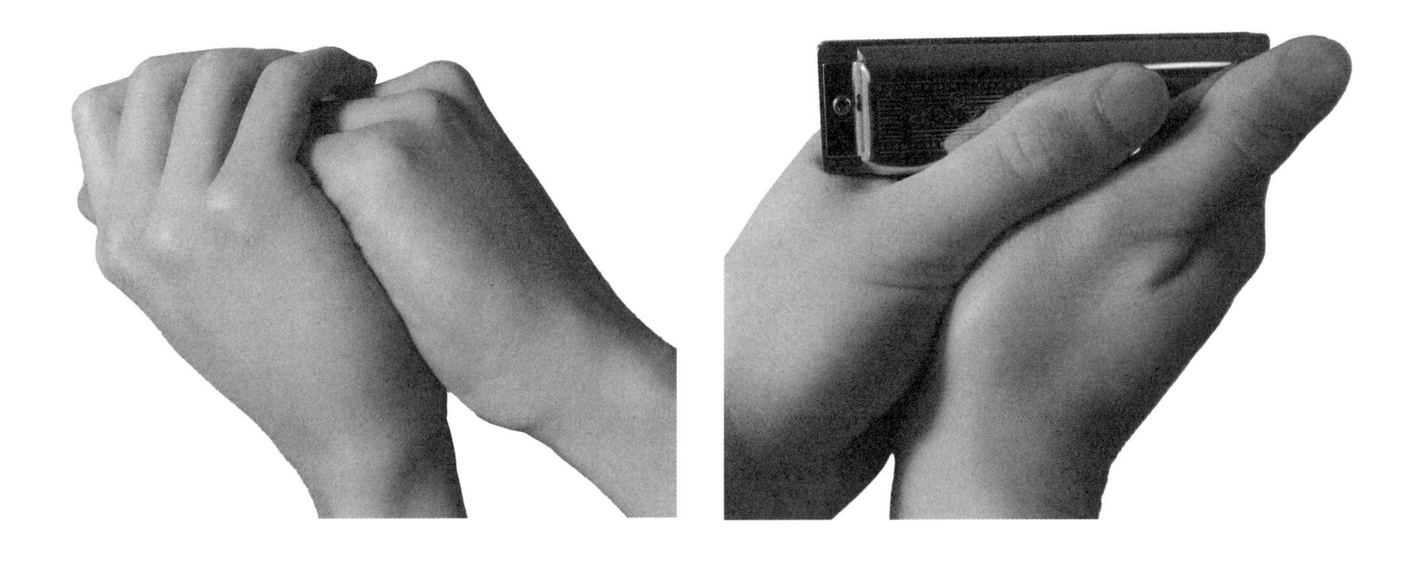

An additional option would be to place your right thumb on the higher, unused holes to make the cup even more airtight.

The following photos show options for opening the cup to create wah-wah and tremolo effects:

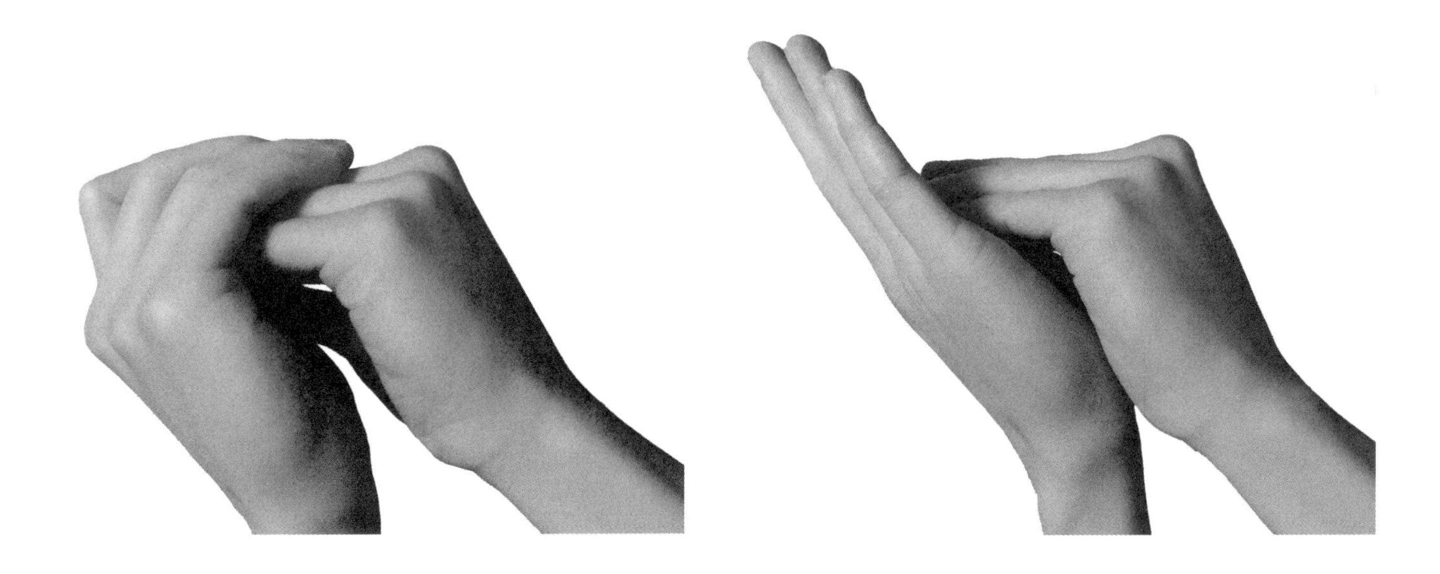

First published in 1931, "Morning Has Broken" is a Christian hymn based on a Scotch folk melody. In 1971, a version was recorded by British singer Cat Stevens, which helped popularize the tune. The melody starts out with a pickup arpeggiating the C major triad. After the first three notes, the guitar enters. Try to keep the air flowing at all times. During the second chorus of the recording, I supported the melody using hand tremolo.

MORNING HAS BROKEN

Traditional Melody

C Harmonica

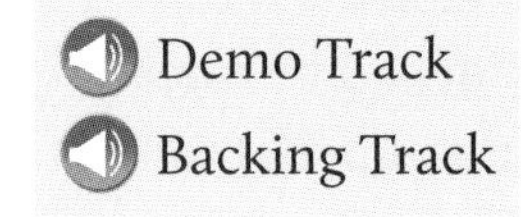

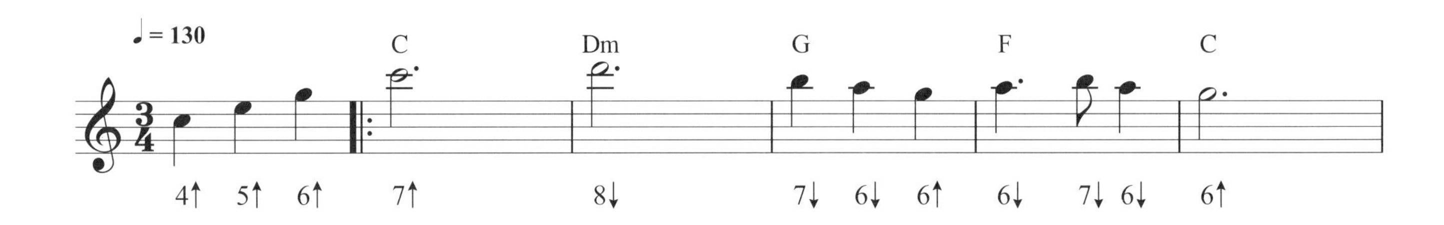

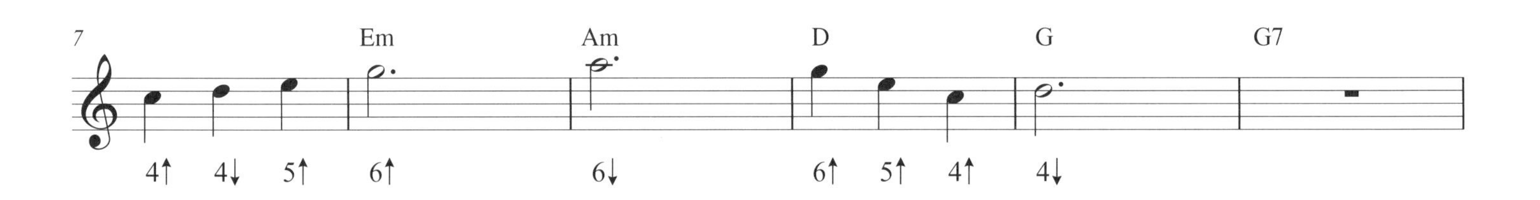

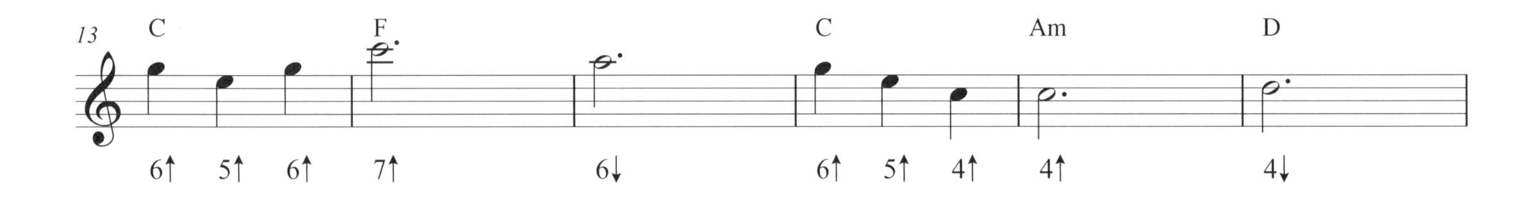

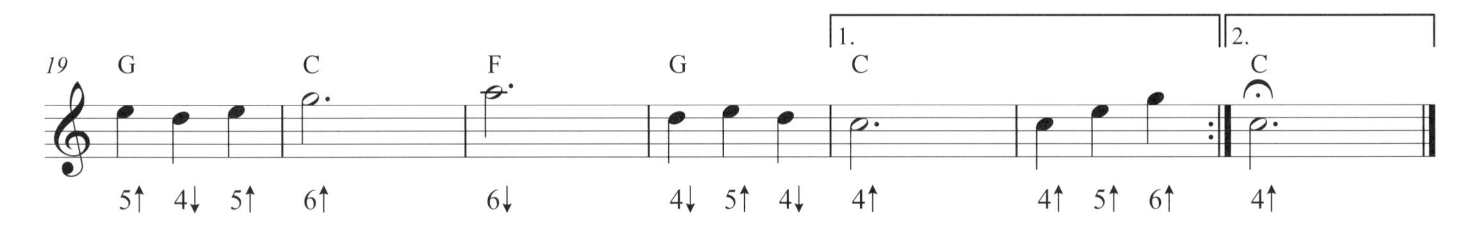

You can also add more life to the following melodies by using hand tremolo. "Time to Say Goodbye"—also known as "Con Te Partirò"—is an Italian song written by Francesco Sartori. The 1996 release of the song paired Andrea Bocelli with British soprano Sarah Brightman and achieved great success, topping charts across Europe.

TIME TO SAY GOODBYE

Original Italian lyrics by Lucio Quarantotto
English lyrics adapted by Frank Peterson
Music by Francesco Sartori
G Harmonica

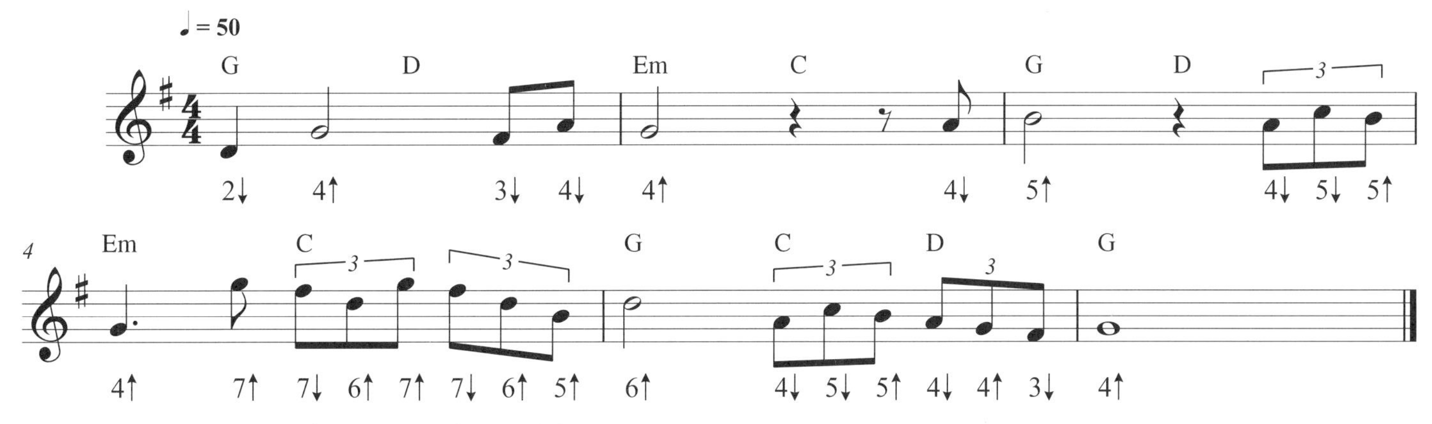

"You Raise Me Up" is a song originally composed by the Norwegian-Irish duo Secret Garden. The song has been recorded by more than a hundred other artists, including the Irish boy band Westlife in 2005. It was the first song that I ever played live onstage. The melody sounds one octave higher than written.

YOU RAISE ME UP

Words and Music by Brendan Graham and Rolf Løvland
F Harmonica

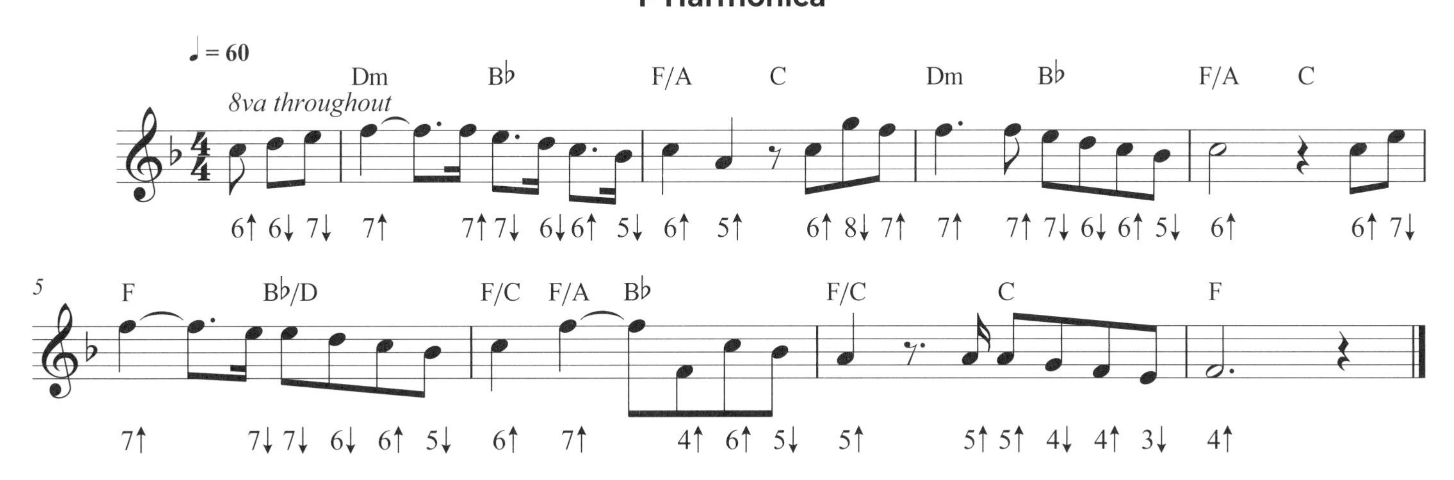

"Moon River" is our first jazz melody. The song was composed by Henry Mancini and was originally performed by Audrey Hepburn. Try to focus on playing the melody as *legato* (smoothly, connected) as possible. I suggest that you slow down the audio and work on smooth transitions between the different holes. For example, isolate and practice the jumps between G, C, and B in bars 4 and 5. The melody sounds one octave higher than written.

MOON RIVER

from the Paramount Pictures feature film
BREAKFAST AT TIFFANY'S

Words by Johnny Mercer
Music by Henry Mancini

C Harmonica

Demo Track
Backing Track

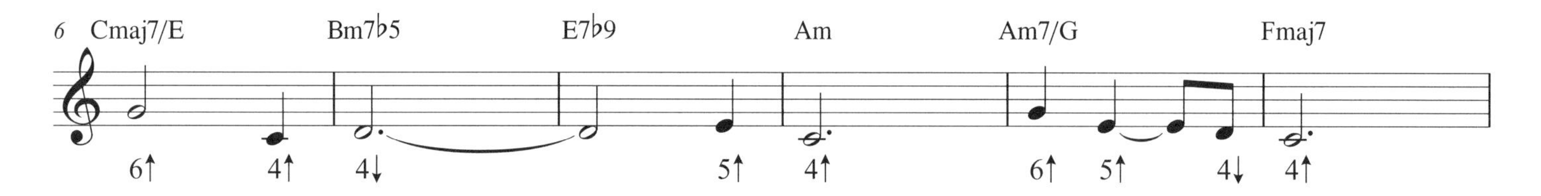

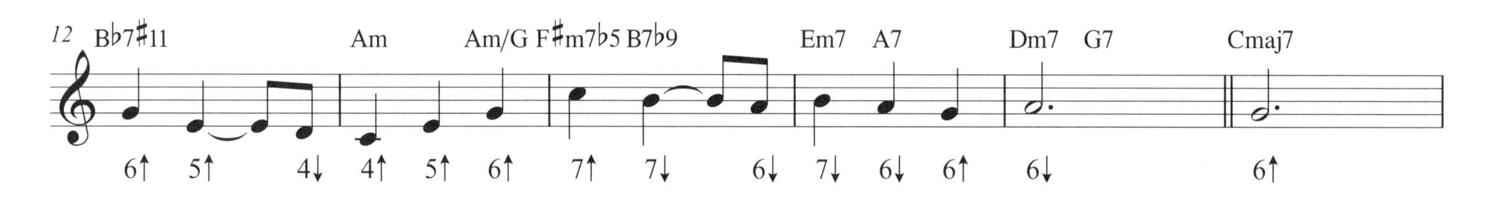

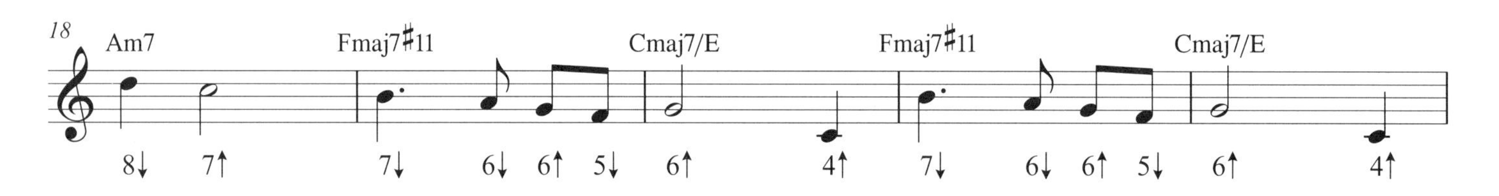

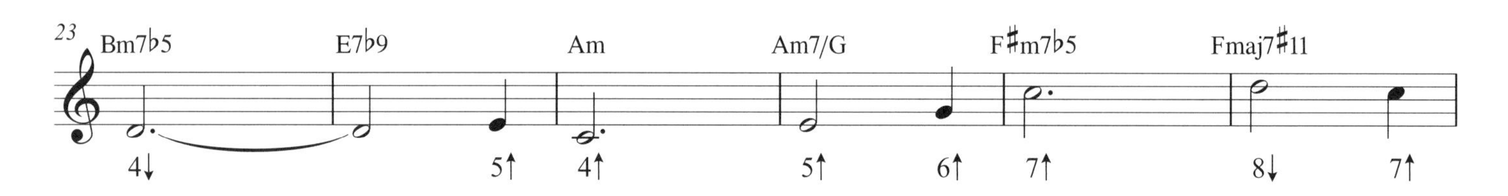

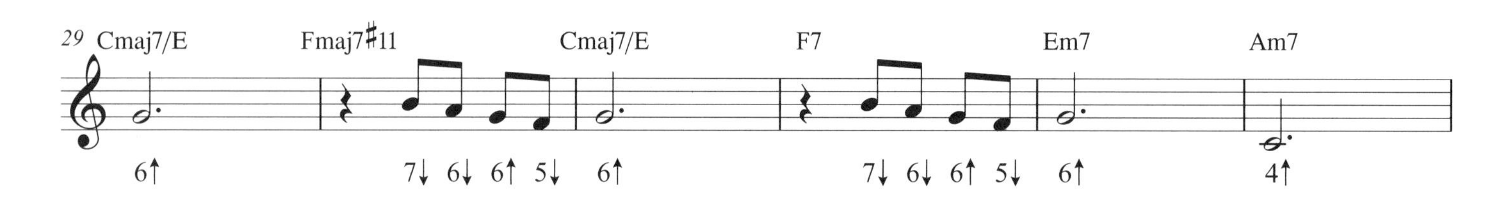

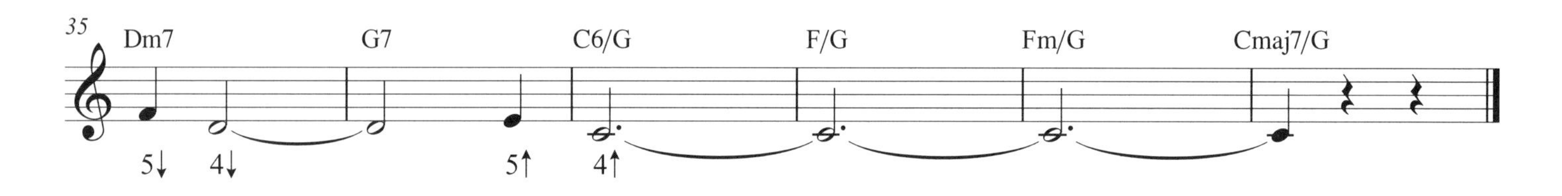

LESSON 12:
The 12-Bar Blues and 2nd Position

TOOLBOX

Diatonic Harmony

Diatonic harmony refers to the chords that belong to a key. A chord can be built on each tone of a scale. The chords built on the notes of a C major scale are C–Dm–Em–F–G–Am–B°. If these were taken one step further and made into 7th chords, they would be Cmaj7–Dm7–Em7–Fmaj7–G7–Am7–Bm7♭5. The chords of a key can be referred to using Roman numerals. The chord built on the tonic is I, the chord built on the 2nd note of the scale is ii, etc. Uppercase Romans are used for major chords and lowercase Romans are used for minor and diminished chords: I–ii–iii–IV–V–vi–vii°.

The *12-bar blues* song form is usually made up of three main parts:

1. The first part of the verse lasts for four bars and generally consists of the I chord. The first musical statement is made here.
2. The second part of the verse consists of two bars of the IV chord followed by two bars of the I chord. In this second part of the verse, you can repeat your musical statement from the first part, or elaborate on it.
3. The third part of the verse provides space for a final answer that prepares for the next verse. There is one bar of the V followed by one bar of the IV chord. (**Note:** Sometimes, this V to IV progression can be replaced with ii to V, as seen in bar 9 of the next song, "Things Ain't What They Used to Be.") The *turnaround*, or last two bars of the structure, generally lands back on the I or V chord. As you can see in the last two bars of the next song, the turnaround can sometimes feature a quick I–VI–ii–V sequence, or similar cadences.

4/4 ||: I | I | I | I |

| IV | IV | I | I |

| V | IV | I | I :||

TOOLBOX

Dominant 7th Chords and the Blues

Very often, all the chords in a 12-bar blues progression are played as dominant 7th chords—that is part of what creates the blues flavor. For instance, in the key of D, the I, IV, and V chords would be D7, G7, and A7.

The 1942 jazz standard "Things Ain't What They Used to Be" is your first melody that follows the regular 12-bar blues progression. Just like chugging rhythms, the blues is usually played in the key of the draw chord.

The melody makes heavy use of the major pentatonic scale (see Lesson 19), applying it to almost every chord. In bars 9 and 10, the *blue note* C (♭7 in the key of D major) comes into play and adds to the blues feeling. You might be able to find a few harmonica recordings of this song online, including a jam by Mark Hummel & The Ultimate Harmonica Blowout, featuring Howard Levy, Jason Ricci, Son of Dave, and Corky Siegel. **Note:** A turnaround/ending "lick" is added to the end of this song, but it includes several bent notes. You can skip the lick for now, but after you've learned how to bend, come back and check it out!

THINGS AIN'T WHAT THEY USED TO BE

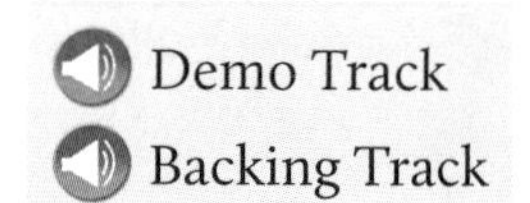

By Mercer Ellington

G Harmonica

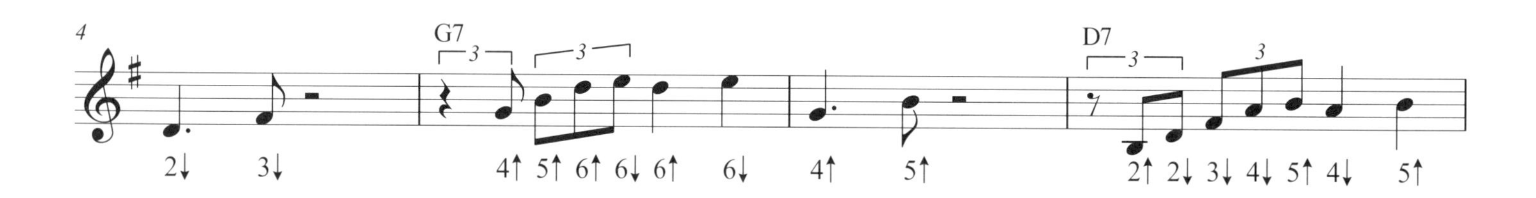

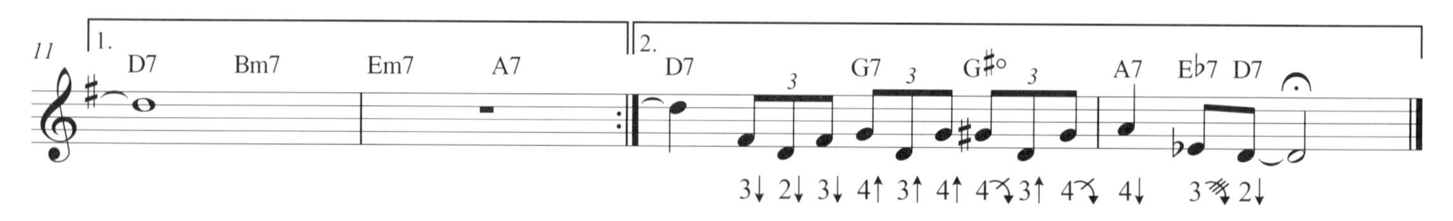

"Juke" is considered a blues harmonica standard. It was recorded by the Chicago bluesman Little Walter Jacobs in 1952, and the originally released recording was the first completed take. "Juke" is played as a swinging shuffle featuring a boogie-woogie guitar pattern. The original key is E. You can find the opening bars of the song notated below, which contain a repeated six-note phrase frequently played by horn players in the 1930s and '40s. This phrase uses the major pentatonic scale (see Lesson 19) in 2nd position. The many advanced tongue-blocked subtleties are excluded from the notation for now and recommended to be picked up by ear.

The harmonica playing in "Juke" is deep-toned and features long saxophone-like phrases. The much-studied head was used most notably in Louis Armstrong's 1941 recording "Leap Frog." The origin of the riff is still unclear.

JUKE

Words and Music by Walter Jacobs

A Harmonica

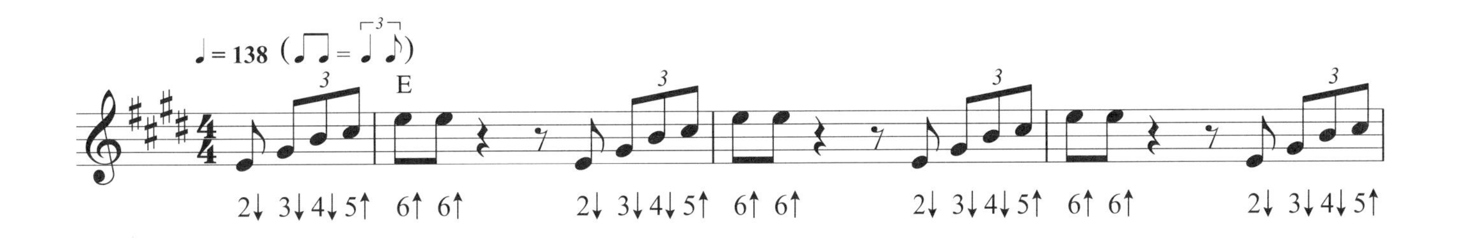

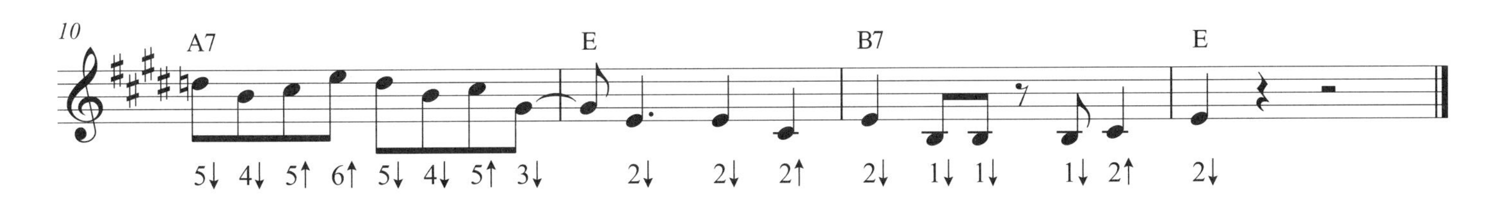

"You Gotta Move" is a rather unusual but wonderful blues melody for beginners. While 95% of all blues recordings rely on a 12-bar blues progression, this 8-bar blues features slightly jazzy harmonies and a memorable melody. The traditional African-American spiritual song has been recorded by a variety of gospel musicians and was popularized with blues adaptions by Fred McDowell and the Rolling Stones. The slow tempo of the song offers great possibilities in terms of expression. You can hear that I used tongue blocking to add quite a few *double stops* (two notes played at the same time) during the second chorus of the recording. Another very tasteful recording can be found on the 1993 album *Blues* by Cuban-Canadian harmonica player Carlos del Junco and Bill Kinnear. **Note:** Another turnaround/ending "lick" is added to the end of this song, and again, it includes several bent notes. Skip the lick for now but return to it once you've learned bending!

"I'm Your Hoochie Coochie Man" is another blues standard written by Willie Dixon and first recorded by Muddy Waters in 1954. The song makes novel use of a stop-time musical arrangement, which was soon absorbed into other styles of music. Again, it features Little Walter on an amplified harmonica playing the riff below. When Bo Diddley adapted it for "I'm a Man," it became one of the most recognizable musical phrases in the blues. This is a great song for practicing your tongue blocking technique with the notated double stops and octaves (see Lesson 14).

I'M YOUR HOOCHIE COOCHIE MAN

Words and Music by Willie Dixon

D Harmonica

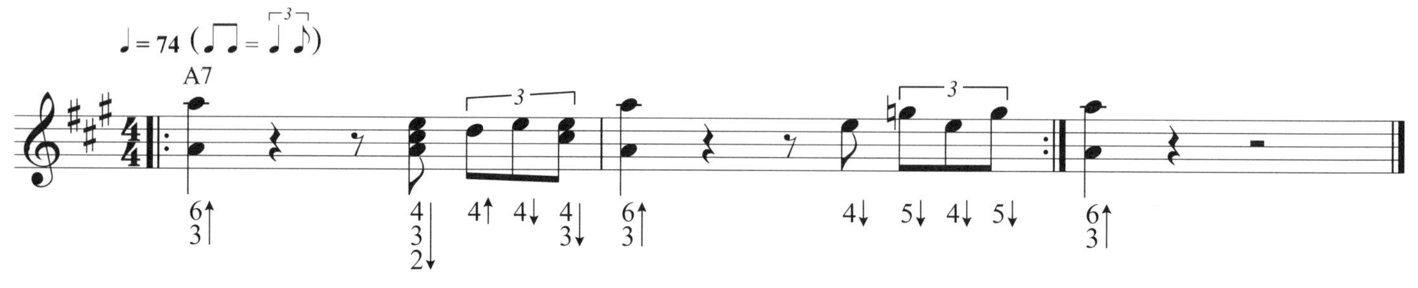

LESSON 13:
More Melodies in Other Positions

Let's move on to some pieces played in the key of the 1-hole draw (3rd position).

"Scarborough Fair" is a traditional English ballad. This incredibly atmospheric song uses the bright D Dorian mode. (**Note:** Modes are covered in Lesson 18.) In London in 1965, Paul Simon learned the song from Martin Carthy. His music duo Simon & Garfunkel released their version of "Scarborough Fair" one year later.

On the C harmonica, the second half of the melody is very high in pitch. In order to make it sound more pleasant, I tried to keep my hands relatively closed on the recording. The audio also includes a 7-bar introduction featuring the iconic guitar accompaniment.

"The Sound of Silence" (1965) is another beautiful melody in 3rd position and an original song by Simon & Garfunkel. Try to get used to the placement of the melody and listen to the original recording a few times. Locking in with the beat and playing very clear eighth notes is essential here.

THE SOUND OF SILENCE

Words and Music by Paul Simon

C Harmonica

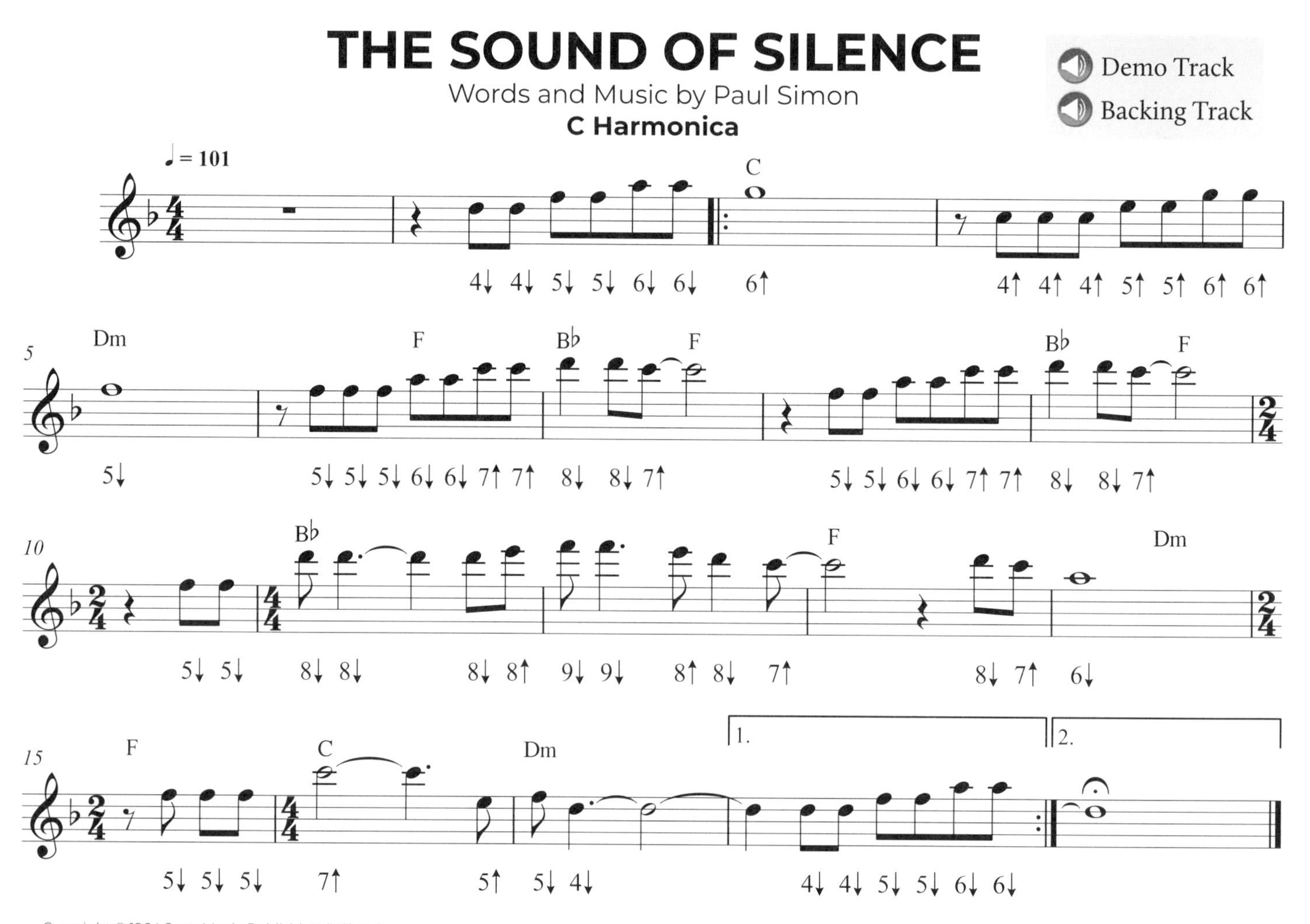

"Move On Up" is a song by Curtis Mayfield from his 1970 debut album *Curtis*. The up-tempo melody, combined with funk and soul elements, turned it into a soul classic over the years.

MOVE ON UP

Words and Music by Curtis Mayfield

A Harmonica

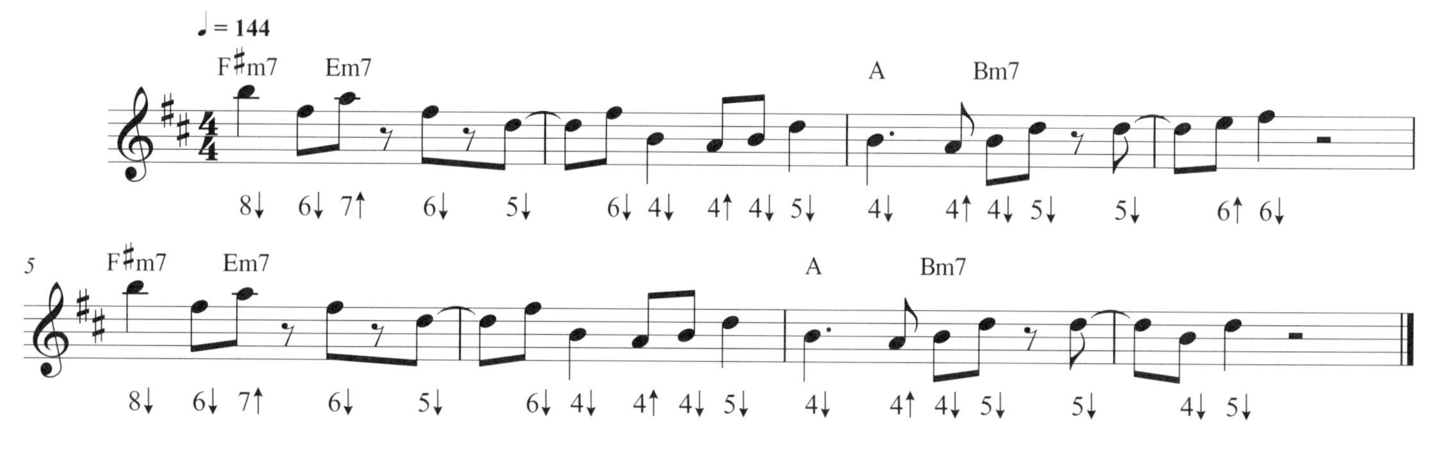

"All That She Wants" is a song by the Swedish group Ace of Base. The final version of the song evolved into a dark fusion of dub reggae with pop.

ALL THAT SHE WANTS

Words and Music by Buddha, Joker, Jenny Berggren and Malin Berggren

B Harmonica

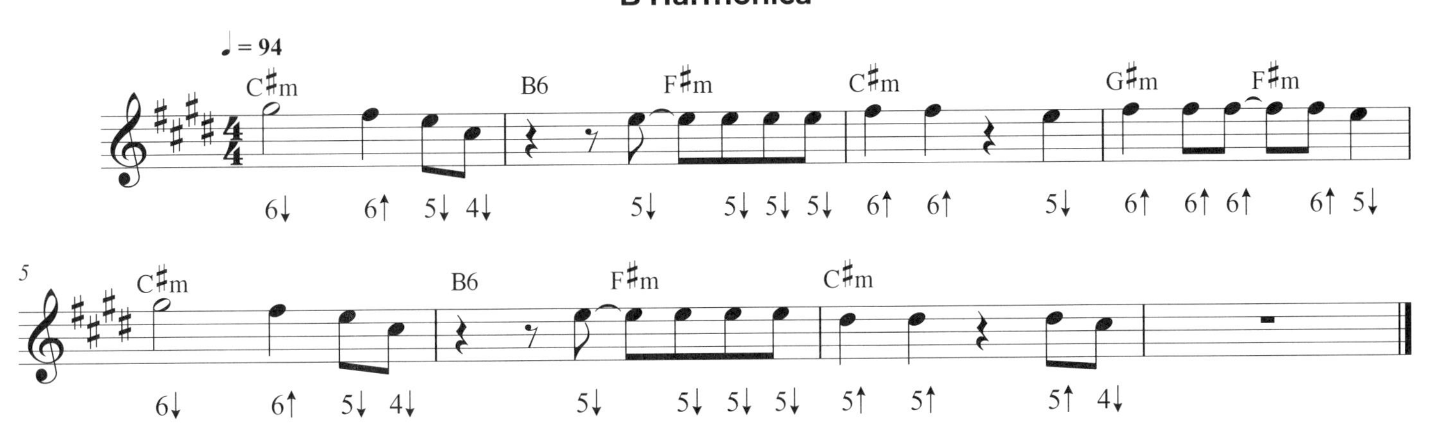

"Sunny" is a soul-jazz song written by Bobby Hebb in 1963. It is one of the most performed and recorded popular songs, with hundreds of versions released. I even uploaded an online harmonica lesson on the song in 2016. "Sunny" is still a wonderful piece to work on, and it will continue to benefit your phrasing and timing. Start the melody by saying "dah-dat" through hole-6 draw to highlight the distinct and defined character of it. The first half of the melody is more rhythmic and articulate, while the second half relies on more connected notes.

SUNNY

Words and Music by Bobby Hebb

G Harmonica

Demo Track
Backing Track

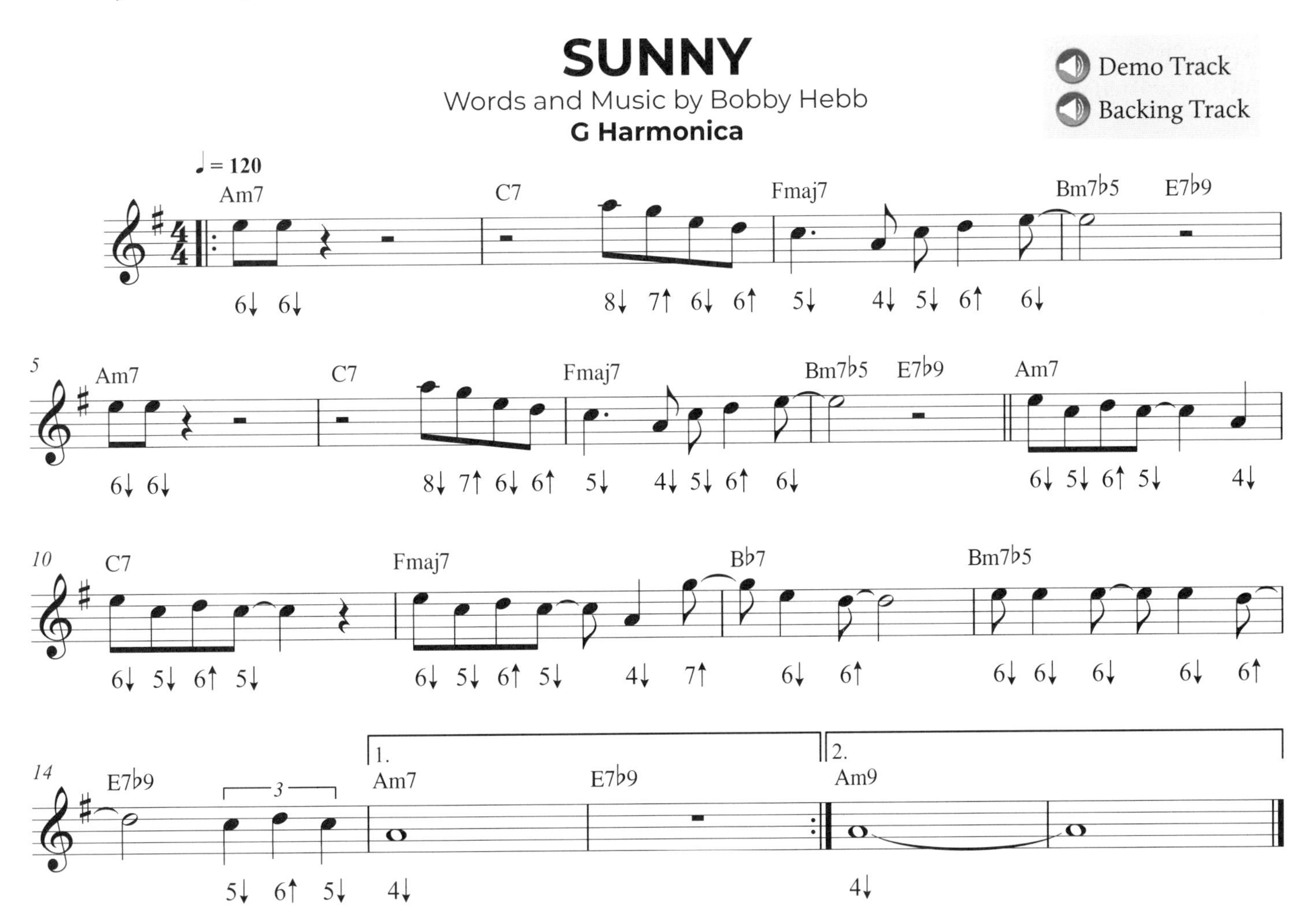

"Killing Me Softly with His Song" was composed by Charles Fox. It became a number-one hit for both Roberta Flack and the American hip-hop group Fugees. It is played in the key a minor 3rd below the key of the harmonica (4th position).

KILLING ME SOFTLY WITH HIS SONG

Words by Norman Gimbel
Music by Charles Fox
G Harmonica

"Amazing Grace" is a Christian hymn that was published in 1779. It is an immensely popular piece that lays out very well in the key a 4th above the key of the harmonica. In this case, the 5-hole draw is your tonic note. This arrangement is written in 9/8 meter, which has nine beats per measure with the eighth note receiving the beat.

AMAZING GRACE

Words by John Newton
Traditional American Melody
G Harmonica

LESSON 14:
Tongue Techniques

Let's take a closer look at tongue blocking and some of the techniques that can be done with this approach.

Octave Playing

Playing two notes an octave apart at the same time on the harmonica can be achieved with tongue blocking. For example, to play both the low and high C notes at the same time, you would need to blow on holes 1 and 4 simultaneously. This can be done by blocking holes 2 and 3 with your tongue.

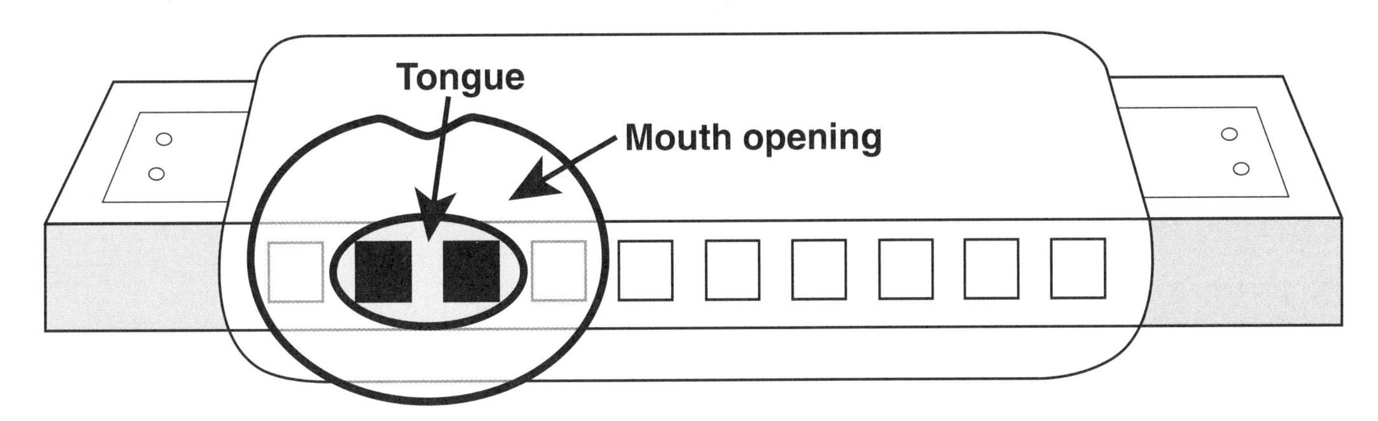

Similarly, if you draw on holes 1 and 4 while blocking 2 and 3, you can play two octave D notes at the same time.

Moving up to holes 2 and 5 while blocking holes 3 and 4 results in octave E notes when blown. However, notice that drawing on holes 2 and 5 gives you a different interval than an octave since you are now producing the notes G and F (technically, a minor 7th). This kind of interval can sound good in a bluesy context, as we'll explore later.

With this in mind, notice that some of the similar drawn note combinations will result in different intervals than an octave. Experiment with this to see what you can come up with!

Tongue Slapping

Using a tongue slap enables you to add a rhythmic element to a melody note, giving it more impact. In other words, it is a chordal *grace note* (or quick embellishment note with no distinct time value) right in front of the melody note. When done correctly, you should hear a quick chord right before the single note sounds. This technique is most frequently used in the blues context, giving melodies an almost jumpy feel.

Application of the tongue slap:

1. Start out by playing a chord with the melody note on the right (a higher note above the chord), for example, with holes 1, 2, and 3.
2. Now flick your tongue against the comb of the instrument, covering the two holes to the left of the hole that plays the melody note. In this example, only hole 3 will be left audible.

Depending on your embouchure and the number of holes that are part of the chord, your tongue might even cover three holes to the left of the hole that plays the melody note.

The tongue slap can also be used to accompany melodies with chords. Start out by playing a clean, tongue-blocked melody note, and then remove your tongue from the instrument to fill the upbeats with chordal material. This technique is most frequently used in the folk genre.

LESSON 15:
General Warm-up for Harmonica Players

This lesson is a general warm-up for harmonica players of all levels. It will help you get to know the instrument and the way to breathe better. At the same time, playing the exercises is a good way to make sure that all the holes are working properly, which is essential before a performance or recording.

Here are some quick reminders before working on the exercises:

- Keep your embouchure firm on the edges, and don't bite down on the top and bottom.
- Don't blow—breathe into the harmonica. Do the same for the inhale.
- The chambers of the harmonica are all separate, and the partitions between the chambers separate the notes.
- Breathe as smoothly as possible and let the harmonica separate the notes for you.

Warm-Up 1

Return to the simple chugging rhythms, and try to apply different techniques to play the blues shuffle:

Break up your breathing from your diaphragm.

Shuffle 1

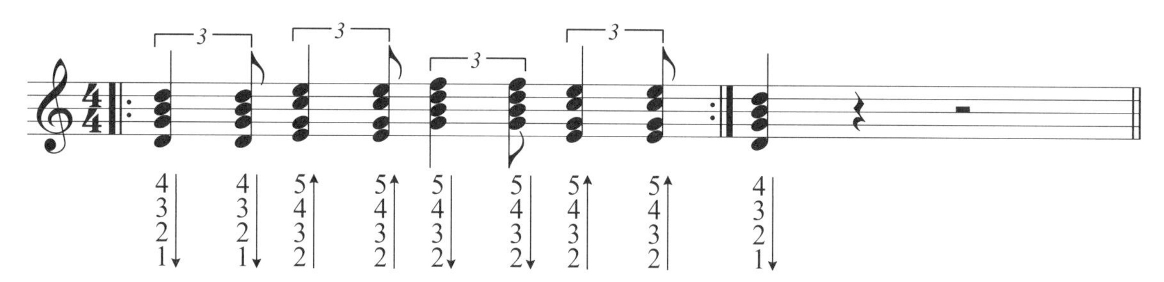

OR

Use your tongue to accent the shorter beat.

Shuffle 2

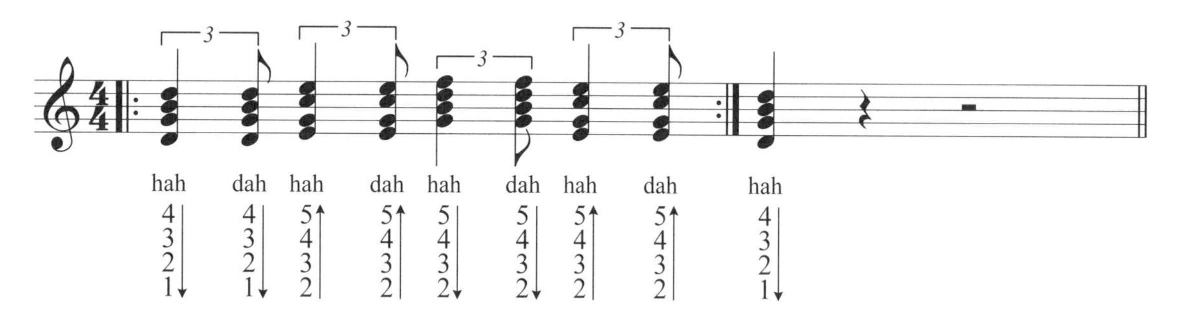

OR

Articulate both beats.

These next shuffle examples include some new tongue techniques to try out.

Shuffle 3 

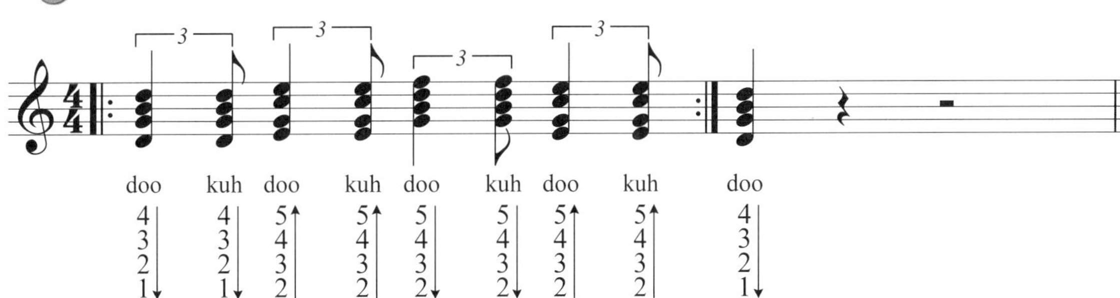

OR
Use tongue blocking.

Shuffle 4

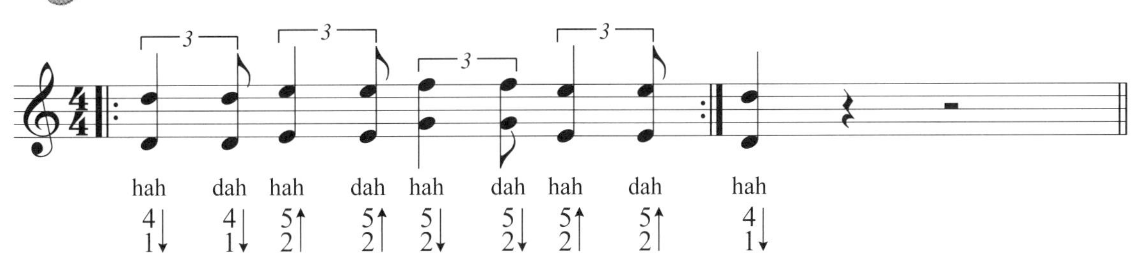

OR
Use tongue slaps.

Shuffle 5

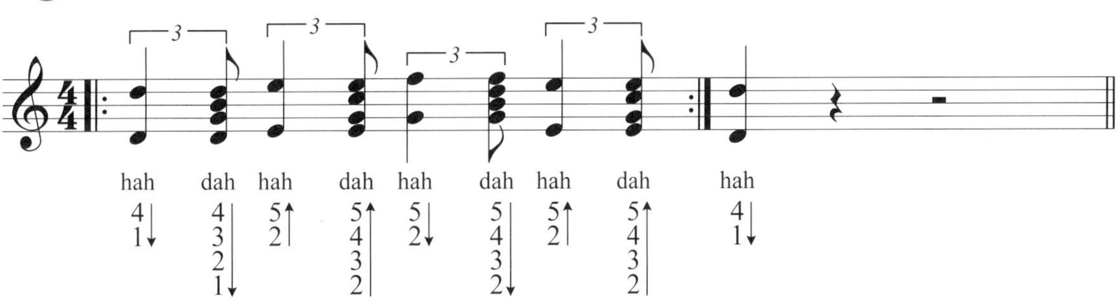

For now, the most important goal is to get air flowing.

Warm-Up 2

Next, you can play a simple scale in the key of C while keeping time. Try to tap your feet with the beat, and start to support the rhythm by accenting some of the notes. Start out by accenting every two notes, then every third note, in order to build up speed.

> Not all notes are equally important. Accenting notes is the foundation for developing facility and speed on the instrument.

Warm-Up 3

Return to the Leapfrog exercise in Lesson 8, playing the notes of the scale in the order of 1st–3rd, 2nd–4th, etc. Accenting every other note (starting with the first) will lay out the scale.

Continue on with four-note groups by going up four notes in the scale from every scale degree.

Warm-Up 4: Drum Rudiments

Drum rudiments organize the strokes of a drummer's hand and can be applied to the harmonica, too. The simplest drum rudiment is the *double-stroke roll*. Right–right–left–left (RLLL) could be a blow–blow–draw–draw pattern on the harmonica. Letting the drumstick bounce corresponds to sliding up or down to the adjacent note on the same breathing direction. Don't think about the notes themselves since rudiments are strictly organizing the breath into patterns. Try to apply the exercise over the whole range of the instrument and invert it, too.

Double-Stroke Roll

The *triple-stroke roll* (RRRLLL) is even easier on the harmonica, while the *paradiddle* (RLRR LRLL) creates some very interesting melodic patterns. Accent the first note of each group of four and support your breath from the diaphragm to build up speed.

Triple-Stroke Roll

Paradiddle

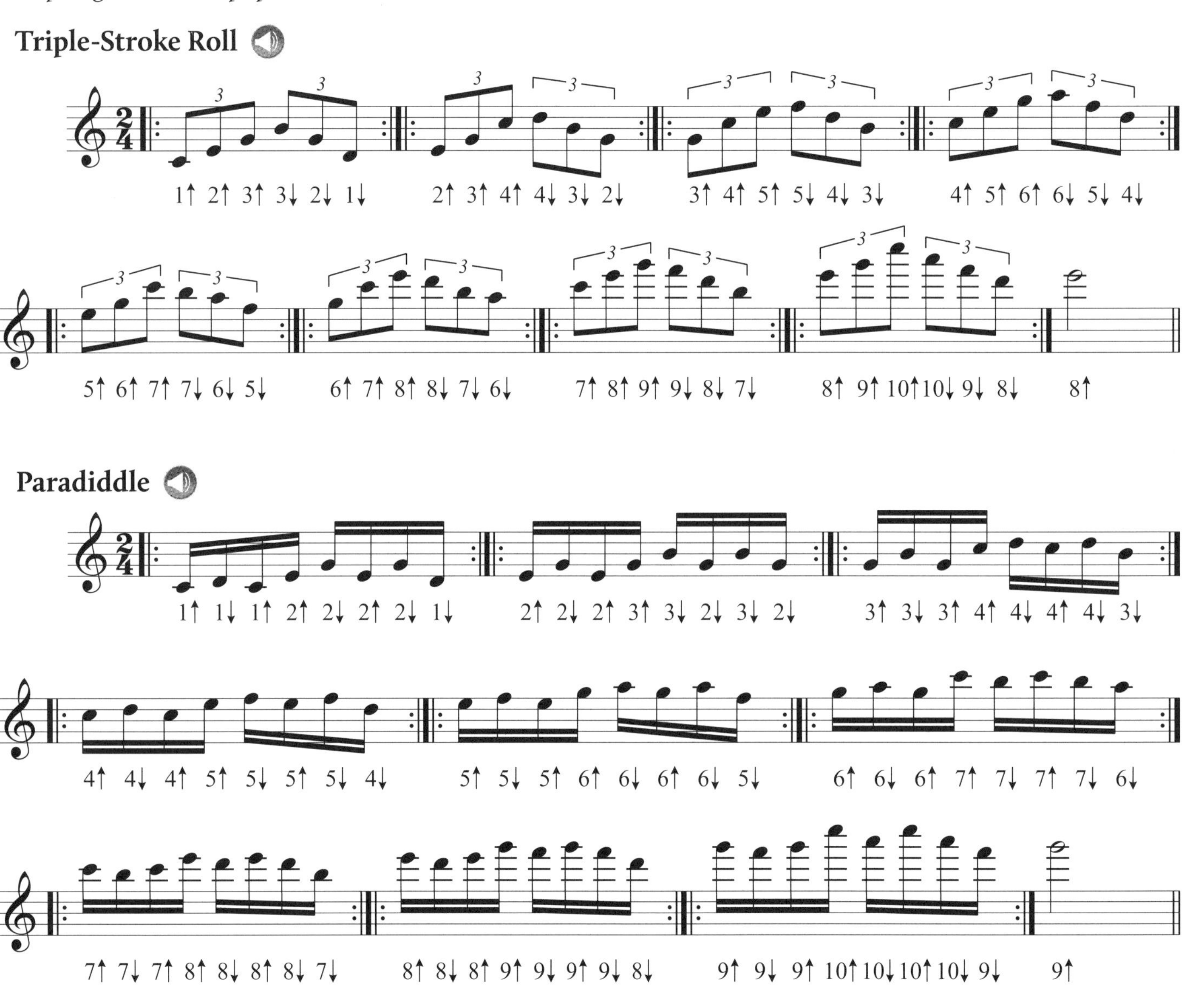

LESSON 16:
Bending

So far, you have learned to play up to seven different notes and 19 different pitches on the harmonica. However, one of the most characteristic sounds of the blues harp is still missing: notes produced by *bending*. Bending is a very expressive and vocal-sounding technique that allows you to create eight additional notes between holes 1 and 6. When you first try to bend notes, you will have difficulties. In fact, improving your bending technique can be a lifelong journey. Intonating bent notes and seamlessly using them in your music might even be harder than intonation on a violin. However, persistence will definitely help you to make your harmonica cry and moan very soon. Despite all the theoretical aspects behind the technique, your ear can sometimes be the best guide for hitting the desired note. Playing the harmonica is still a feel.

As mentioned earlier, the harmonica reeds were never meant to be bendable. The discovery of the additional notes is just a happy little accident. Bending changes the pitch of a note, making it vibrate slower for a lower note or faster for a higher note.

Before we dive into the invisible process of bending, I would like to encourage you to experiment with many different tongue positions. Sometimes this can provide you with first results even earlier. You can start by whistling a random note; after doing it the first time, alter your airflow and whistle the note again. You will notice that the pitch of your whistle just changed. With this concept, you will soon be able to make your draw and blow reeds vibrate simultaneously on certain holes.

Of course, it is essential to get an idea of what's going on inside your mouth, and experimenting with breathing and vocal noises might get you closer to your goal faster than expected.

Following is an illustration of possible tongue positions and vowels in phonetic spelling for you to think about while playing a bend. I adapted the graphic from my very first online harmonica teacher Ralf Fuckardt. It is important to keep in mind that we want to redirect our airflow to the blow note. In order to do so, you usually raise some part of your tongue to a place along the contour of the roof of your mouth. Depending on the pitch of the note, the size of your oral cavity has to be adjusted. A tongue raised back in the mouth creates a big space and can be applied to low notes. A tongue raised forward in the mouth creates a small space and can be applied to high notes.

To bend a note, you have to narrow the airflow between your tongue and your palate.

The illustration also gives you an overview of the formerly missing notes that you can now try to produce. The eight additional pitches will not only enable you to play many melodies in the lower octave of the instrument, but they also offer you endless means of expression. Blues and rock playing almost doesn't exist without the bending technique.

Bending allows you to access half-step increments below your regular draw notes.

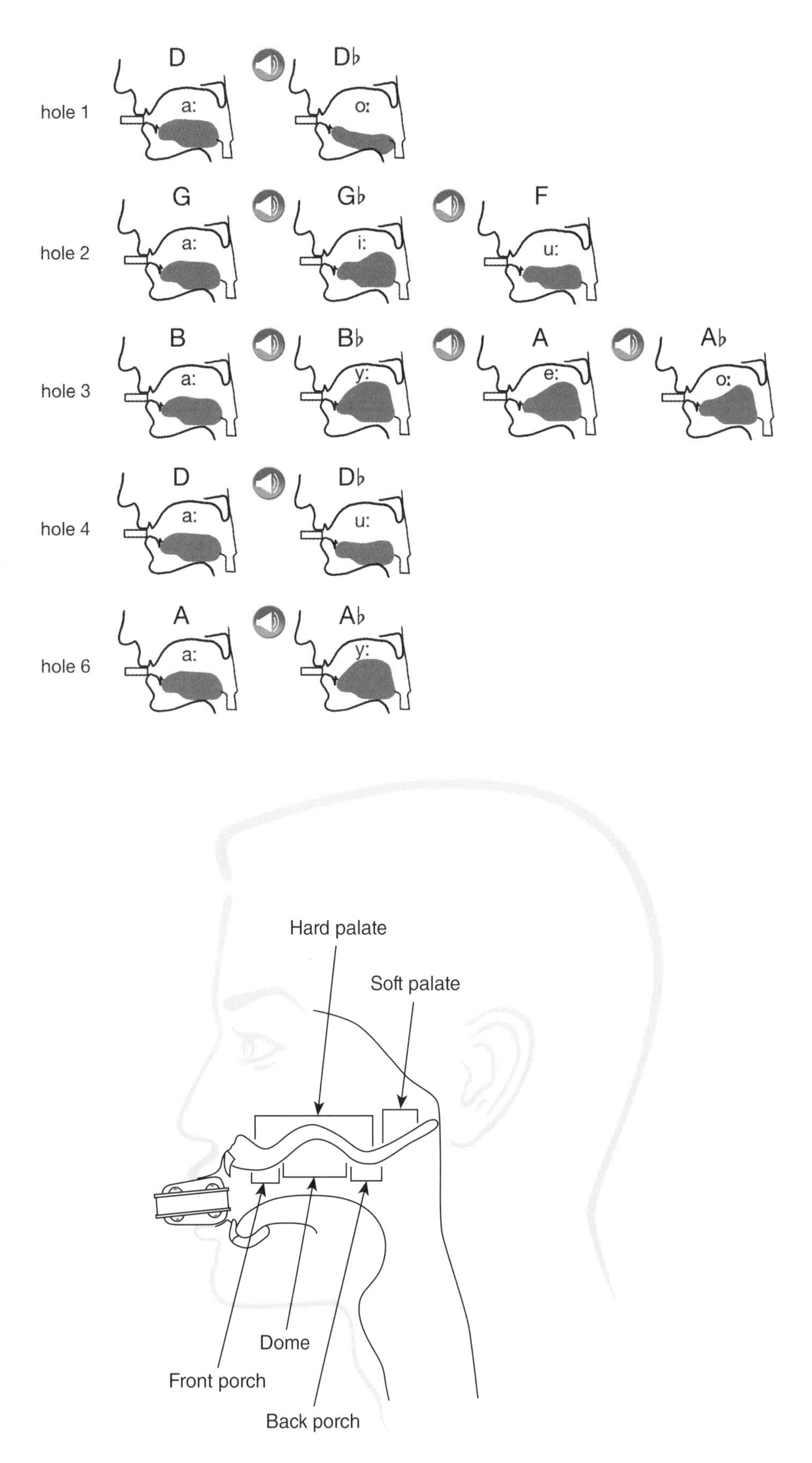

You can start out practicing your bending technique on hole 1. While inhaling, try to expand the opening of your throat. Lower your tongue toward the base of your mouth at the same time. It is recommendable to stay relaxed while maintaining a regular airflow. This will ensure that you are using the right technique to change the pitch of the note.

It is helpful to have an idea of the note in your mind and maybe even be able to sing it using the vowels. Try to sing the note D using the corresponding vowel and lower the pitch as slowly as possible while transitioning into the vowel that corresponds to the note D♭. It is always helpful to work with a reference note. This could be a tuned guitar, a piano, or even an app on your phone.

I like to work with drones played by cellos or a tanpura, which is an Indian instrument. The D♭ drone in the accompanying audio (shown later in this lesson) gives you the opportunity to practice the lowest playable bends on your harmonica. The low D♭ should sound just like the D♭ drone. To go a step further, D♭, F, and A♭ on holes 1–6 form the D♭ major triad, which will sound very consonant when played along with the drone. The D♭ major triad consists of a 1-draw half-step bend, 2-draw whole-step bend, 3-draw one-and-a-half-step bend, 4-draw half-step bend, 5-hole draw, and 6-draw half-step bend.

Keep in mind that holes 2 and 3 offer two or more pitches to play with. Generally, the more you lower your tongue, the lower the pitch of the note you'll produce. Gaining more and more control over these two holes can be a real challenge. However, holes 2 and 3 contain the most expressive notes on the harmonica.

Don't give up if you struggle with the bending technique at first. Mastering all these pitches can be a lifelong journey; but at the same time, the new means of expression are very rewarding. You are in complete control over all imaginable parameters as a player. Being extremely close to the source of sound production will feel really good and motivating. It allows you to create your own sound, your individual voice.

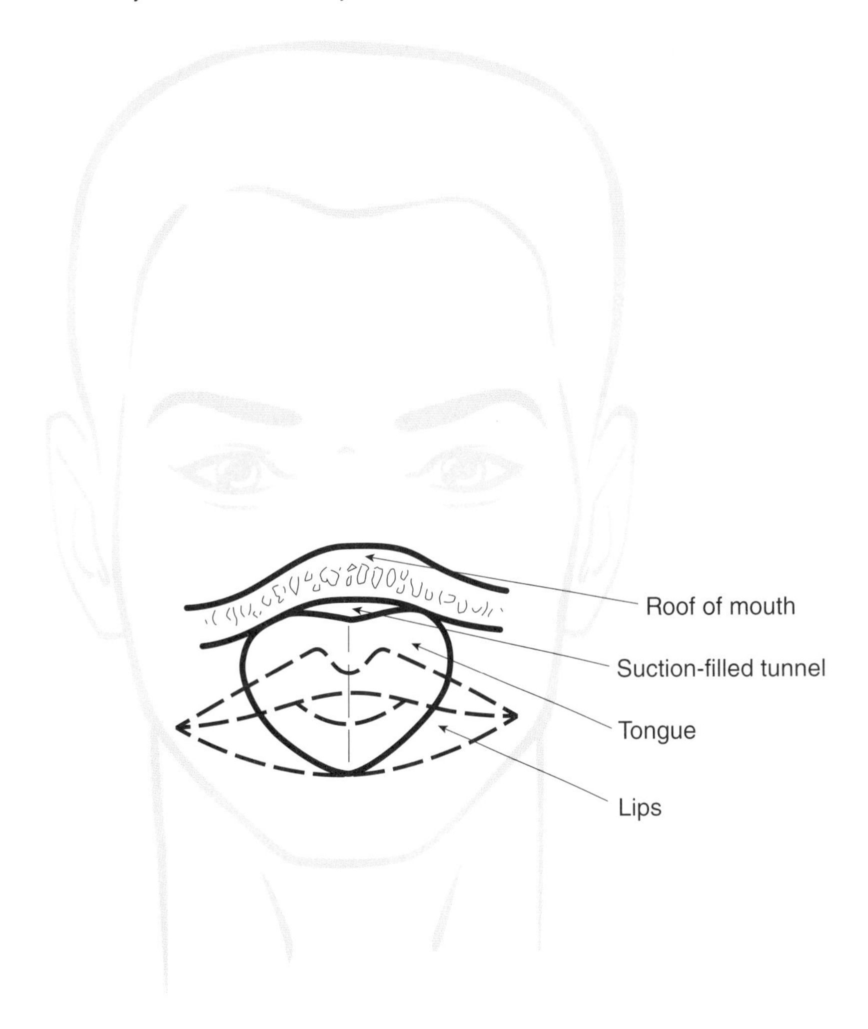

The 3-Hole Draw

The bends on hole 3 are probably the hardest notes to play on the diatonic harmonica. However, step by step, they will develop into the most expressive notes on the instrument. They can be important for many different musical styles, so let's give them a little more attention.

You can play a G by blowing on hole 3 and a B by drawing on hole 3. With that said, hole 3 offers the biggest distance between the blow note and the draw note on the harmonica. There are four half steps in between G and B.

You can produce the missing notes on hole 3 by bending down the B to B♭ to A to A♭. Before you start hitting these notes individually, it is important to explore the whole range of the bend.

For this first exercise, you'll start on a 3-hole draw and then try to bend the note down as slowly as possible in linear motion. Try to maintain a consistent volume and timbre (tone) over the whole range.

> The lowest note you can produce on a bent hole-3 draw is even a little lower than A♭!

3-Hole Bend: The Whole Range

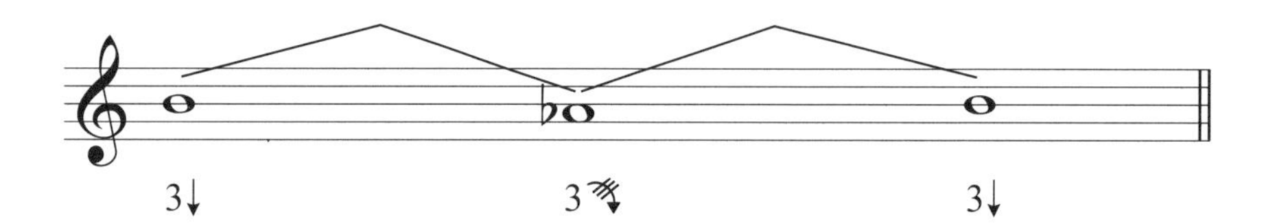

In the second step, start out on B again. This time you want to bend it down as slowly as possible until you reach the note you want to reach—the target note.

Try to hold on the target note for a long time while keeping the timbre consistent.

3-Hole Bend: Target Note

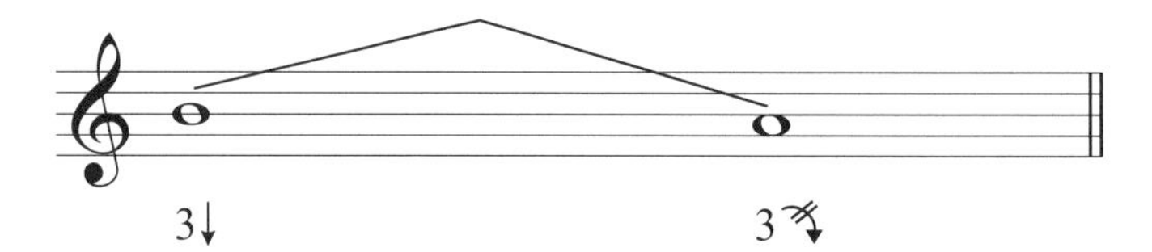

If you feel comfortable with this exercise, you can try to stop the airflow on the target note and then try to play the note again while keeping your embouchure the same. The supreme discipline would be to take the harmonica out of your mouth in between.

3-Hole Bend: Target-Note Articulation

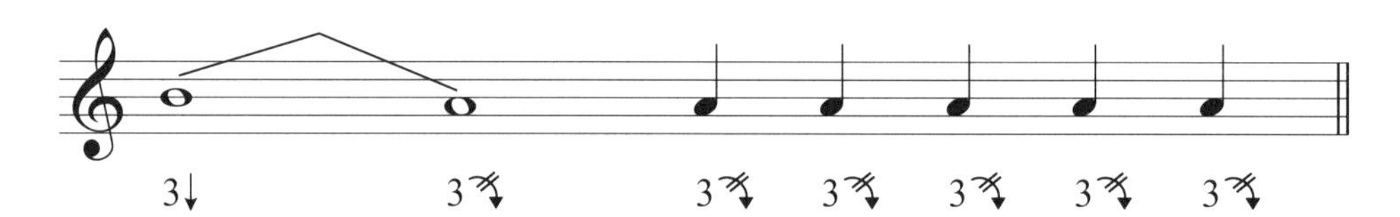

The next step is to incorporate these notes into your playing. The following exercise is a little more musical. It takes advantage of the fact that there are two ways to play a G note on the C harmonica.

3-Hole Bend: Drone Exercise

The great thing about this sequence is that you will always hear your 3-hole-draw note in reference to the G, which is great for your ear and also good for your intonation.

In general, it is always helpful to incorporate ear training when practicing your bends. Having access to a reference note like in these audio examples can help a lot. However, any other tuned instrument can be your reference. I like to work with drone backing tracks that you can find in the accompanying audio material or online in the remaining keys. Pick the one that corresponds to the note of the bend you want to practice.

Bending to Drone Track Example

D♭ Drone Track

The following two diagrams show the complete layout of the C harmonica. You can always refer to them to find all the notes of the chromatic scale and the techniques used to create them.

All the Notes on the C Harmonica

Overblows (holes 1–6) / Blow bends (holes 8–10)

										B♭
	E♭			E♭	G♭/F♯	B♭		E♭	G♭/F♯	B
Blow	C	E	G	C	E	G	C	E	G	C
Hole	1	2	3	4	5	6	7	8	9	10
Draw	D	G	B	D	F	A	B	D	F	A
	D♭	G♭/F♯	B♭	D♭		A♭	D♭		A♭	D♭
		F	A							
			A♭							

Draw bends (holes 1–6) / Overdraws (holes 7–10)

Techniques for Playing All C Harmonica Notes

Overblows (holes 1–6) / Blow bends (holes 8–10)

										10⤴⤴
	1⤴°			4⤴°	5⤴°	6⤴°		8⤴	9⤴	10⤴
Blow	1↑	2↑	3↑	4↑	5↑	6↑	7↑	8↑	9↑	10↑
Hole	1	2	3	4	5	6	7	8	9	10
Draw	1↓	2↓	3↓	4↓	5↓	6↓	7↓	8↓	9↓	10↓
	1⤵	2⤵	3⤵	4⤵		6⤵	7⤵°		9⤵°	10⤵°
		2⤵⤵	3⤵⤵							
			3⤵⤵⤵							

Draw bends (holes 1–6) / Overdraws (holes 7–10)

LESSON 17:

Playing One Harp in Many Keys

A *position* is the relationship between the key of the harp and the key of the tune you play on it. Most diatonic harmonica players play more than one key of harp and play each harp in more than one key. Although harmonicas are tuned to major scales (exceptions and special orders notwithstanding), you can play other scales on them. Every position has its own unique possibilities, and thinking about them enables you to transfer what you know on a harp in one key to a harp in any other key. The blow-draw patterns remain the same, even though all note names will be different. You don't need to know what the note names are; you just need to be familiar with the sequence of moves that produces the desired sound.

Positions are numbered 1 through 12. Each time you count up five scale steps (a *5th*) starting from the tonic, or the key of the harp, you reach the next position. 1st position is when you play in the key of the blow chord that the harmonica is tuned to; for example, playing the C harp in the key of C. However, the draw chord is another great starting point for playing, and it is called 2nd position. 2nd position is five scale steps up from the C blow chord, and it is G.

The *circle of 5ths* can help you figure out the relationship between the key of the harp, the key of the tune, and the position. The following diagram shows you the different positions on a C harmonica.

Circle of 5ths and Positions on C Harmonica

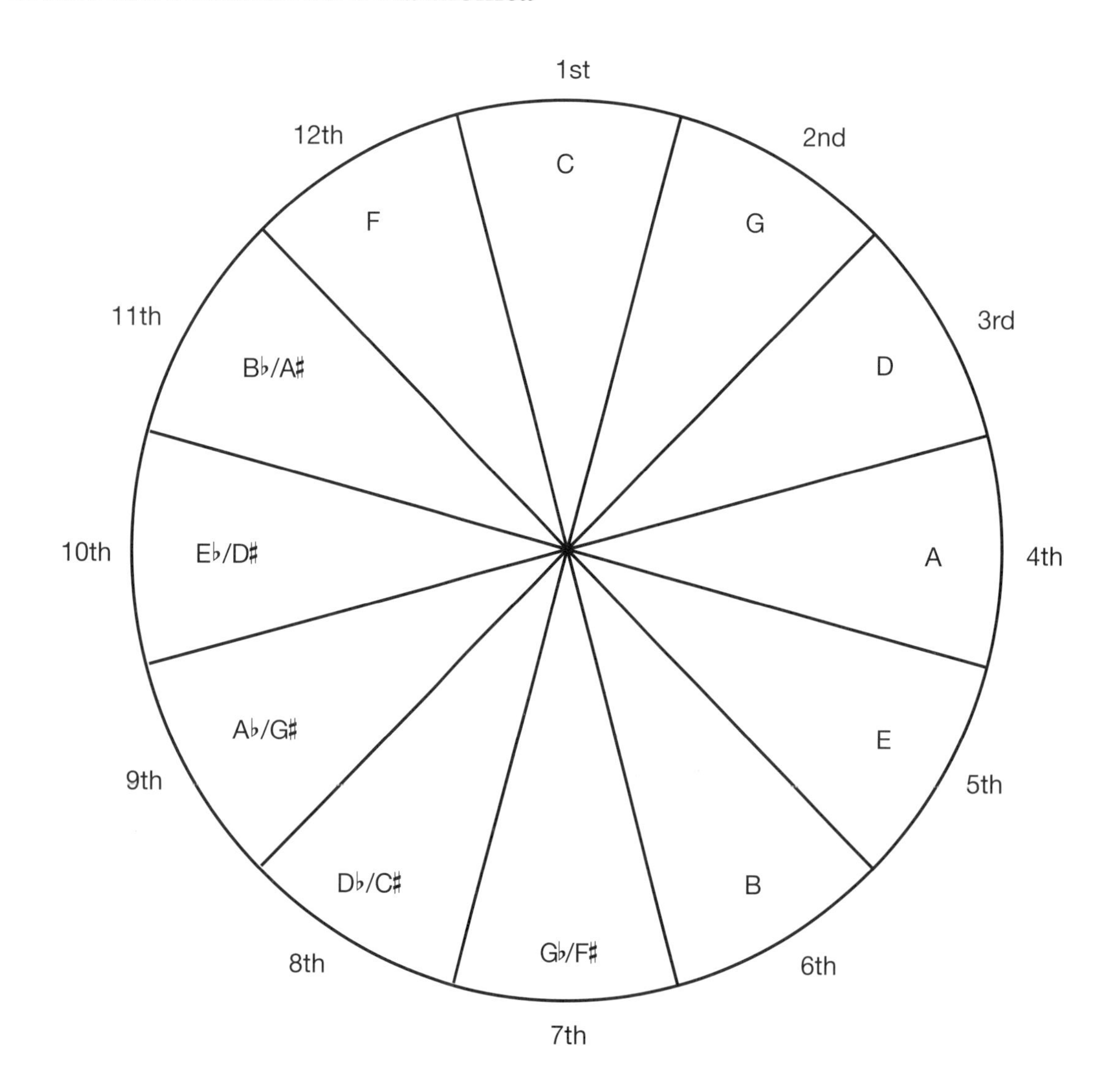

LESSON 18:
Modes of the C Major Scale

What is a *mode*?

A mode is a type of scale. The modern modes consist of seven scales that relate to the familiar major and minor scales. In the next examples, you will see that each mode has the same set of notes as the major scale, but with different starting and ending points.

Each mode has characteristic intervals and chords that give it its distinct sound.

- *Ionian* is another name for our modern major scale, and its associated sound is a suspended chord—created by the ♮4—that makes all of the scale notes sound consonant, or pleasing to the ear. A possible chord vamp would be Cmaj7 to Fmaj7.
- *Dorian* is a minor scale with a ♮6 and is commonly used in jazz. (**Note:** The minor scale being referred to here is actually the Aeolian mode discussed below.) As one of the brightest minor scales, you will also encounter it in folk music (e.g., "Scarborough Fair"). A possible chord vamp would be Dm7 to G7.
- *Phrygian* is a minor scale with a ♭2, which gives it its Middle Eastern flavor. It's one of the darkest minor scales, and a possible chord vamp would be Em7 to Fmaj7.
- *Lydian* is a major scale with a ♯4, and it is the brightest major scale. It actually originates from stacking up 5ths and is widely used in film music. A possible chord vamp would be Fmaj7 to G7.
- *Mixolydian* is a major scale with a ♭7, which gives it its bluesy color. A possible chord vamp would be G7 to F.
- *Aeolian* is the *natural minor scale*, and its characteristic note is the ♭6. A possible chord vamp would be Am7 to Fmaj7.
- *Locrian* is a minor scale with a ♭2 and ♭5. It sounds very dark and unstable because of the missing perfect 5th. However, it is commonly used on the 2nd scale degree in a minor ii°–V–i progression.

In the audio, you will hear each basic mode played to a drone track and then some brief improvising using the notes of the mode. There is also a drone track for each mode, so you can practice the mode, improvise, and really get the sound of each mode in your ear.

> **TOOLBOX**
>
> **Blow Bends**
> In addition to the draw bends you've learned on holes 1–6, there are also some more challenging bends that can be achieved on holes 8–10, called *blow bends*. All the aforementioned techniques for draw bends apply to blow bends, only much farther toward the front of your mouth. A couple of the following scales include a blow bend on hole 10 to try out, but feel free to skip it for now if it's too difficult!

C Ionian (major)

C Drone

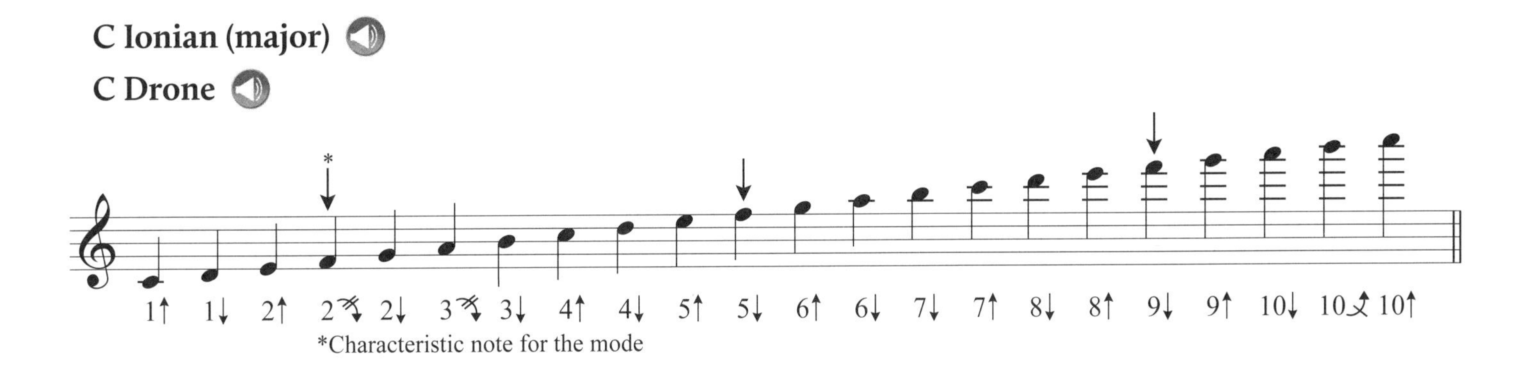

*Characteristic note for the mode

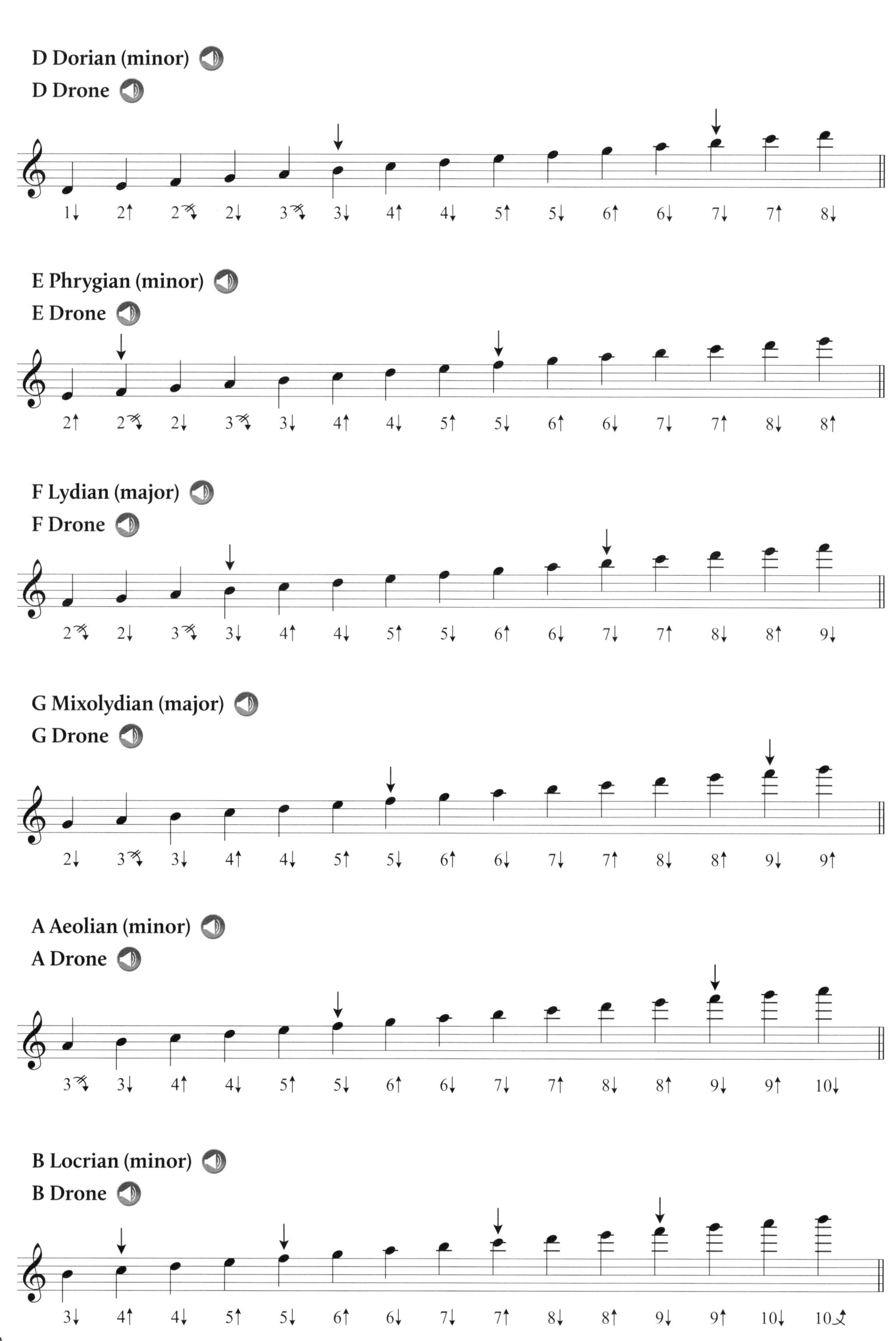
D Dorian (minor)
D Drone
E Phrygian (minor)
E Drone
F Lydian (major)
F Drone
G Mixolydian (major)
G Drone
A Aeolian (minor)
A Drone
B Locrian (minor)
B Drone

LESSON 19:

Pentatonic Scales

The *pentatonic scale*, which has five notes, is a very common scale used in many types of music. When compared to the major scale, the notes of the *major pentatonic* are 1–2–3–5–6. The notes of the *minor pentatonic* are 1–♭3–4–5–♭7. The following examples show the six easiest pentatonic scales to play on the diatonic harmonica, and they are in the six most useful keys. Use the C harmonica for these. If you discover a new song and want to improvise or play along with it on the harmonica, you can now refer to these options.

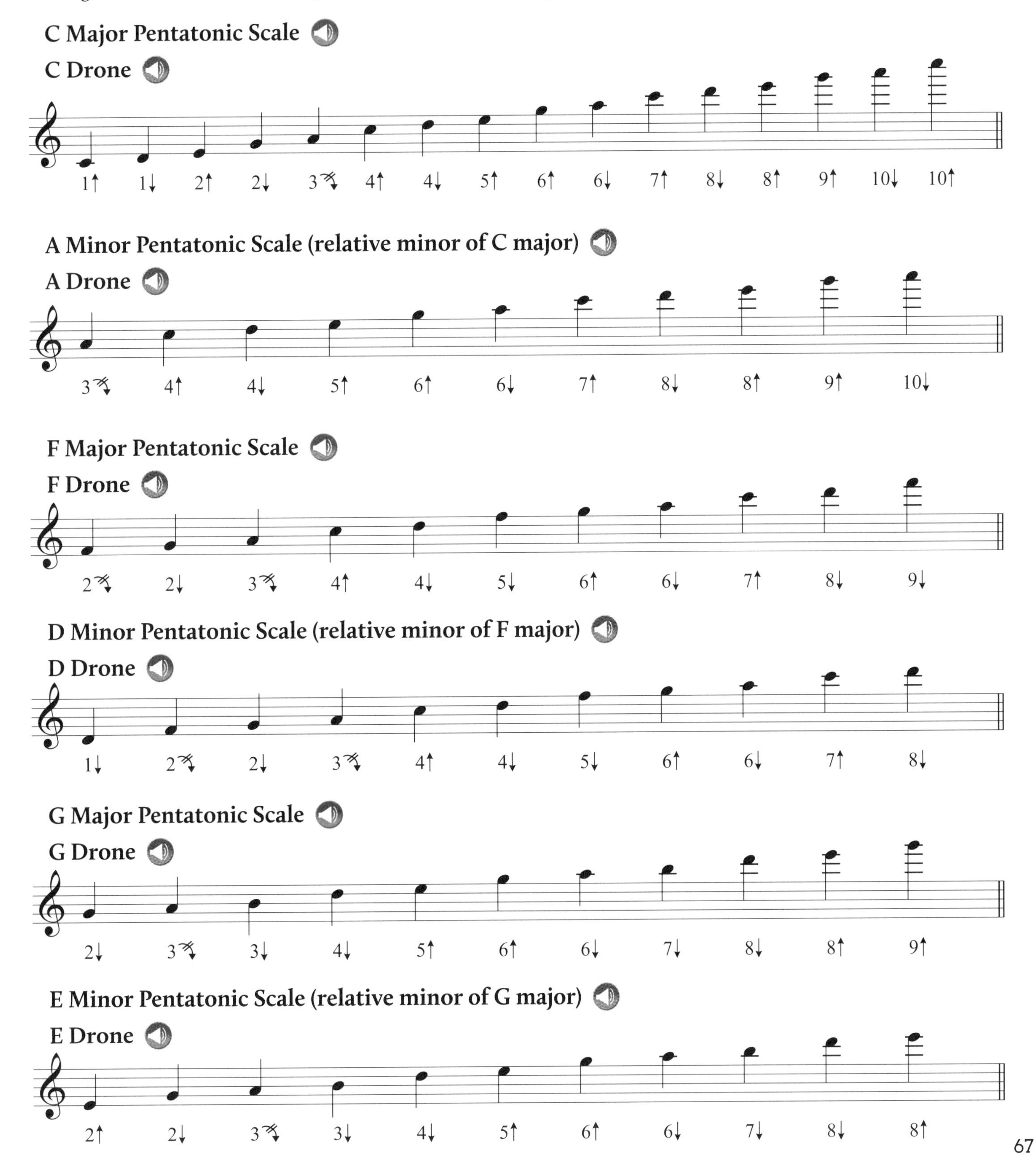

LESSON 20:
Melodies with Bends

"My Heart Will Go On" is a song recorded by Canadian singer Celine Dion. The song serves as the main soundtrack to James Cameron's blockbuster film *Titanic*. Listening to the recording, you will probably notice the comparably warm tone of the harmonica; you can achieve this by using your hands to dampen the overtones of this high-pitched melody. Also, the goal is to connect the notes as much as possible by making the volume of the notes swell.

MY HEART WILL GO ON

from the Paramount and Twentieth Century Fox Motion Picture TITANIC

Music by James Horner
Lyric by Will Jennings
C Harmonica

"Imagine" is a song by English rock musician John Lennon from his 1971 album of the same name. The lyrics encourage listeners to imagine a world of peace, without borders separating nations, without religion, and without materialism. You can listen to a harmonica recording of the song on Reinberg's album *Old Friend*. To play the G note, try to use 3-hole blow instead of 2-hole draw. The transition between E and G on two adjacent blow notes sounds more natural than a change of breathing directions.

"Gonna Fly Now," also known as "Rocky Theme," is the theme song from the movie *Rocky*, and it was composed by Bill Conti. The song is often played at sporting events, especially in Philadelphia. Playing the melody on the harmonica is great fun, and it can help you perfect your articulation on the instrument.

GONNA FLY NOW

Theme from ROCKY

By Bill Conti, Ayn Robbins and Carol Connors

C Harmonica

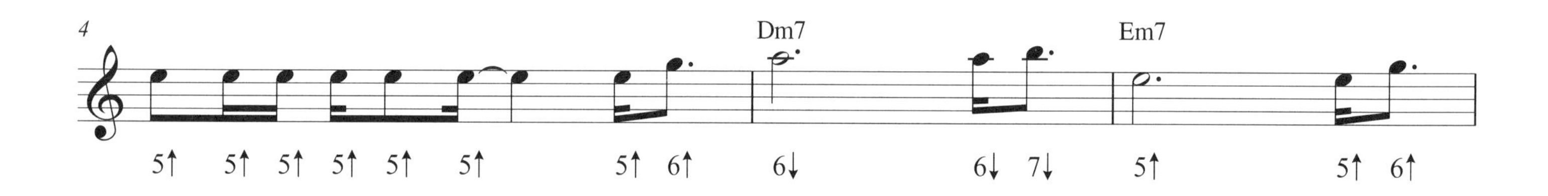

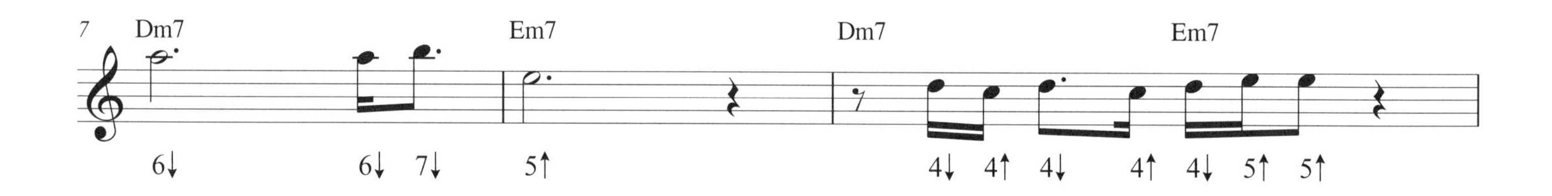

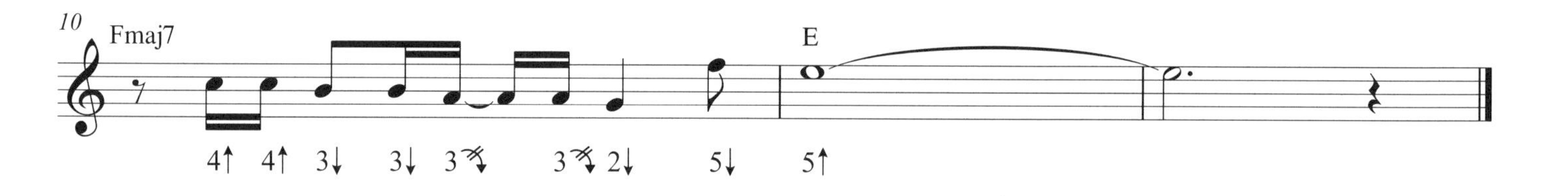

"Heart of Gold" is the only U.S. number-one single by Canadian singer-songwriter Neil Young. The song is one of a series of soft acoustic pieces that were written partly as a result of a back injury.

The harmonica is played during the three instrumental portions, including the introduction of the song. Neil Young uses a 3-hole blow instead of a 2-hole draw to play the note G.

HEART OF GOLD

Words and Music by Neil Young

G Harmonica

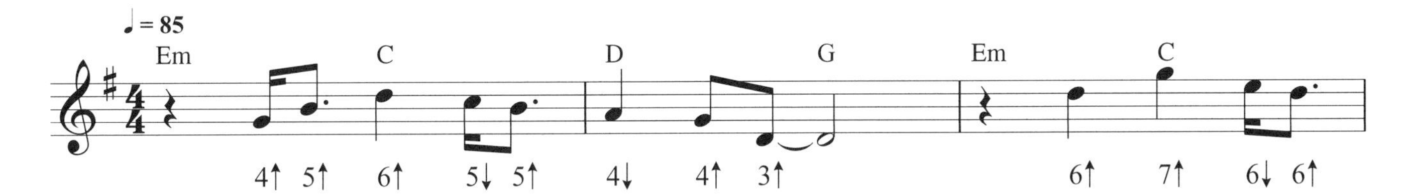

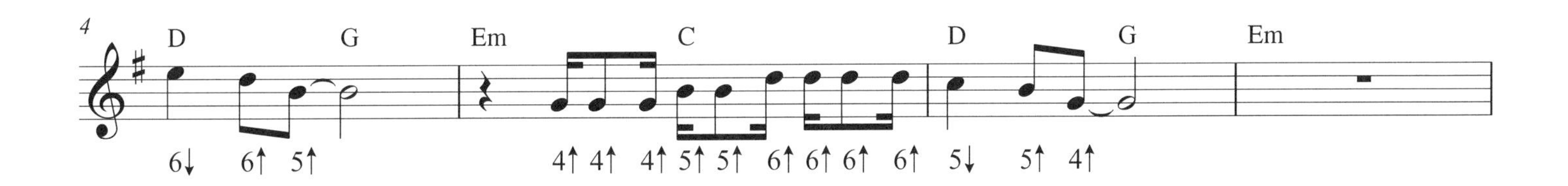

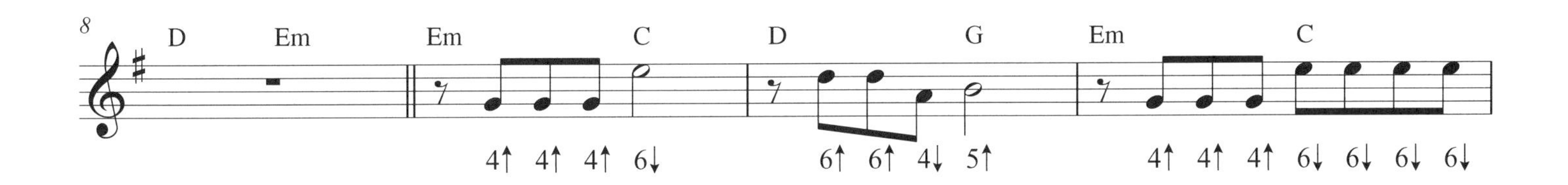

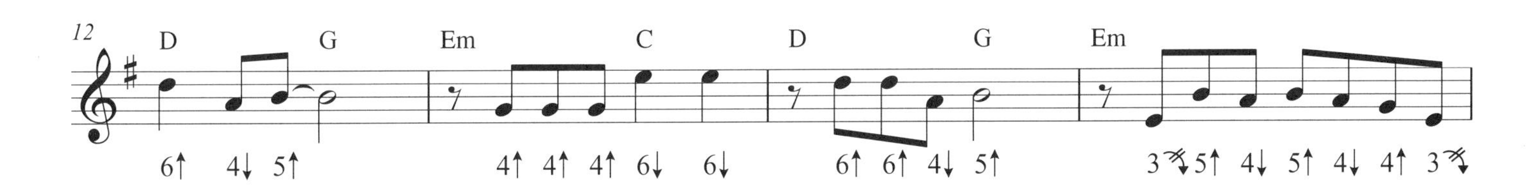

"There Must Be an Angel (Playing with My Heart)" is a song by the British musical duo Eurythmics, and it features a harmonica solo by American musician Stevie Wonder. Try to emulate Stevie Wonder's chromatic harmonica sound. Also, try to play along with the original recording, focusing on clear articulation during the chorus.

THERE MUST BE AN ANGEL (PLAYING WITH MY HEART)

Words and Music by Annie Lennox and David Stewart

C Harmonica

"Mary's Little Boy Child" is a 1956 Christmas song written by Jester Hairston. It is widely performed as a Christmas carol but can also be reinterpreted in many other musical styles. Playing it with a calypso feel creates new rhythmic possibilities and a wonderful playground for improvisations.

MARY'S LITTLE BOY CHILD

Words and Music by Jester Hairston

B♭ Harmonica

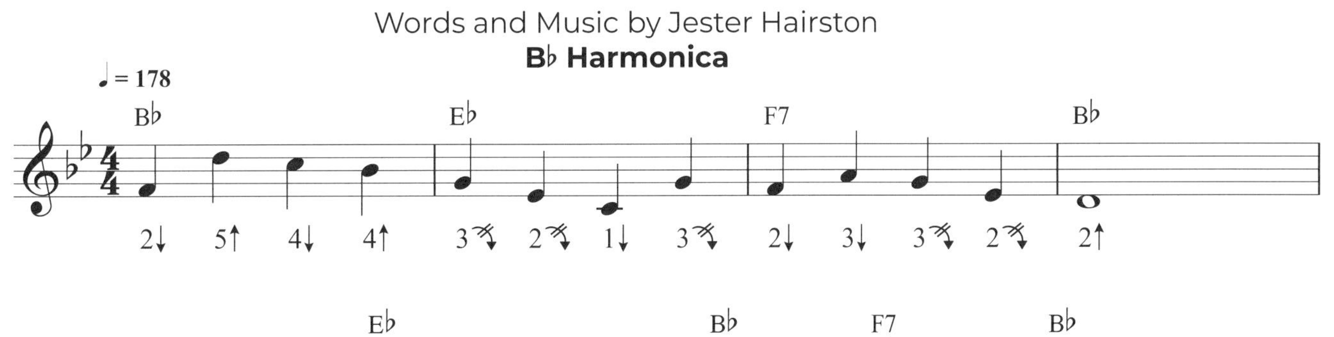

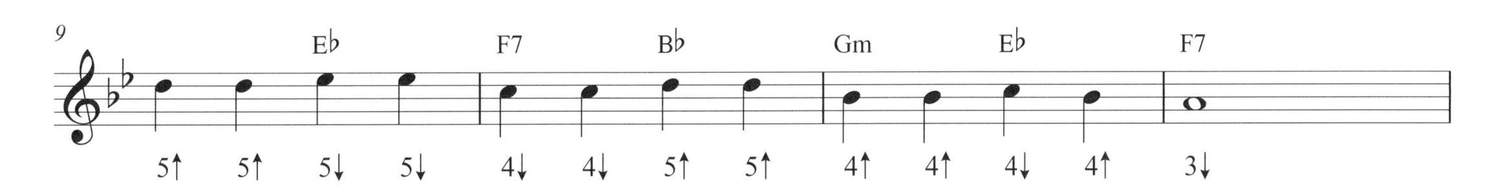

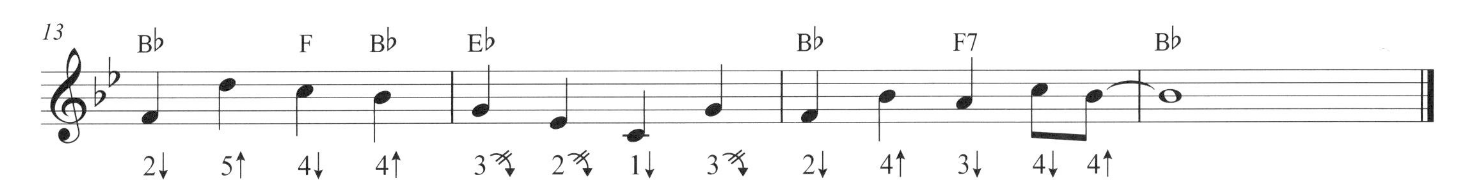

"Auld Lang Syne" is a popular song, particularly in the English-speaking world. Traditionally, it is sung to bid farewell to the old year at the stroke of midnight on New Year's Eve. I remember discovering a recording of harmonica virtuoso Jason Ricci performing the melody amplified and in 2nd position. The melody consists of notes from the major pentatonic scale exclusively.

AULD LANG SYNE

Words by Robert Burns
Traditional Scottish Melody
C Harmonica

♩ = 76

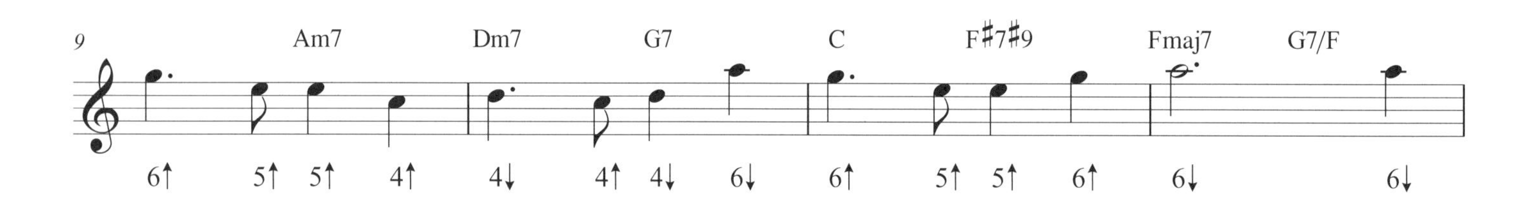

"The Morning Star" is a traditional Irish melody that I learned from Brendan Power's book *Play Irish Music on the Blues Harp.* Brendan Power is a New Zealand harmonica player, composer, and inventor who currently lives in Britain. Many of his online videos are very inspirational and could also give you ideas on how to incorporate ornaments and decorations into Irish music. Additionally, his recordings with Tim Eddy on guitar and accordion are phenomenal. The continuous stream of eighth notes could also serve as a great preparation before diving into playing jazz on the harmonica.

THE MORNING STAR

Traditional Irish

G Harmonica

"Danny Boy" is a ballad written by English songwriter Frederick Weatherly in 1913, and it is set to the traditional Irish melody of "Londonderry Air." The melody is played as the victory sporting anthem of Northern Ireland at the Commonwealth Games. Focus on the exact intonation of your 3-draw whole-step bend to make the melodic phrases end strongly.

DANNY BOY

Words by Frederick Edward Weatherly

Traditional Irish Folk Melody

C Harmonica

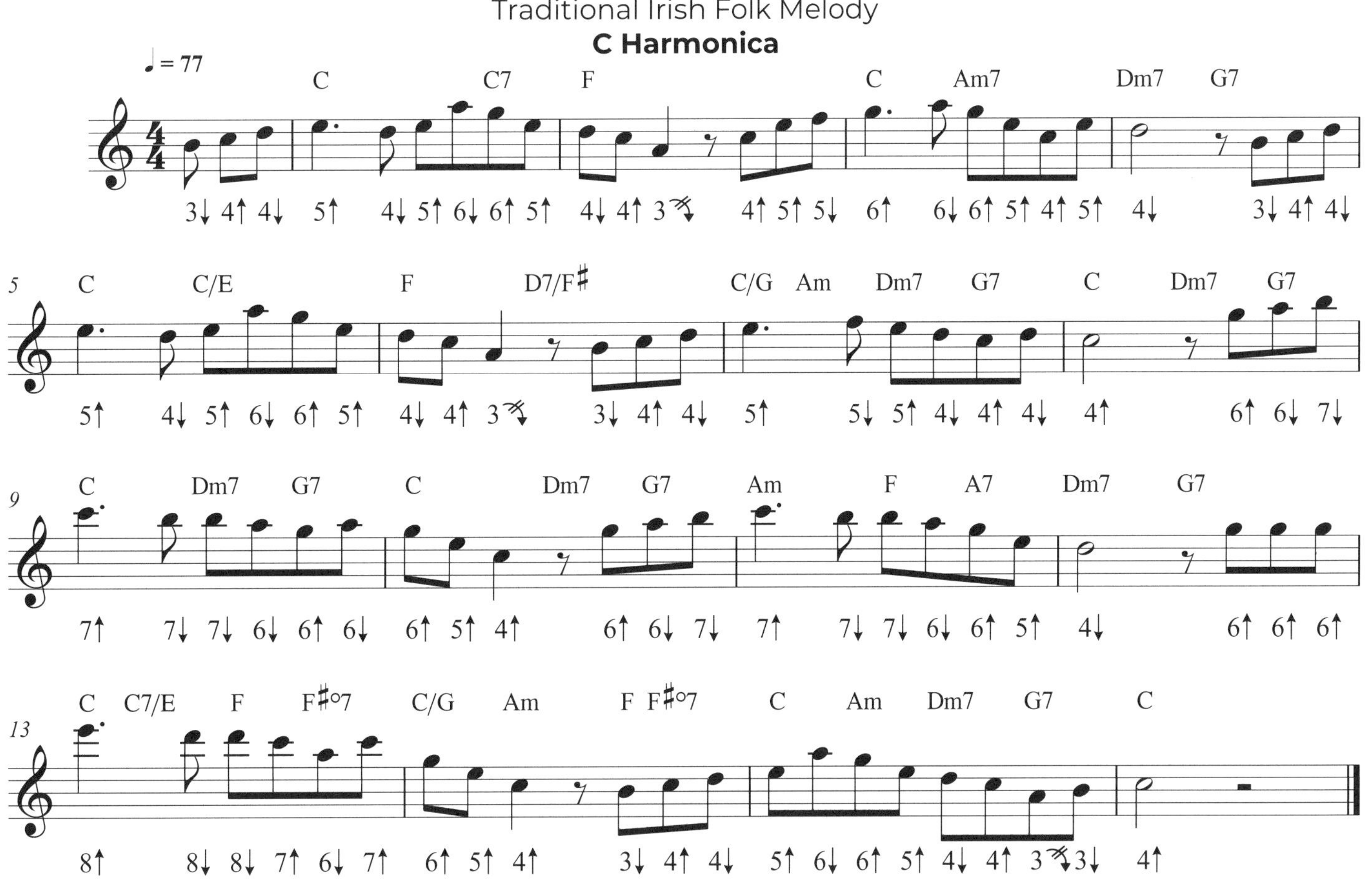

"Fly Me to the Moon" is one of the great jazz melodies in the key of C and uses almost no bent notes at all. It was written in 1954 by Bart Howard, and Frank Sinatra's 1964 version was closely associated with the Apollo missions to the moon. The two bends on holes 4 and 6 are very sensitive. Be careful about not intonating them too low. Another inspirational recording of the song by British chromatic harmonica player Philip Achille can be found online. The melody here sounds one octave higher than written, and the recording has some jazzy embellishments that give you a feel for how this can sound when mastered.

FLY ME TO THE MOON (IN OTHER WORDS)

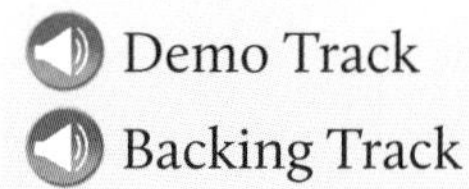

Words and Music by Bart Howard

C Harmonica

"Over the Rainbow" is a ballad composed by Harold Arlen. It was written for the 1939 film *The Wizard of Oz* and was sung by actress Judy Garland. You may also be familiar with Hawaiian musician Israel Kamakawiwo'ole's version of the song, which has been featured on countless film and TV soundtracks. Besides a beautiful, amplified harmonica version in 2nd position by Canadian harmonica player Roly Platt, you can listen to a harmonica recording of the song—played in 12th position—on Reinberg's album *Old Friend*. The melody sounds one octave higher than written.

OVER THE RAINBOW

from THE WIZARD OF OZ

Music by Harold Arlen

Lyric by E.Y. "Yip" Harburg

C Harmonica

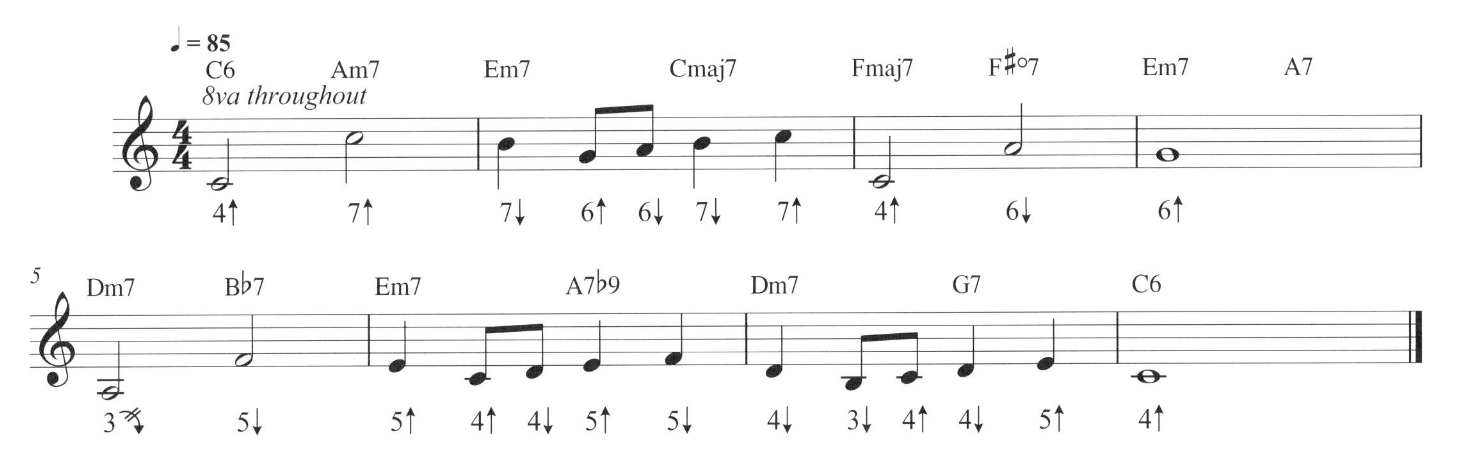

The opening octave jump in "Over the Rainbow" is characteristic for the piece and is a wonderful opportunity to practice all diatonic octave jumps on the harmonica. There are two demo audio tracks for this example: one played at regular tempo and the other at a slow tempo.

Octave Jumps

Regular Tempo

Slow Tempo

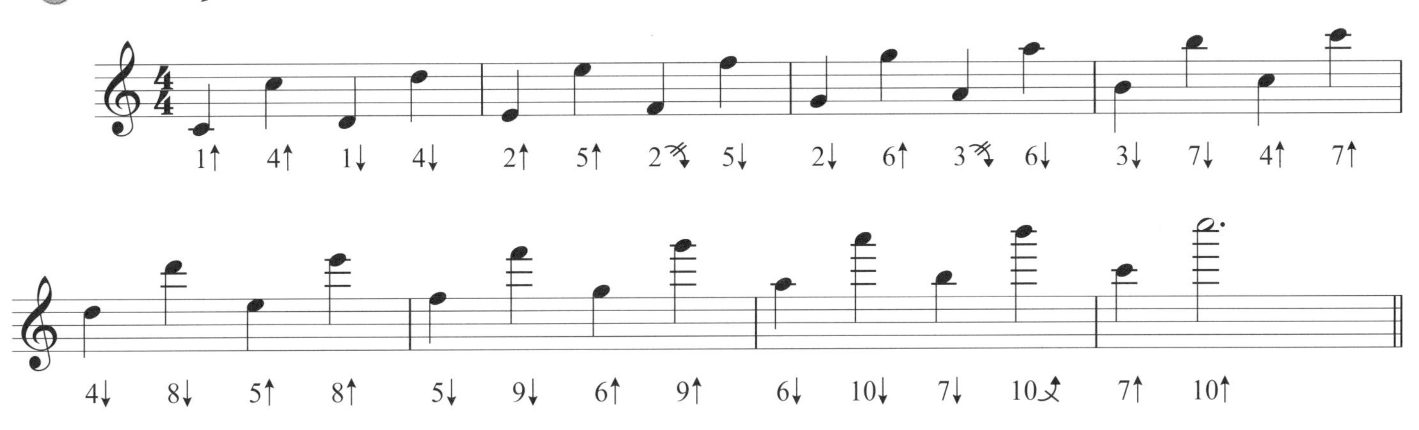

Playing classical music on the diatonic harmonica is a challenge in and of itself. It requires extreme precision and control over the expressiveness of the instrument. "Jesu, Joy of Man's Desiring" is derived from a chorale setting of a cantata composed by Johann Sebastian Bach in 1723. It is often performed slowly and reverently at wedding ceremonies, as well as during Christian festive seasons like Christmas and Easter. Diatonic harmonica pioneer Howard Levy popularized a solo harmonica arrangement of the melody that uses advanced tongue-blocking techniques; this version can be heard on his album *Tango & Jazz*, with Anthony Molinaro on piano. Additionally, Carlos del Junco integrated the melody into his solo recording of "Amazing Grace" on the 2008 record *Steady Movin'*.

JESU, JOY OF MAN'S DESIRING

By Johann Sebastian Bach

G Harmonica

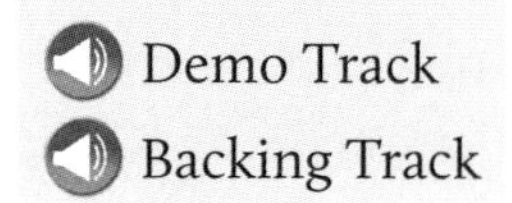

"St. Thomas" is probably the most recognizable instrumental in the repertoire of American jazz tenor saxophonist Sonny Rollins. The tune is based on the traditional Bahamian folk song "Sponger Money" and the traditional English song "The Lincolnshire Poacher." The joyful calypso rhythm popularized the tune and led Rollins to release 12 different versions of the song.

ST. THOMAS

By Sonny Rollins

C Harmonica

The 1968 film *Once Upon a Time in the West* is a western directed by Sergio Leone. The soundtrack, which was composed by Ennio Morricone, sold about 10 million copies worldwide and features the harmonica extensively. The theme music has wordless vocals by Italian singer Edda Dell'Orso. It would be a great challenge to play along with the original recording and try to replicate the vocal expression on the harmonica. Try to keep the long notes in the upper octave alive by making them swell and by using the hand tremolo technique.

ONCE UPON A TIME IN THE WEST

from the Paramount Picture ONCE UPON A TIME IN THE WEST

Words and Music by Ennio Morricone

D Harmonica

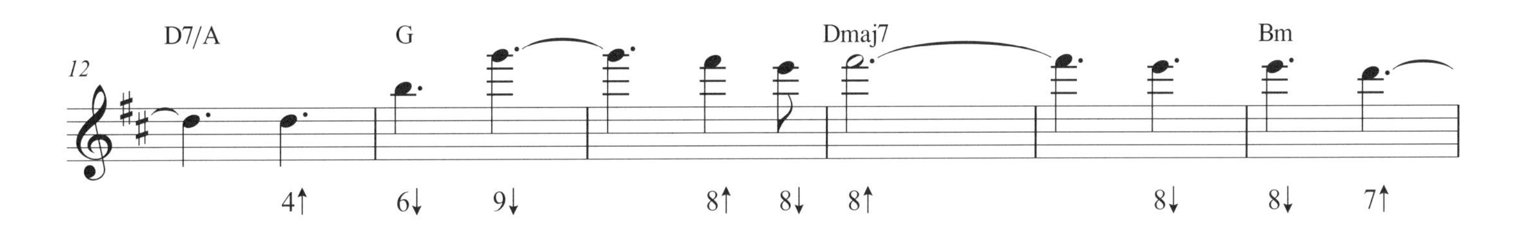

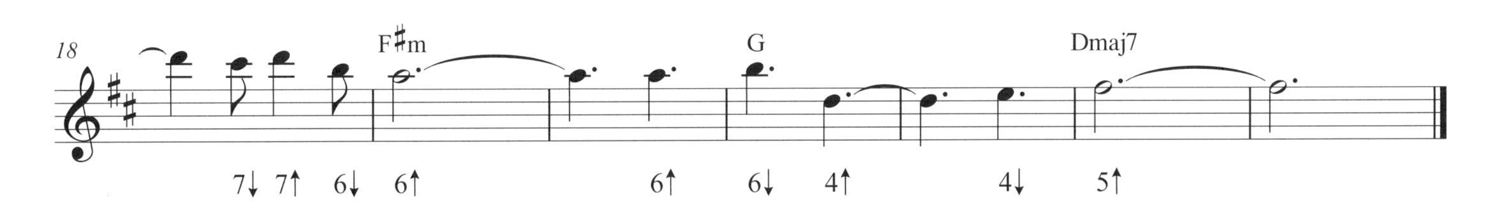

"Let It Be" is a song that doesn't need any further introduction. The Beatles released the song in 1970. You can find a recording online of an impromptu performance by the late and great German harmonica player Igor Flach. His signature sound on the high-pitched F harmonica and his rhythmic variation let the melody shine in 2nd position.

LET IT BE

Words and Music by John Lennon and Paul McCartney

C Harmonica

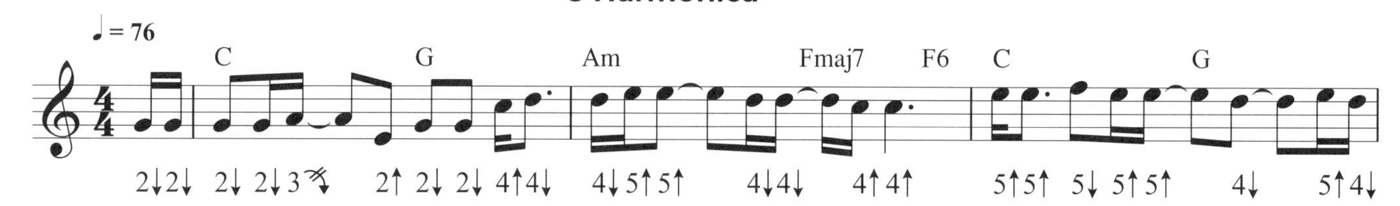

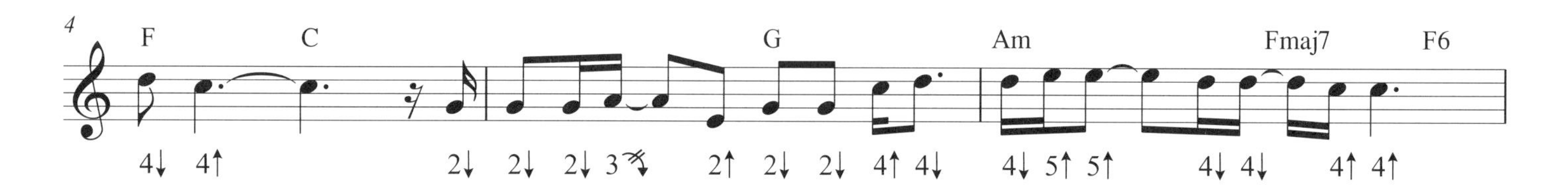

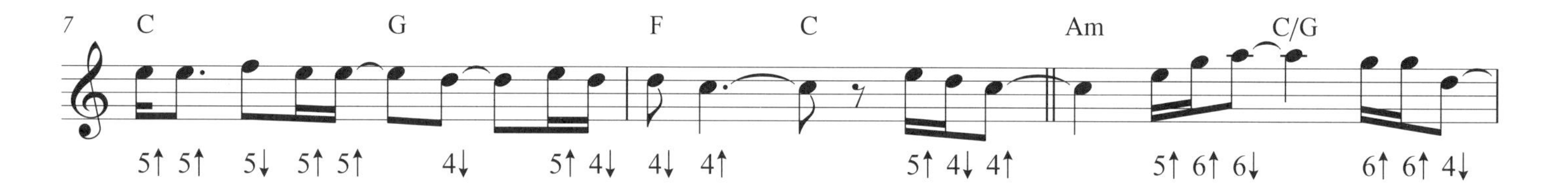

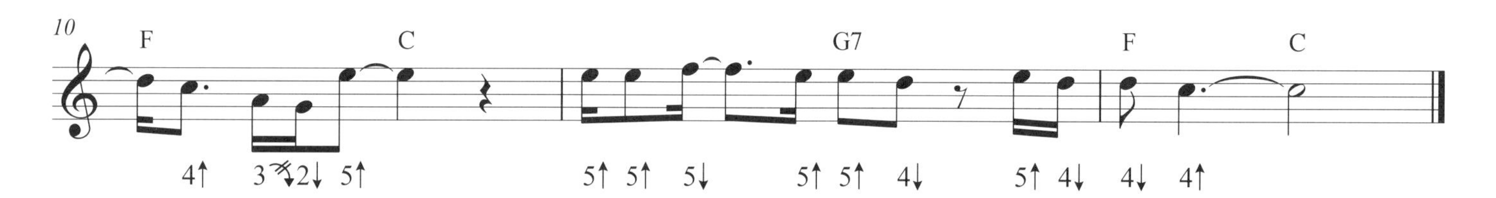

"(They Long to Be) Close to You" is a song written by Burt Bacharach and Hal David. The best-known version was recorded by American duo the Carpenters in 1970. The melody sounds one octave higher than written.

(THEY LONG TO BE) CLOSE TO YOU

Lyrics by Hal David
Music by Burt Bacharach

E♭ Harmonica

"You Are the Sunshine of My Life" is a 1973 single released by Stevie Wonder. The song became his third number-one single on the Billboard Hot 100 chart. It starts out in the key of B (1st position) before briefly modulating to G♯ major (4th position).

YOU ARE THE SUNSHINE OF MY LIFE

Words and Music by Stevie Wonder

B Harmonica

"The Bare Necessities" is a jazz song, written by Terry Gilkyson, from the animated 1967 Disney film *The Jungle Book*. The song was also sung by Louis Armstrong.

THE BARE NECESSITIES

from THE JUNGLE BOOK

Words and Music by Terry Gilkyson

C Harmonica

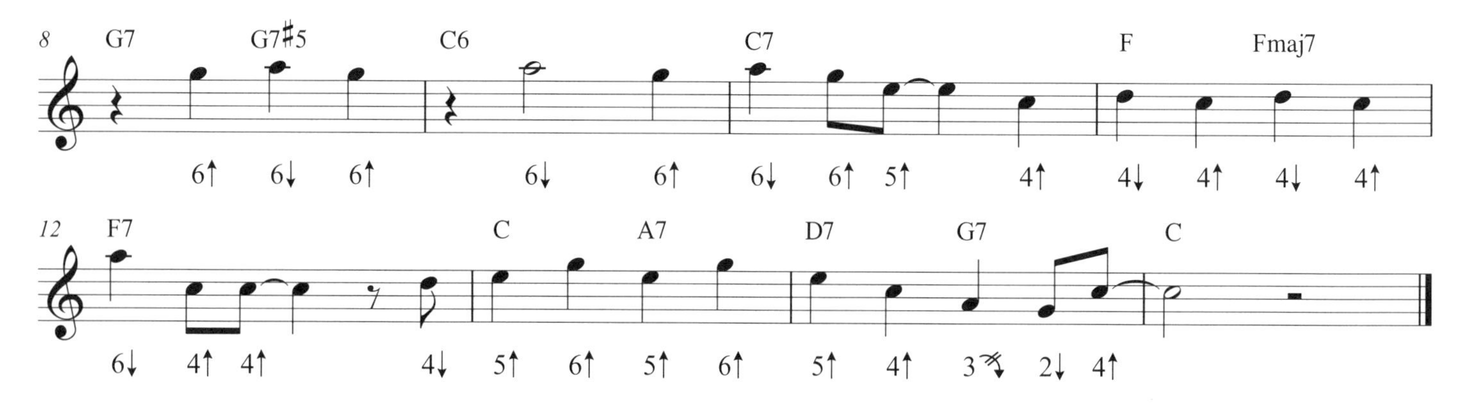

Playing "On the Sunny Side of the Street" will immediately put you in a good mood. The song was composed in 1930 by Jimmy McHugh. Dizzy Gillespie made one of the most notable recordings of the tune, and it features a great saxophone solo by Sonny Rollins.

ON THE SUNNY SIDE OF THE STREET

Lyric by Dorothy Fields
Music by Jimmy McHugh
C Harmonica

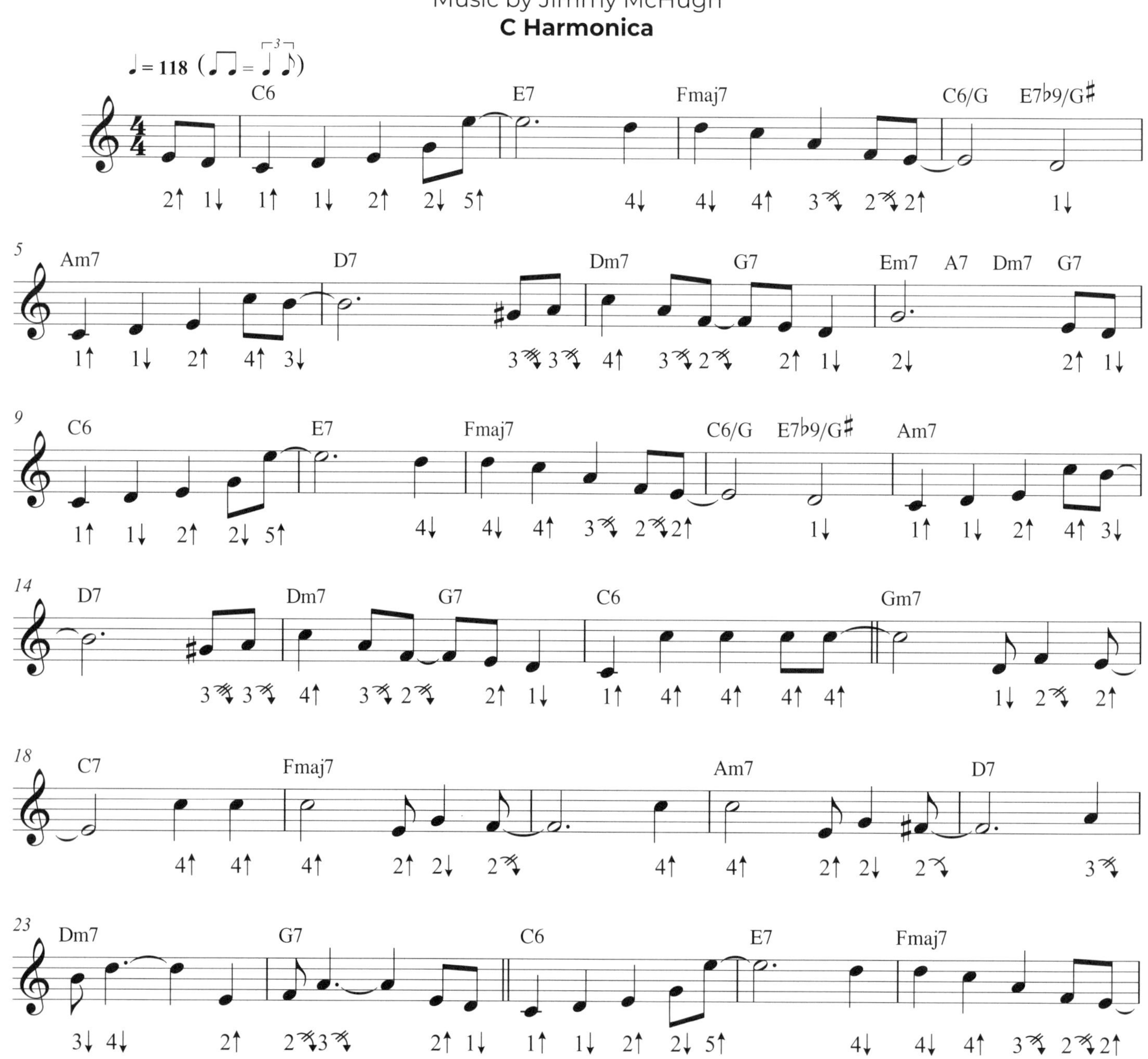

"Misirlou" is a folk song from the Eastern Mediterranean region, with origins in the Ottoman Empire. It gained worldwide popularity through Dick Dale's 1962 American surf rock version. Quentin Tarantino used it in his 1994 film *Pulp Fiction*, and the melody gained renewed popularity, being used as a sample in the Black Eyed Peas' song "Pump It" (2006). It introduces you to a new scale and will strengthen your "brainstrument" by doing so.

The *double harmonic major scale* makes use of both the 4-hole draw bend and the 6-hole draw bend, giving it its dark and distinct sound.

Double Harmonic Major Scale

Here's the scale in E, the key of the song.

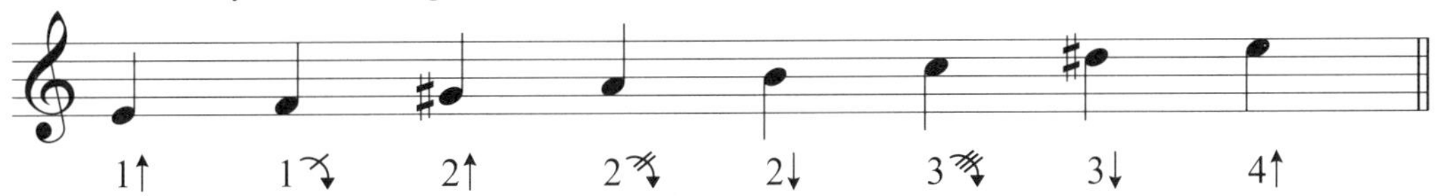

MISIRLOU

Words by Fred Wise, Milton Leeds, Jose Pina and Sidney Russell
Music by Nicolas Roubanis

"Can You Feel the Love Tonight" is a song from Disney's 1994 animated film *The Lion King* and was composed by English musician Elton John. It won the 1995 Academy Award for Best Original Song. Good intonation on your 3-hole-draw whole-step bend is absolutely crucial in order to make the melody sound good.

CAN YOU FEEL THE LOVE TONIGHT

from THE LION KING

Music by Elton John

Lyrics by Tim Rice

B♭ Harmonica

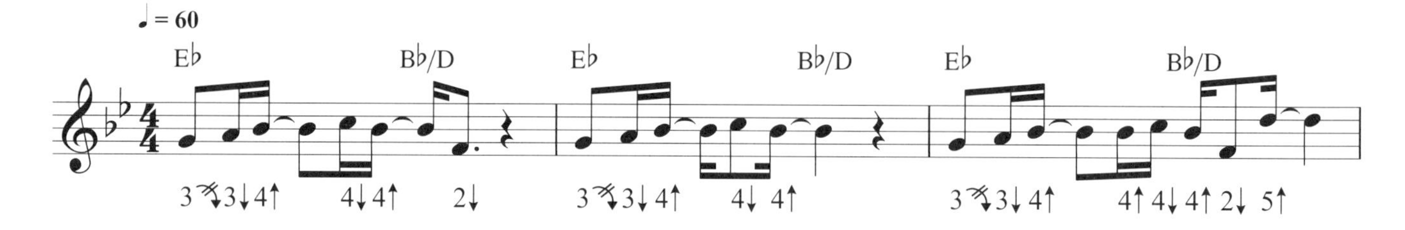

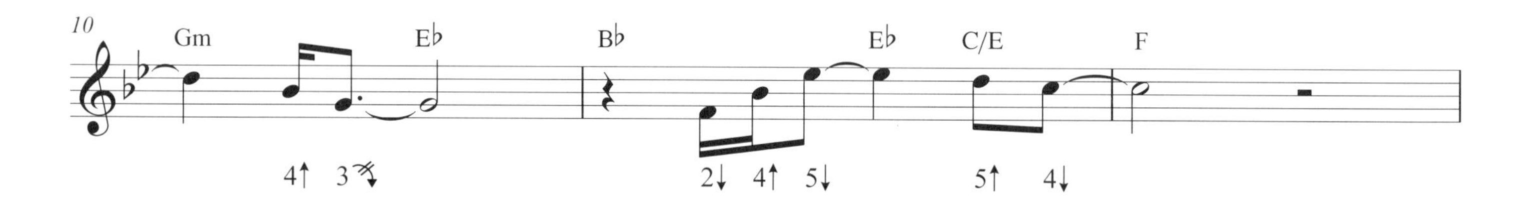

"Satin Doll" (1953) is a jazz standard written by Duke Ellington. The song has been recorded by many famous artists including Ella Fitzgerald. Its chord progression is well known for its unusual use of chords and opening with a ii–V–I turnaround just like "Honeysuckle Rose."

SATIN DOLL

By Duke Ellington

C Harmonica

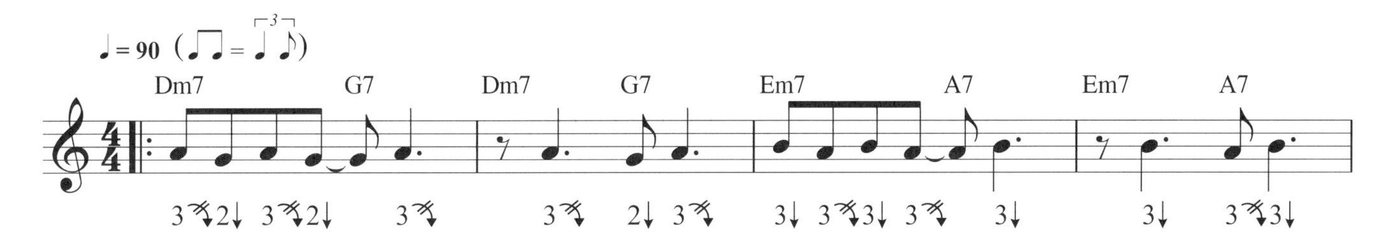

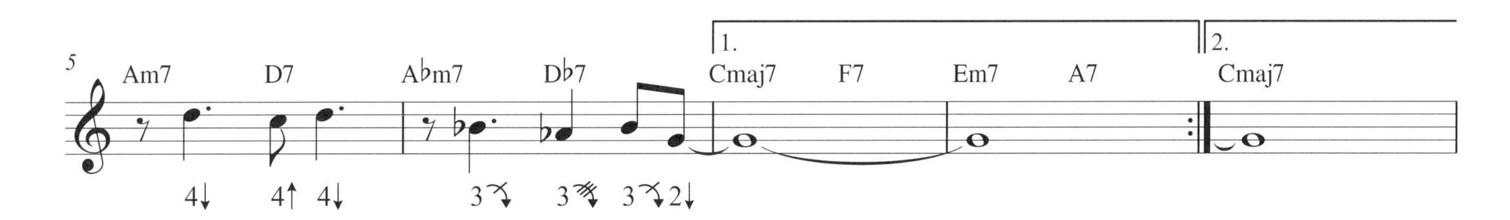

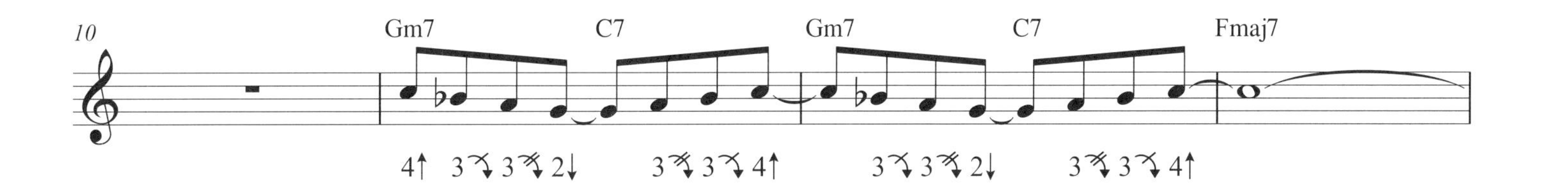

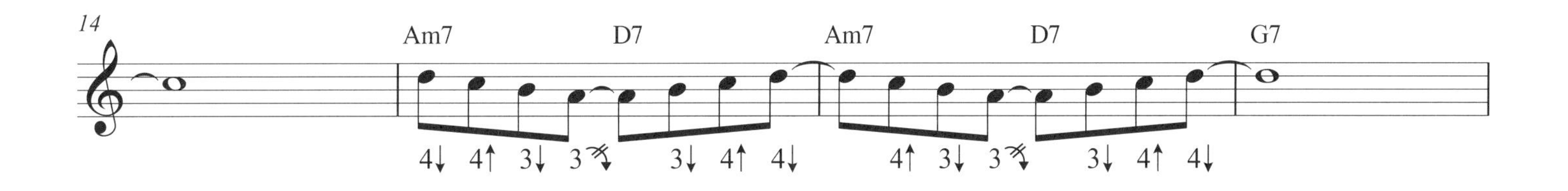

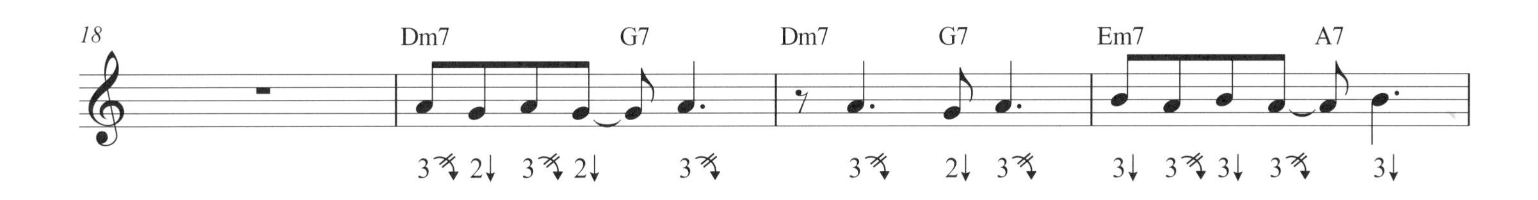

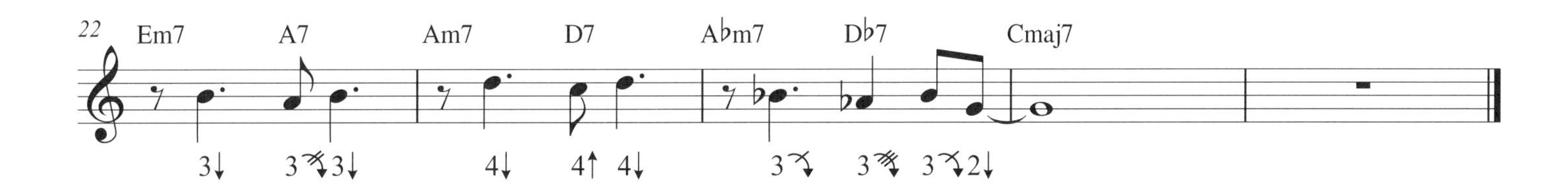

"All of Me" is a popular song and jazz standard written by Gerald Marks and Seymour Simons in 1931. The melody almost exclusively follows the chord progression and its arpeggios. It also serves as a great introduction to secondary dominant chords, which are beyond the scope of this book; however, you might be able to find a harmonica tutorial online that explains the chord progression in greater detail. Mariano Massolo includes a version of the song on his debut album.

> Replace the notes D♯ and E♭ (both 1-hole overblow) by playing E (2-hole blow) for now.

ALL OF ME

Words and Music by Seymour Simons and Gerald Marks

"I Got Plenty o' Nuttin'" is a song composed in 1934 by George Gershwin for the "folk opera" *Porgy and Bess*. The B7 chord, which appears several times, is a secondary dominant that leads to the temporary key of E major (4th position).

I GOT PLENTY O' NUTTIN'

from PORGY AND BESS®

Music and Lyrics by George Gershwin, DuBose and Dorothy Heyward and Ira Gershwin

"Take the 'A' Train" is a jazz standard by Billy Strayhorn and was a signature tune of Duke Ellington and His Orchestra. The piece is written in C major and follows an AABA structure. However, the melody is comparably advanced, using 6ths and 4ths in the A section and 7ths and 5ths in the B section. The secondary dominant chord in bar 3 (D7♯11) is characteristic of the song and highlights the 3-draw one-and-a-half-step bend.

TAKE THE "A" TRAIN

Words and Music by Billy Strayhorn

C Harmonica

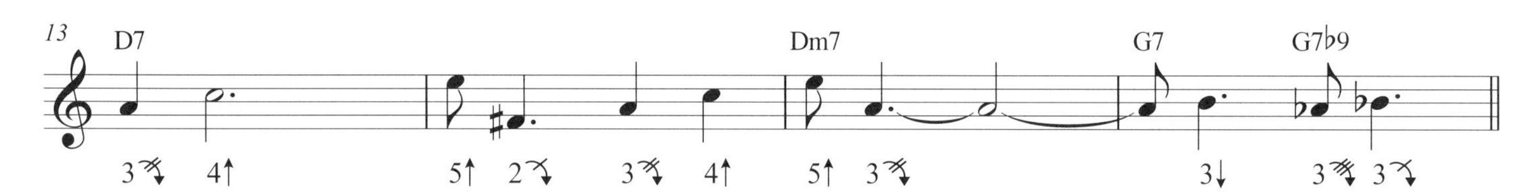

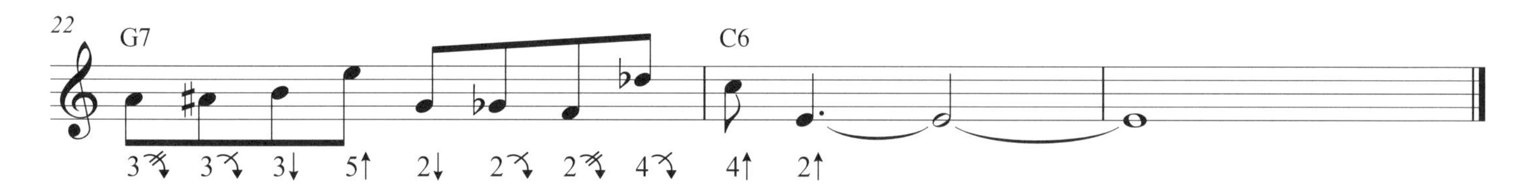

"Some Day My Prince Will Come" is a song from Walt Disney's 1937 animated movie *Snow White and the Seven Dwarfs*. The waltz became popular as a jazz standard, and it was performed by jazz musicians such as Dave Brubeck. Another great recording of the song came from Miles Davis in 1961.

SOME DAY MY PRINCE WILL COME

from SNOW WHITE AND THE SEVEN DWARFS

Words by Larry Morey
Music by Frank Churchill

B♭ Harmonica

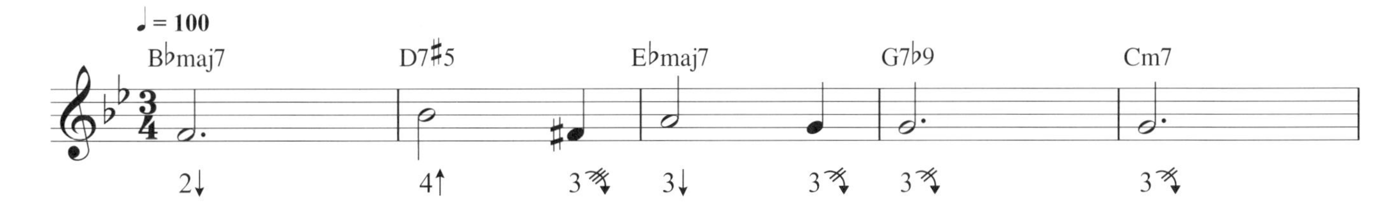

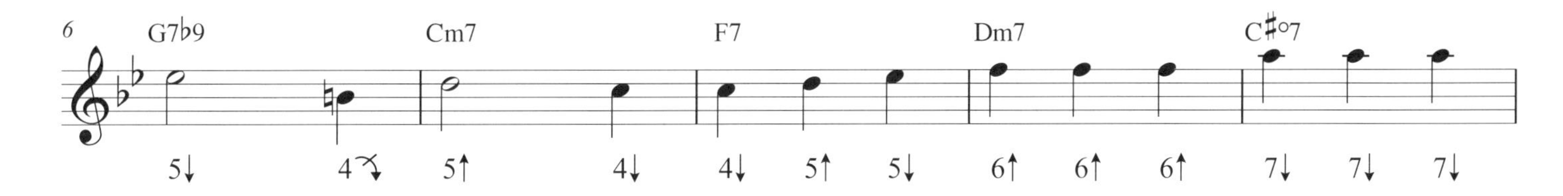

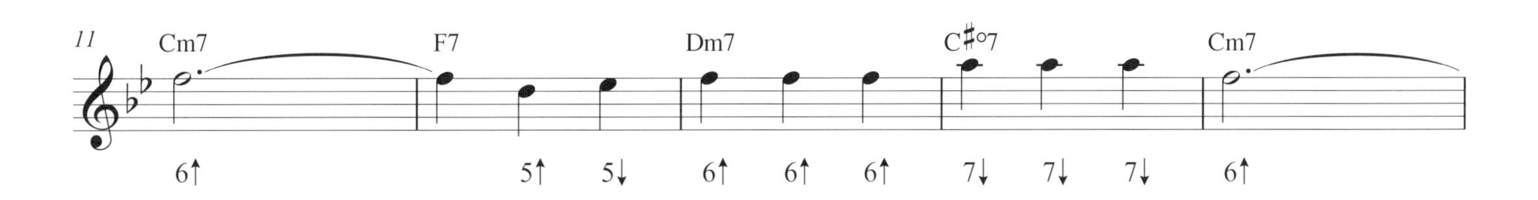

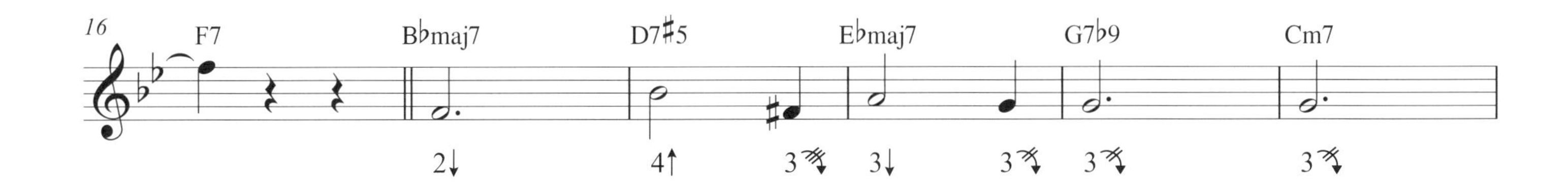

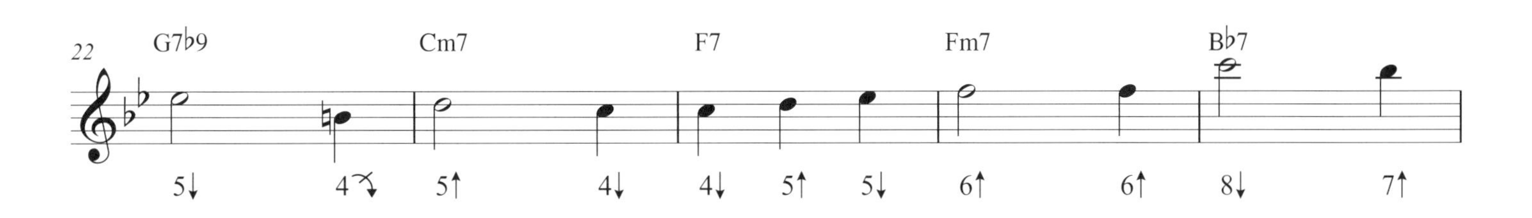

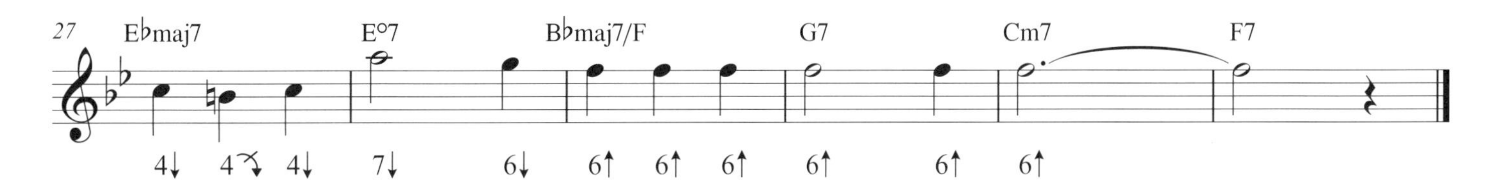

LESSON 21:

Vibrato

You can bring your melodies to life even more by pulsating sustained notes using *vibrato*. The two most common techniques use the same motions as when you start and stop notes, but they are done more gently. In both cases, a series of gentle pulses is responsible for the pitch variation, usually moving slightly below the pitch of the regular note before bringing it back up.

Throat vibrato is the most widely favored sound by blues players, while more melodic and jazz-oriented players tend to use *tongue vibrato* more often.

Throat Vibrato

Throat vibrato can influence both the pitch and loudness of a note. Your goal is to narrow the air passage while pulsing the note with your glottis. Try to whisper "ah.ah.ah.ah.ah" on a single breath. Each dot is a glottal stop that breaks the breath into a series of distinct puffs. The challenge is to connect all those puffs while air continues to flow. Your glottis only narrows and doesn't stop the airflow. As soon as you can do this at a lower volume, you can be sure that you have mastered the technique. Try it on the harmonica as soon as it is possible for you to sustain a continuous, uninterrupted flow of air. Think about massaging the air.

Your glottis "coughs" very softly while your abdomen moves smoothly without pulsing. As your bending technique improves, you will also be able to gain more and more control over the pitch variation accompanying your throat vibrato. Each pulsation will lower the pitch and let it rise again.

Pulsation

Now, you can move on to synchronizing the pitch variation of your vibrato to the divisions of the beat. In most cases, the beat is divided into three or four pulsations. It is even possible to layer both abdominal and throat pulsations. While your throat moves at a faster rate, your diaphragm can highlight some of the pulsations.

The rhythmic combination does just that. In the notated music, the abdominal pulses indicated with accent marks (>) over the notes are layered on top of the steady rhythm provided by your throat. The vowels "Ah" and "Oh" are preceded with exclamation points representing glottal stops, and the arrows tell you to draw on the first two measures and blow on the next two measures.

Pulsation

Pulsation with Harmonica

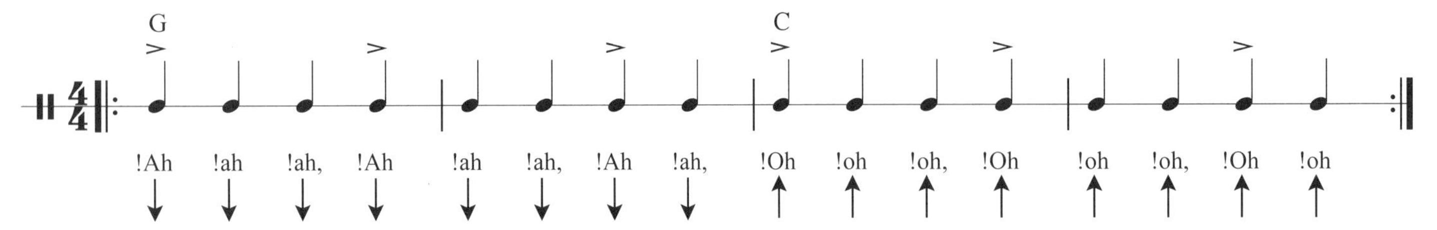

Tongue Vibrato

Tongue vibrato can influence both the pitch and tone color of a note. In order to create the tonal changes with your tongue, you can start out by making a subtle "yoyoyo" sound. Since pitch variation can get very extreme in this case, you could try to say "ayayayaya" using one continuous breath. The "y" sound really enables you to control the sound of the note. You will feel air pressure that presses your tongue away from the roof of your mouth. When you try this with a harmonica, you'll want to minimize the vowel change.

LESSON 22:
Overbending

In some of the following songs, you will encounter a few *overbends*, an advanced bending technique. Most of the overbends can be replaced for now, but here is a guide to coax these sounds out of your instruments for the sake of completeness.

In recent years, the overbending technique has completely transformed the landscape of diatonic harmonica performance. Overbending enables you to play any chromatic note within the three-octave range of the diatonic harmonica, providing a new expressive tool for musical styles. Some of the overbent notes are available by exhaling and others by inhaling. This is why they are often referred to as *overblows* and *overdraws*. I would like to focus on the few overblows that occur in this book.

When playing these notes, you basically use the same technique as bending a note down. However, the results come out backward. As soon as you apply your regular bending technique on a blow note between holes 1–6, an overblow can pop out.

This technique works much better with reed adjustment, but many of the current mid-priced harmonica models overblow reasonably well in holes 4, 5, and 6.

An overblow is always one half step higher than the draw note of the same hole, and it is important to mention that this technique does not have to do with air pressure. Considering the inside workings of the instrument, it is all about redirecting the airflow.

Here are a few more pointers to consider during the learning process:

- Overblows can be played very softly and are easier to control then, too. Using too much force or pressure will not help, but rather, will stress the reeds.
- Keep every part of your body relaxed. Tension just tires you out and can make your overblow practice session a frustrating experience.
- Start out learning overblows with a pucker before trying to incorporate tongue blocking. Even though tongue-blocked overblows are possible, the pucker embouchure will give you more direct control and an earlier sense of achievement.
- Train your ears and practice with an audible reference. That could be a drone backing track or another instrument. Hearing your target note will make it easier to find the right tongue position. At some point, you will be able to anticipate and hear the target note in your mind without any external source.
- Be very conscious about your tongue placement and the airflow. Do not be afraid of experimenting. In the end, it is all about the constriction of the airflow back in your throat (low overblows) or more up front between your tongue and palate.

Approach 1

Start out by practicing on hole 6. Applying the bending technique to one of the six blow notes might lead to no sound coming out of the instrument at all. If you solely hear the air flowing through the instrument but the reed is silent, then congratulations—you are halfway there! Immobilizing the blow reed so no sound comes out of it is your subgoal. Try to think about the target note now.

This might frequently cause squeaky noises. If you carefully increase the volume of air, a clear note starts to sound. Your redirected breath pushed the draw reed away from the slot and unveiled the overblow literally out of thin air.

TOOLBOX

Overblow Cheat

The blow reeds are attached to the upper reed plate. Use a screwdriver to unscrew the cover plates of the harmonica. Prevent the blow reeds from swinging by covering the slots above with your forefinger. This way you can basically skip the first subgoal, and an overblow is the only sound that can come out of the instrument.

Approach 2

Because the sound of the overblow note comes from the draw reed, it can be helpful to set that very reed in motion before starting the overblow. In order to do so, start out by playing the 6-hole draw. Bend the note down and hold it before reversing the breathing direction. At the same time, try to keep everything else in your mouth the same. A higher note should pop out. If you do not get the overblow, try to slightly increase your breath volume. Carefully moving the constriction of the airflow forward or backward inside your mouth can also help.

Do not be bound to hole 6 during the whole process. Try out holes 1, 4, and 5, too. You might be surprised and succeed on one of these lower holes first.

Your first overblow will take some concentrated effort, and you are not alone if the process to get there includes a few frustrating moments. Remember that regular bendings are an important foundation to get started with overbending. Stay patient. Soon you will be able to incorporate overblows in your melodies all over the harmonica.

LESSON 23:
Songs in 2nd Position and the Blues Scale

"Love Me Do" is the debut single by the Beatles, and it begins with probably one of the most popular harmonica melodies ever. The single features John Lennon's prominent harmonica playing with a bluesy, dry "dockside harmonica" riff. The melody strongly highlights the offbeats and uses the Mixolydian mode for its melodic material.

LOVE ME DO

Words and Music by John Lennon and Paul McCartney

C Harmonica

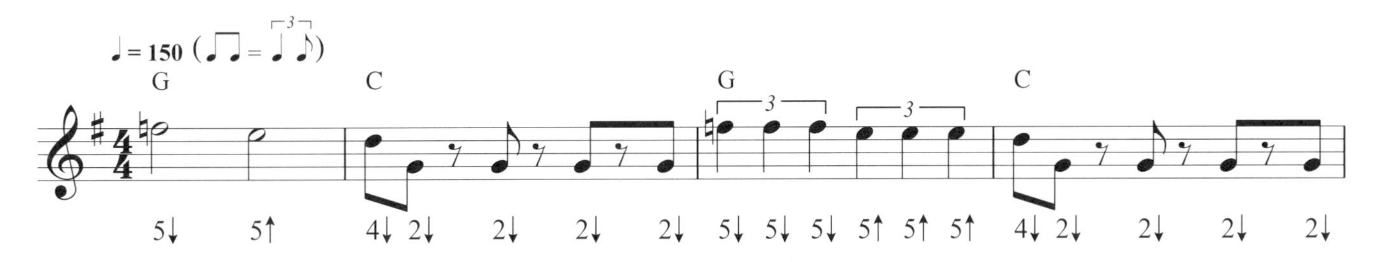

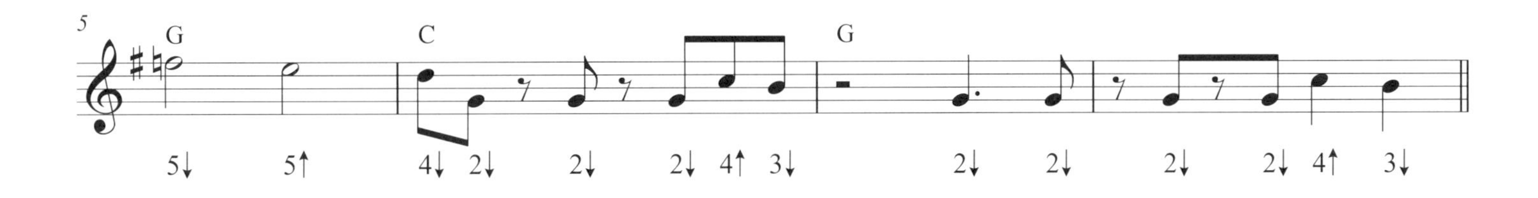

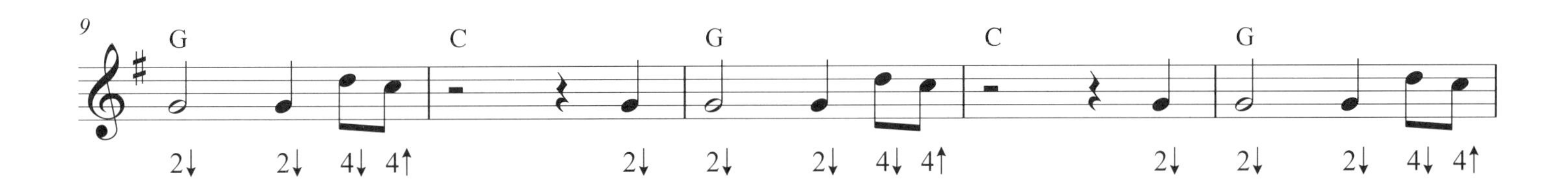

"All Blues" is a jazz composition by Miles Davis first appearing on the influential 1959 album *Kind of Blue*. It is a 12-bar blues in 6/8. The chord sequence is that of a basic blues and is made up entirely of 7th chords, with a ♭VI (a 7th chord built from the minor 6th degree of the scale) in the turnaround instead of just the usual V chord; in the composition's original key of G, this chord is an E♭7. A distinctive feature of the piece is the bass line that repeats throughout.

ALL BLUES

By Miles Davis

C Harmonica

"Timber" is a dance-pop/EDM/folktronica song by American rapper Pitbull featuring Kesha. The song interpolates Lee Oskar's 1978 single "San Francisco Bay" and features harmonica player Paul Harrington, who plays through the entire song and was told to emulate Oskar. The sound of the high-pitched E harmonica really supports the country feeling of the melody.

TIMBER

Words and Music by Steve Arrington, Charles Carter, Greg Errico, Waung Hankerson, Lee Oskar Levitin, Keri Oskar, Roger Parker, Armando Christian Perez, Priscilla Renea, Breyan Isaac, Kesha Sebert, Jamie Sanderson, Lukasz Gottwald and Henry Walter

E Harmonica

"Birdland" is a jazz/pop song written by Joe Zawinul of the legendary band Weather Report as a tribute to the Birdland nightclub in New York City. The highly syncopated melody is a lot of fun to play in 2nd position on the C harmonica.

BIRDLAND

By Josef Zawinul

C Harmonica

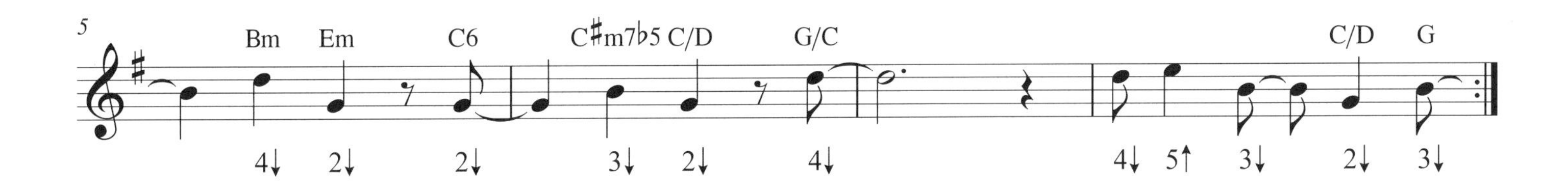

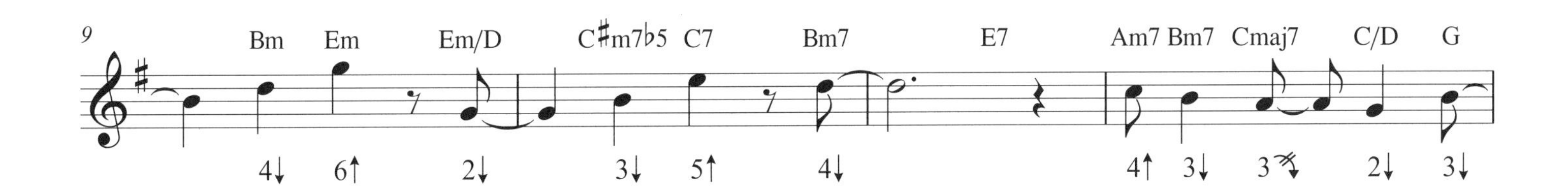

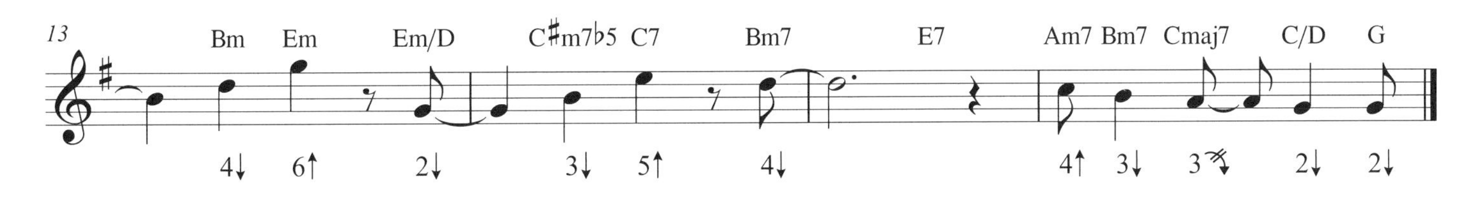

"Honeysuckle Rose" (1929) is a song composed by Fats Waller. Try to be very precise when playing your 3-hole draw bends in this tune. It is up to you how much bluesiness you want to add by using double stops. You can listen to a very playful harmonica recording of the song on Reinberg's album *Old Friend*.

> Replace the note D♭ (4-hole overblow) in bar 14 by playing D (5-hole blow) for now.

HONEYSUCKLE ROSE

Words by Andy Razaf
Music by Thomas "Fats" Waller
B♭ Harmonica

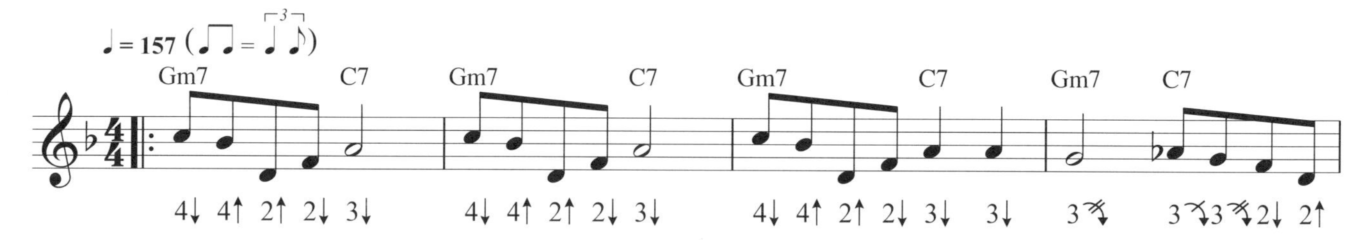

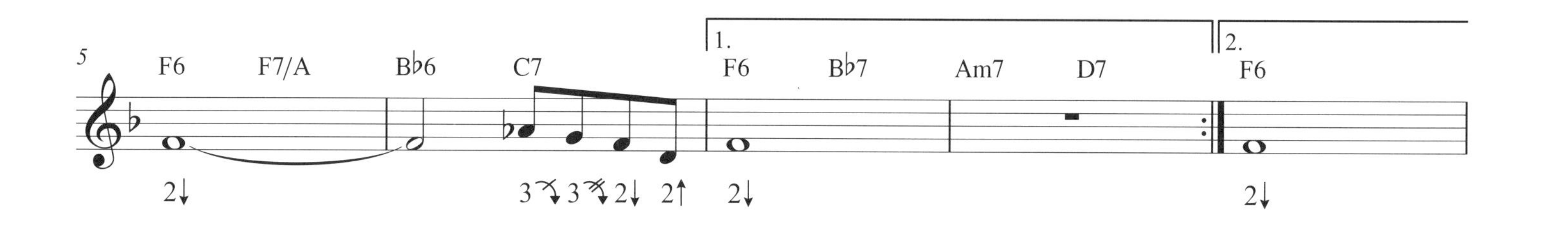

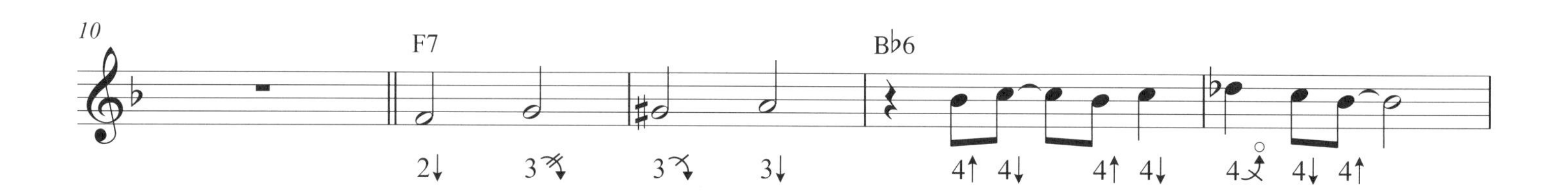

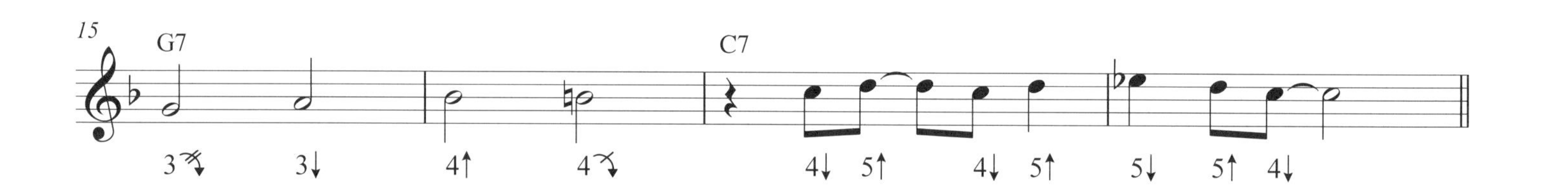

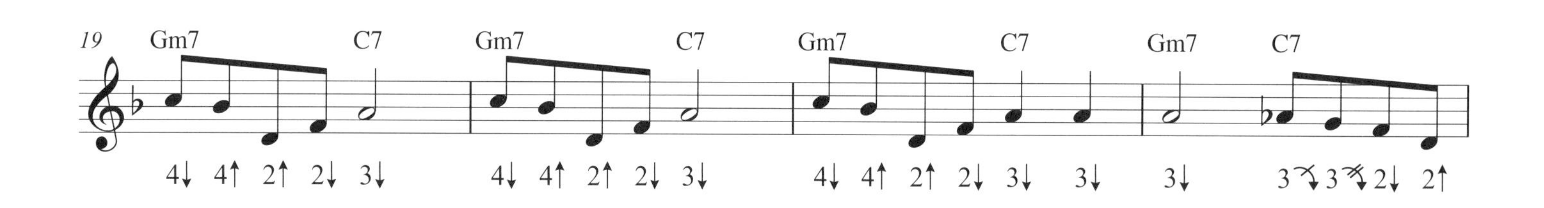

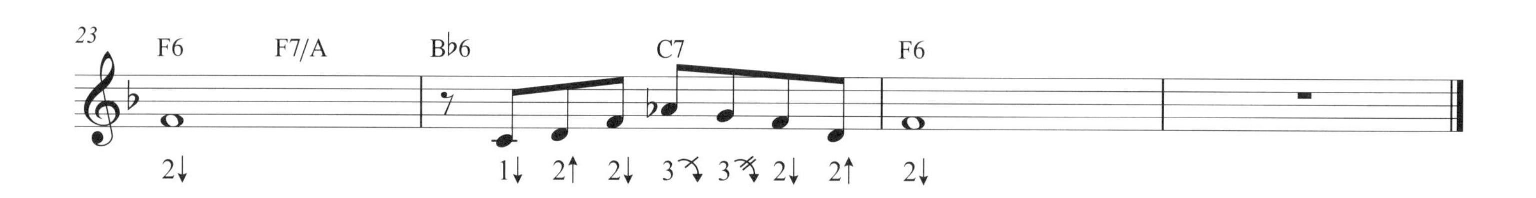

"I'm Yours" is a song written and recorded by Jason Mraz. It had already become a crowd favorite before its release in 2008. Because it was such a huge commercial success, many harmonica players started to cover the song online. I highly recommend checking out Kif Valentine's and Aiden N Evelyn's interpretations of the song on YouTube. You can hear chromatic harmonicas on both versions, but the melody is very expressive on the diatonic harmonica, too.

I'M YOURS

Words and Music by Jason Mraz

E Harmonica

The next two songs essentially follow the same chord progression. Both of them are great exercises to get even more familiar with the arpeggios for the I and V7 chords in 2nd position.

"La Cucaracha" is a popular Mexican folk song about a cockroach who cannot walk. The song's origins are unclear, but it dates back at least to the 1910s during the Mexican Revolution and belongs to the Mexican corrido genre. Mentionable recordings include interpretations by Louis Armstrong and Charlie Parker, whose bebop improvisation showcases more elaborate melodic ideas over the simple chord progression. Try to focus on the exact intonation of the C7 arpeggio (C–E–G–B♭) using the 2-hole-draw half-step bend and 3-hole-draw whole-step bend.

"El Jarabe Tapatío," often referred to as the "Mexican Hat Dance," is the national dance of Mexico. The original music for the song was composed by Jesús González Rubio in the 19th century. However, its more common instrumental arrangement dates from the 1920s. Nowadays, its music is most commonly performed by either mariachi groups or string ensembles. The song features chromatic (half-step) approach notes being played below their target notes. Always articulate the note that follows a bend with the syllable "dah."

EL JARABE TAPATÍO

Traditional Mexican

A♭ Harmonica

"Mo' Better Blues" is the title track of a collaborative album by the Branford Marsalis Quartet and Terence Blanchard. It was released in 1990 as the soundtrack to Spike Lee's eponymous film. The 8-bar blues is driven by an eighth-note rock groove and features an easy-to-play melody.

MO' BETTER BLUES

By William E. Lee

B♭ Harmonica

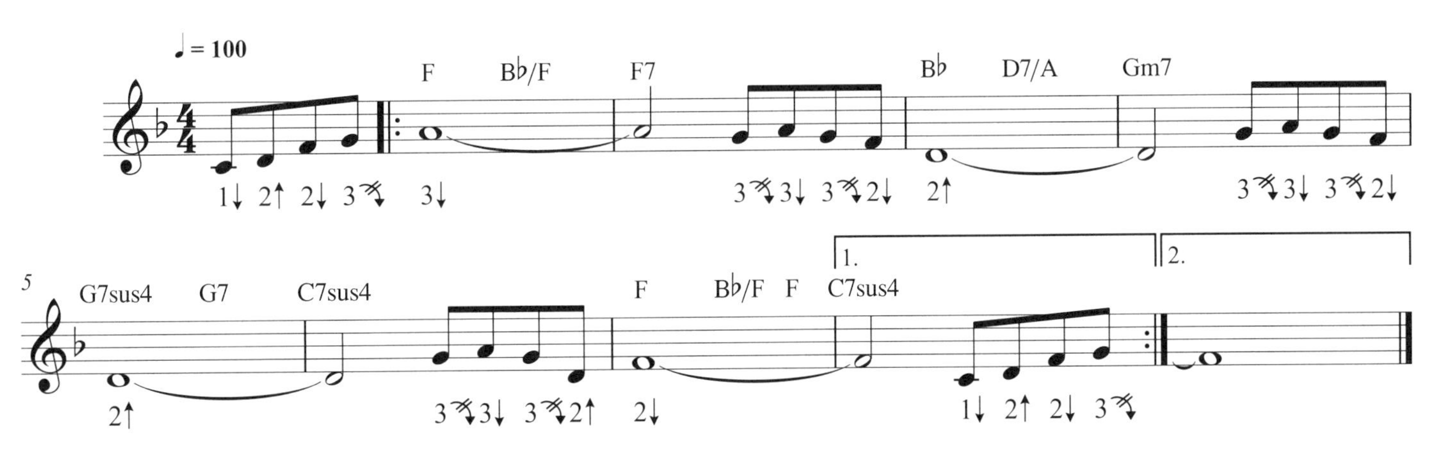

Even though "Breezin'" became even better known for a successful re-recording by singer and guitarist George Benson, the composition by Bobby Womack was first recorded by the influential Hungarian jazz guitarist Gábor Szabó. It is always beneficial to imitate other instruments on the harmonica—and in this case, the challenge is to groove along to the song while playing the bass line. Playing the remaining parts of the melody is a great way to work on your articulation. To play bar 5, say "hah-dah-dah-dah, dah-dah-dah-dah" through the instrument.

BREEZIN'

Words and Music by Bobby Womack

G Harmonica

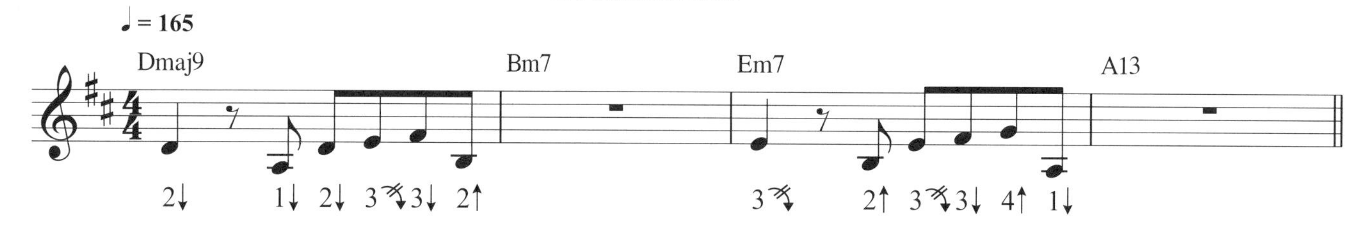

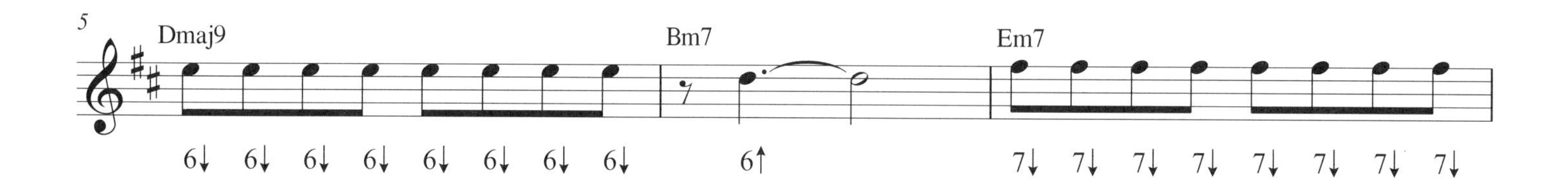

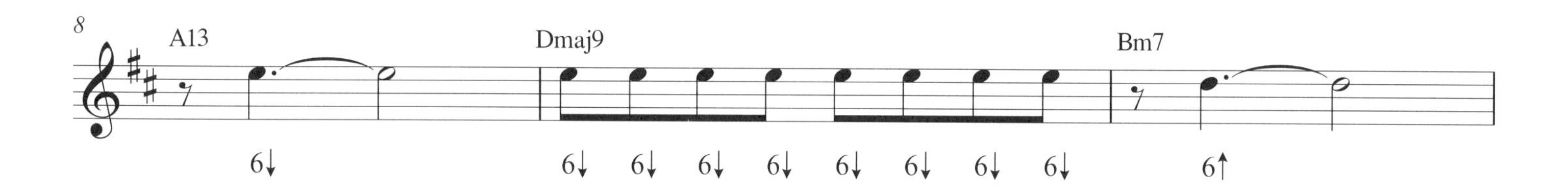

"If I Ain't Got You" (2004) is one of the most famous songs by Alicia Keys. The introduction makes a wonderful exercise for practicing your arpeggios. The arpeggios outline the chords Cmaj7, Bm7, Am7, and Gmaj7; for each chord, the 3rd, 7th, and 5th are played in descending order. Try to play along with the original recording of the song and replicate the phrasing of Alicia Keys.

IF I AIN'T GOT YOU

Words and Music by Alicia Augello Cook

C Harmonica

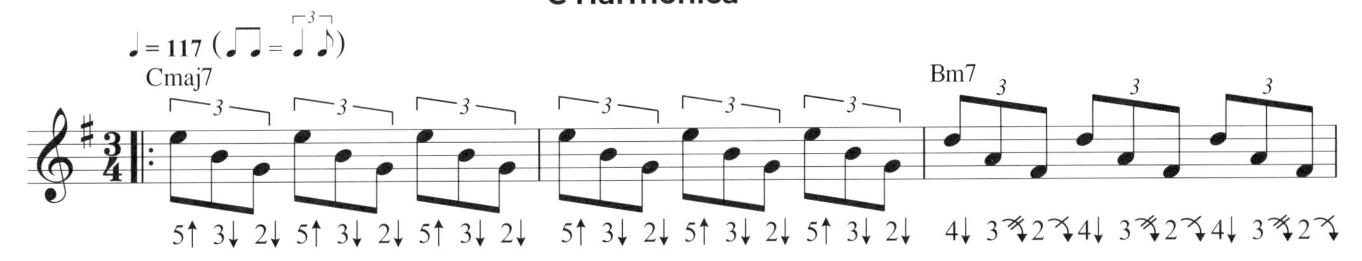

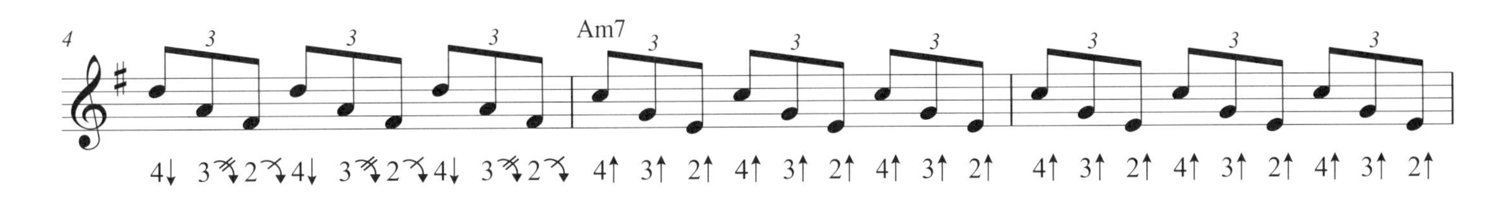

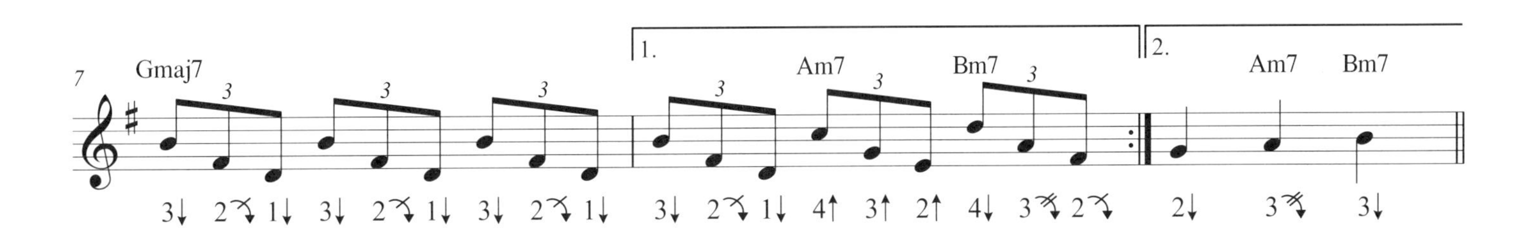

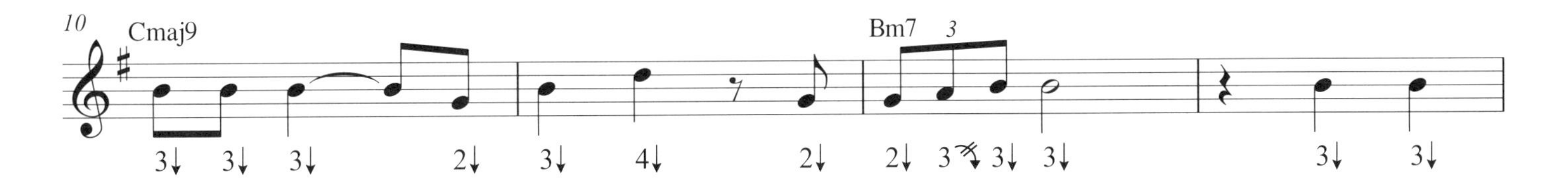

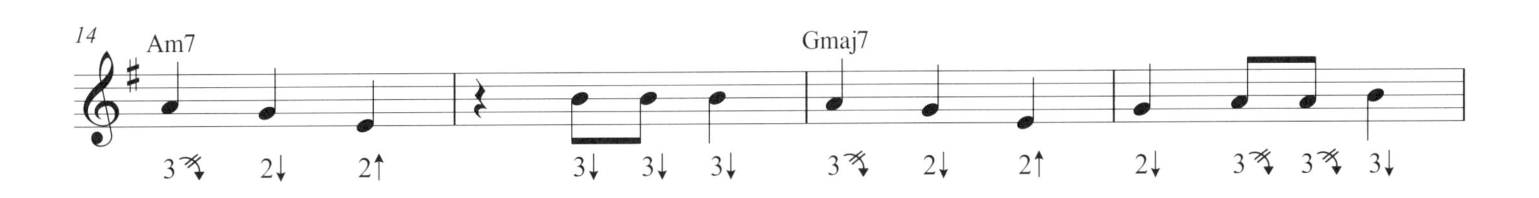

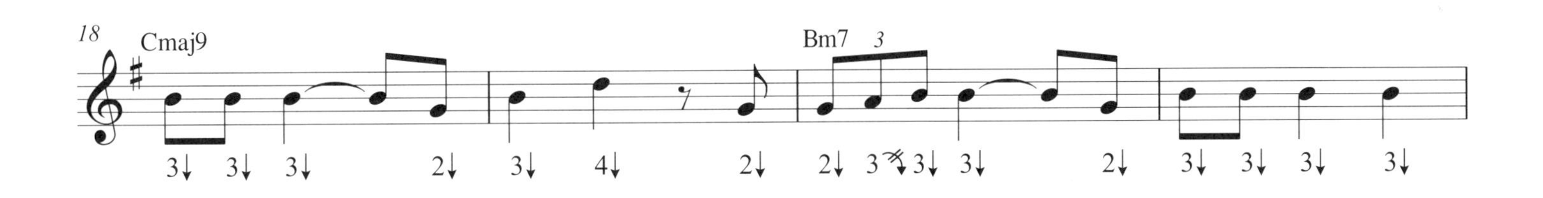

Bobby McFerrin's "Don't Worry, Be Happy" (1988) was the first a cappella song to reach number-one on the Billboard Hot 100 chart. Playing the melody on a high-pitched E harmonica supports the overall mood of the song.

DON'T WORRY, BE HAPPY

Words and Music by Bobby McFerrin

E Harmonica

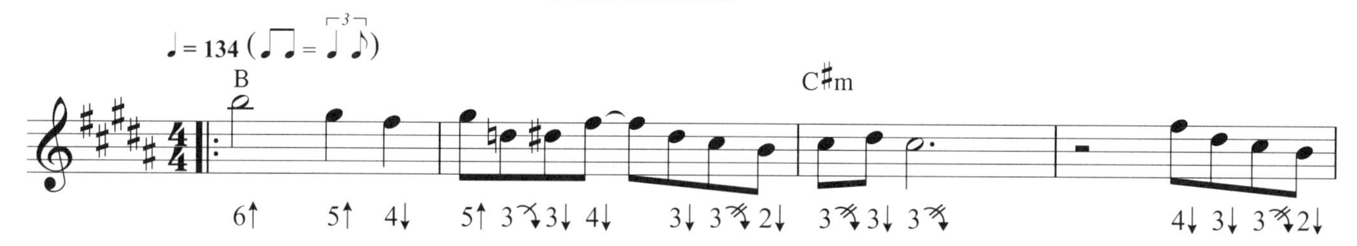

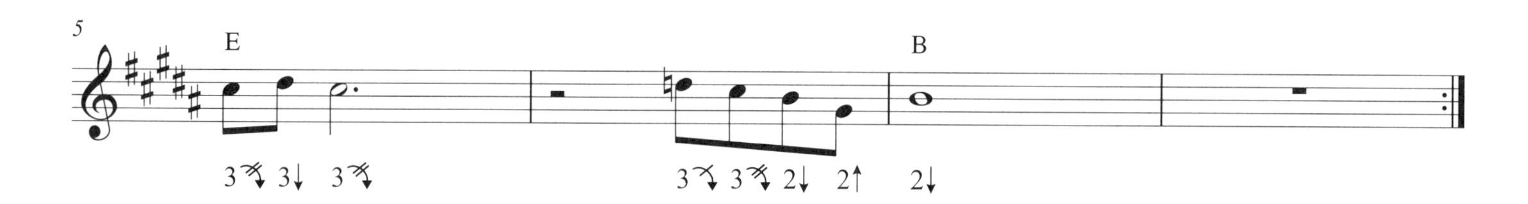

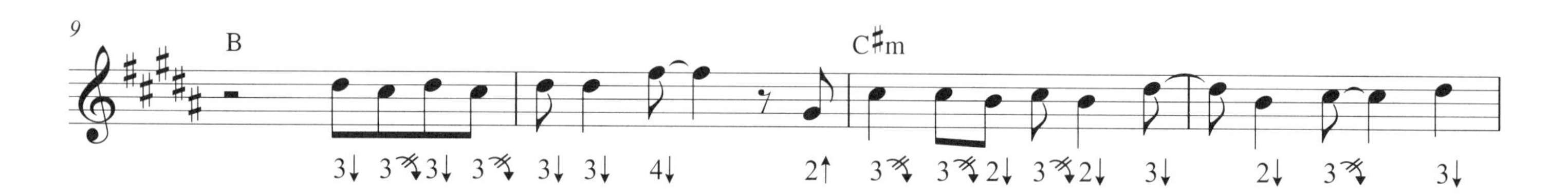

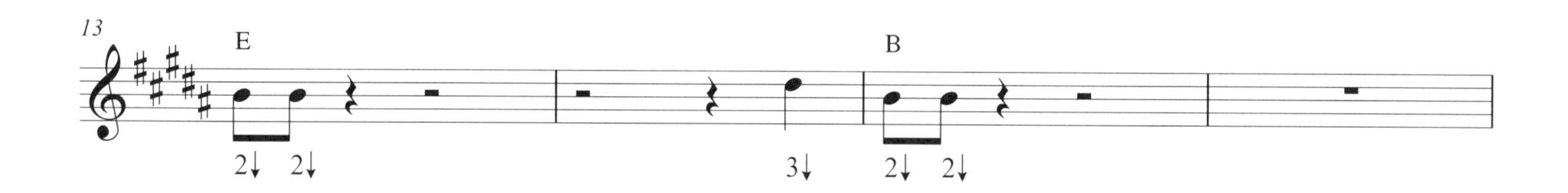

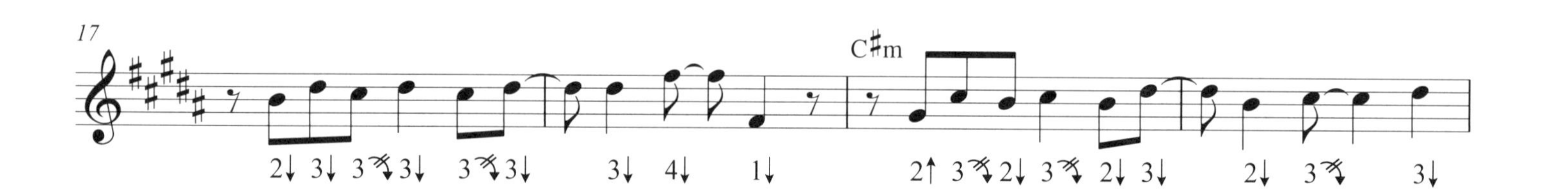

"Oh, Lady Be Good!" is a 1924 song by George Gershwin introduced in the eponymous Broadway musical. A 1947 recording of the song became a hit for Ella Fitzgerald, notable for her scat solo. Howard Levy recorded a beautiful version on the album *Howard Levy's Acoustic Express—Time Capsules*. Even though the melody lays out well with almost no bends on the C harmonica, on Levy's recording, he improvises the solo in 11th position on the A harmonica.

The overblow in bar 9 can be neglected since bars 9 and 13 are usually just played by the rhythm section.

OH, LADY BE GOOD!

from LADY, BE GOOD!

Music and Lyrics by George Gershwin and Ira Gershwin

C Harmonica

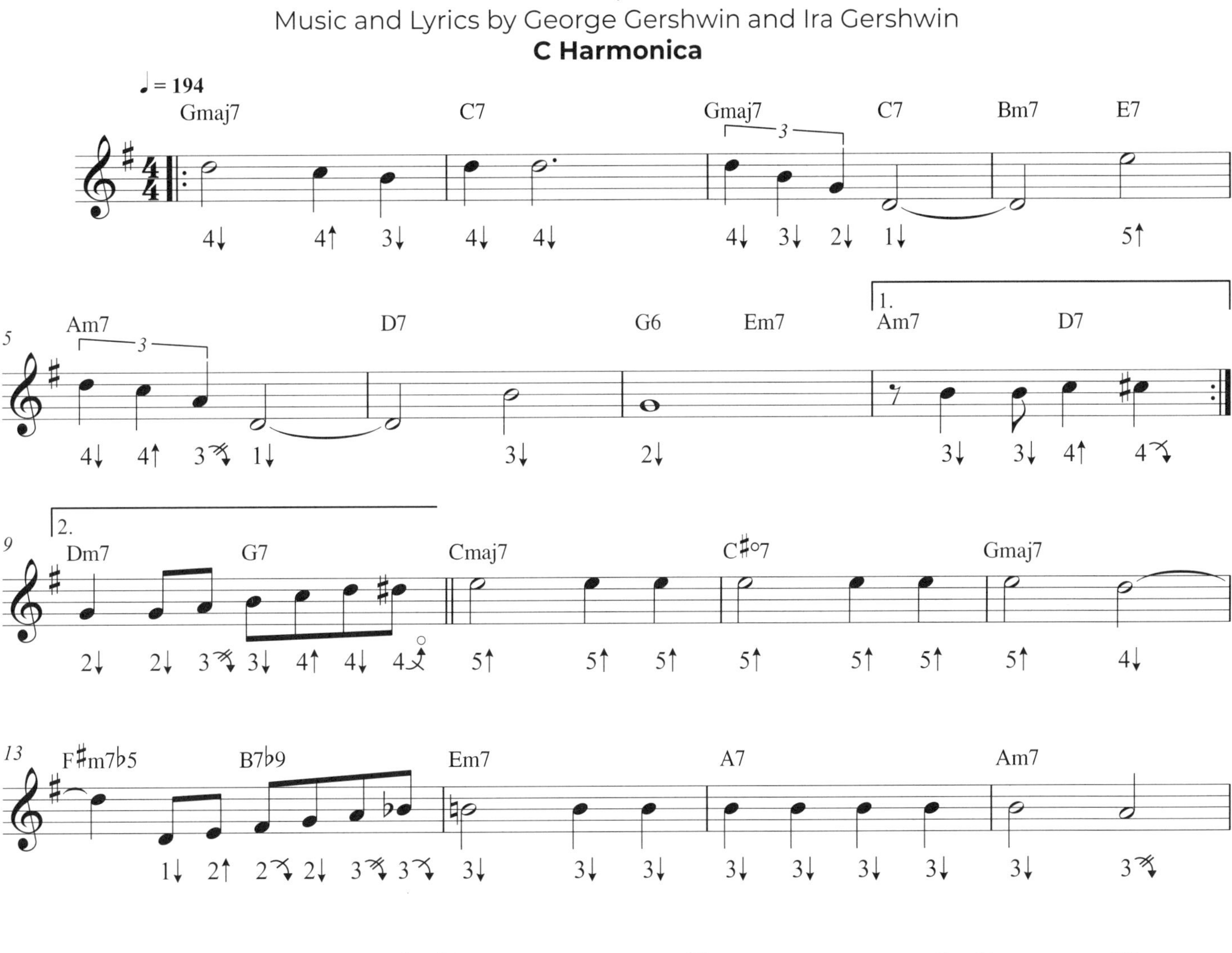

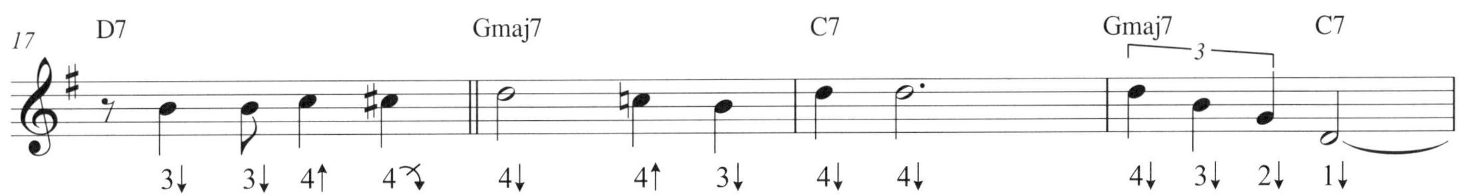

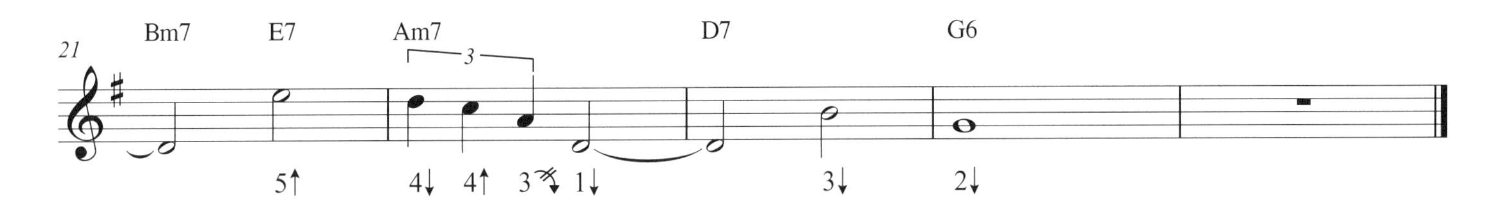

"Mercy, Mercy, Mercy" is a jazz song written by Joe Zawinul for Cannonball Adderley. The first part of the theme is played twice and is completely made of notes from the major pentatonic scale. Even though the song doesn't follow a typical blues progression, the subdominant (IV) chord in the beginning section emphasizes a bluesy and laid-back feeling. You can experiment with different gradations of the 3-hole-draw half-step bend according to your taste here.

MERCY, MERCY, MERCY

By Josef Zawinul

E♭ Harmonica

"Doxy" is an early composition by jazz saxophonist Sonny Rollins, originally recorded with Miles Davis on trumpet. The song was written during a stopover in England on a European tour. It was named after a bread-spread the band was eating in the hotel. The harmonic progression almost exclusively relies on dominant chords, which give the song a lightweight feel. The difference between the 3-hole draw and the 3-hole-draw half-step bend really distinguishes the flavor of the phrases here.

DOXY

By Sonny Rollins

E♭ Harmonica

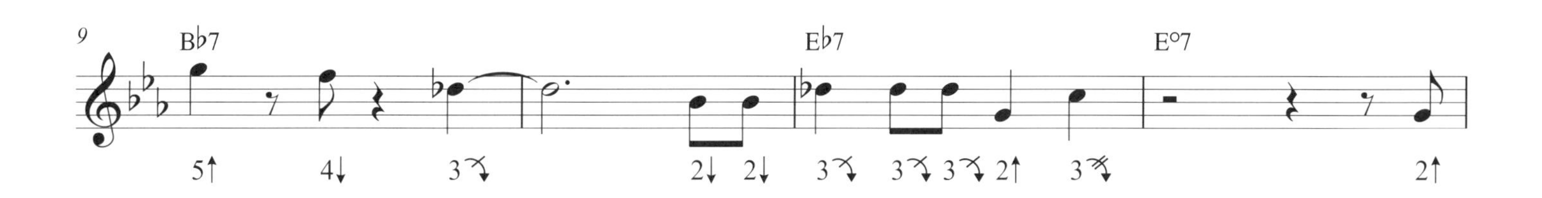

"Sweet Sue, Just You" is an American popular song from 1928. It's also widely popular among jug bands and works well in a jazz manouche setting, too. You can listen to a great harmonica recording of the composition on Mariano Massolo's album *Dark Eyes*. The song doesn't start out on the tonic. It alternates between the ii and V chords, creating an interesting harmonic progression and buildup before resolving to G6 on the 2-hole blow.

Replace the note E♭ (4-hole overblow) in bar 23 by playing D (4-hole draw) for now.

SWEET SUE, JUST YOU

from RHYTHM PARADE

Words by Will J. Harris
Music by Victor Young
C Harmonica

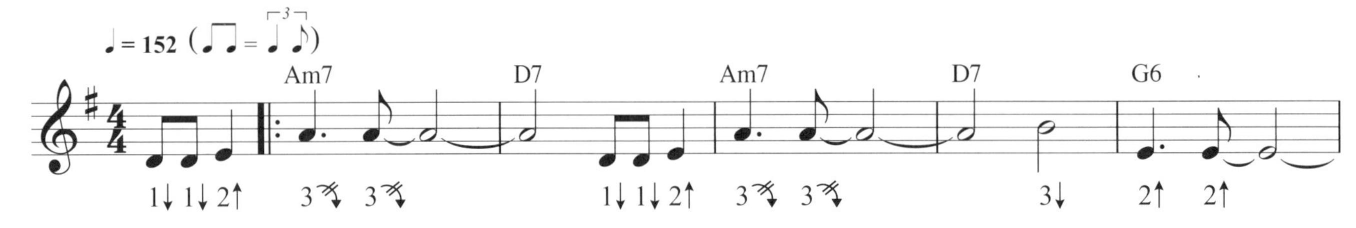

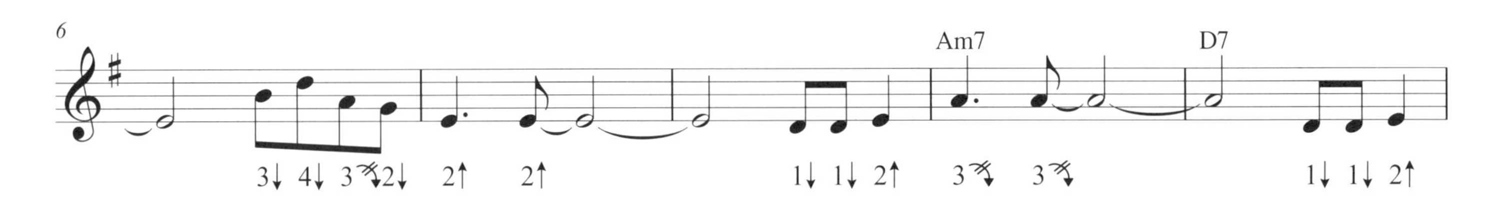

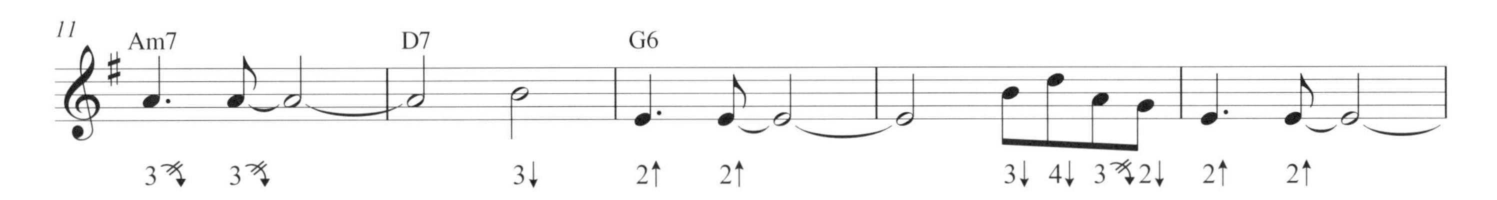

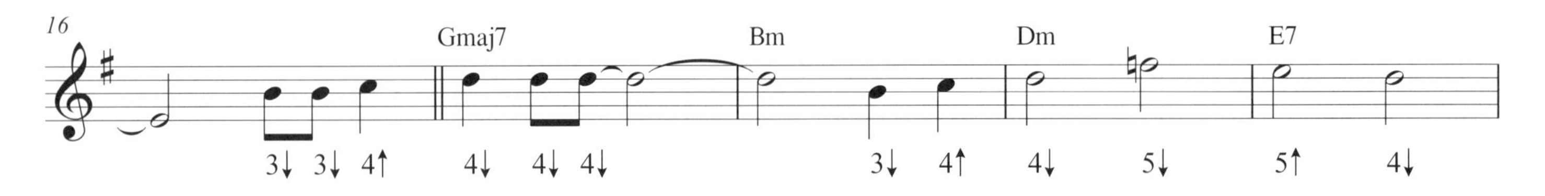

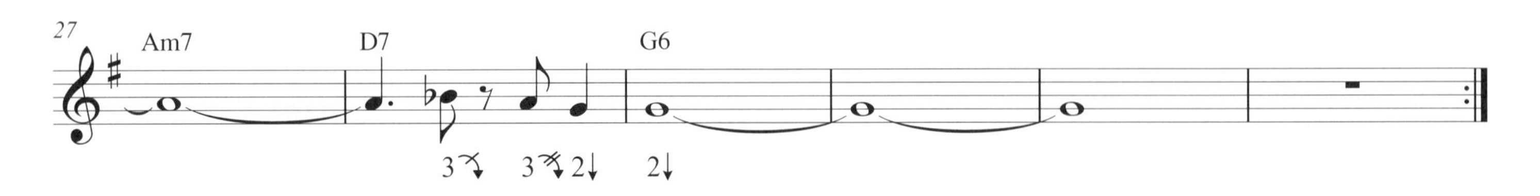

"Basin Street Blues" is a ballad often performed by Dixieland jazz bands. Louis Armstrong recorded the song for the first time in 1928. Basin Street refers to the Main Street of Storyville, the red-light district of early 20th-century New Orleans. The chromatically ascending opening of the melody is a wonderful addition to your blues lick vocabulary. This and a few of the following tunes feature multiple overblows to try out!

BASIN STREET BLUES

Words and Music by Spencer Williams

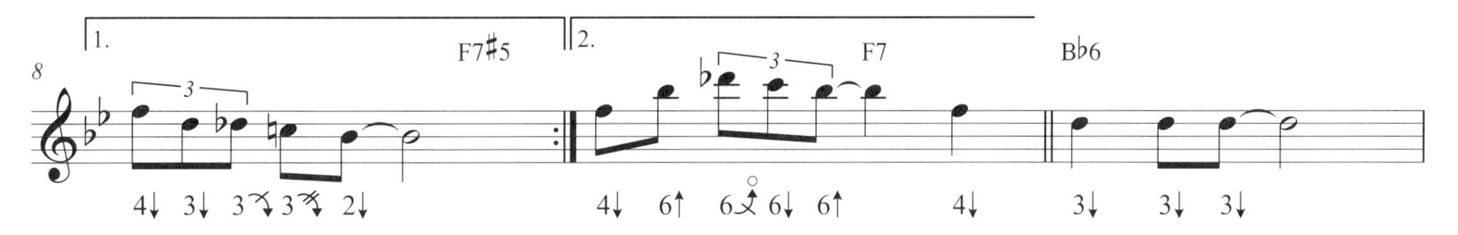

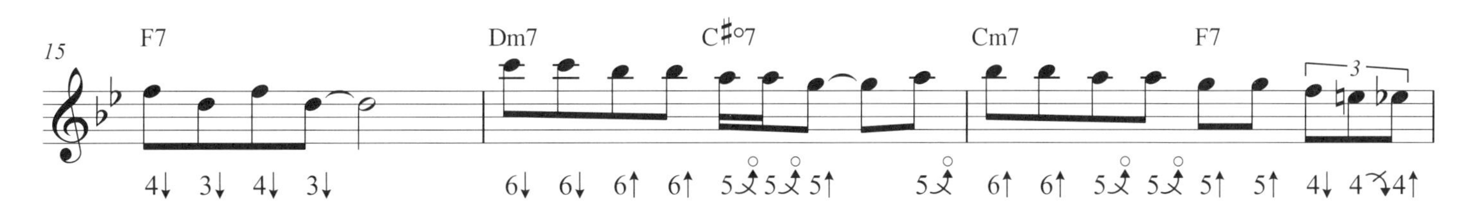

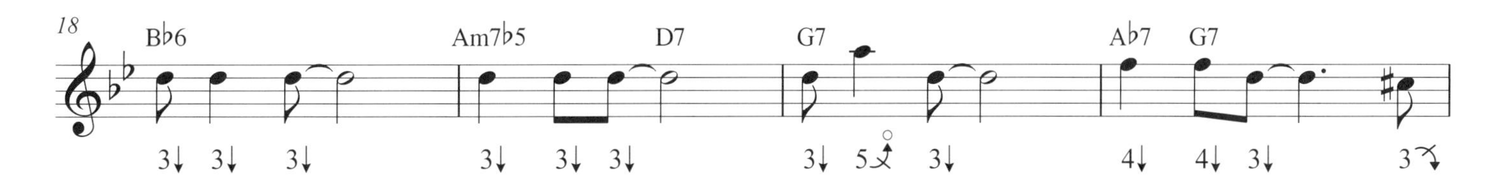

"Au Privave" by Charlie Parker is a great example of combining a 12-bar blues with a fast bebop melody. The chord changes are a little more elaborate, adding a ii–V of the IV chord in bar 4 and the ii chord in bar 9. Playing the melody even at a slow tempo is a challenge, so take your time with this one.

AU PRIVAVE

By Charlie Parker

B♭ Harmonica

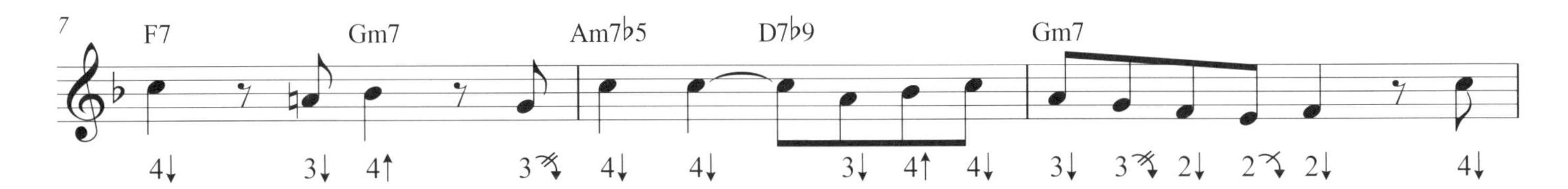

"Walking by Myself" was Jimmy Rogers's sole R&B chart appearance. You will most likely hear or play this song at a blues jam session, even though it is a somewhat unorthodox example of the 8-bar blues chord progression. Gary Moore recorded another well-known version of the song on his 1990 album *Still Got the Blues*.

WALKING BY MYSELF

By James A. Lane

A Harmonica

"Scotch and Soda" is a song recorded by the Kingston Trio in 1958. The composer still remains unknown. Independently, you can find an inspiring recording of the song by Jimi Lee playing guitar and harmonica in a rack on YouTube. The melody is heavily characterized by the 1-hole-draw half-step bend, giving it a bittersweet feel.

SCOTCH AND SODA

Words and Music by Dave Guard

B♭ Harmonica

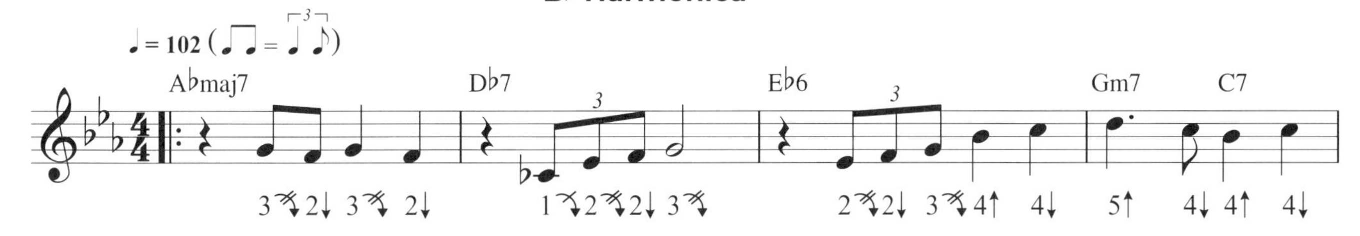

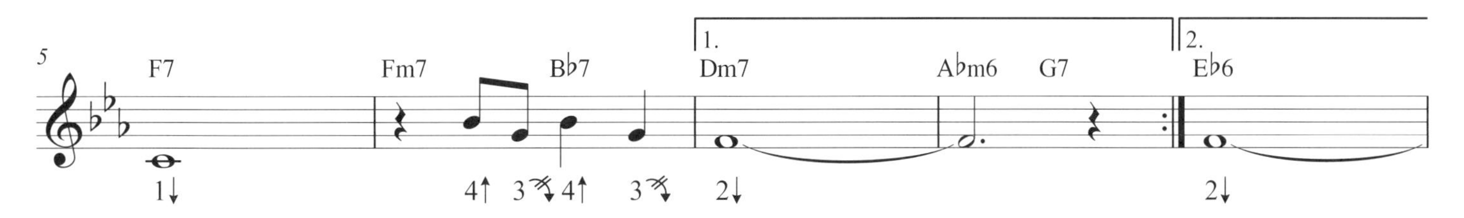

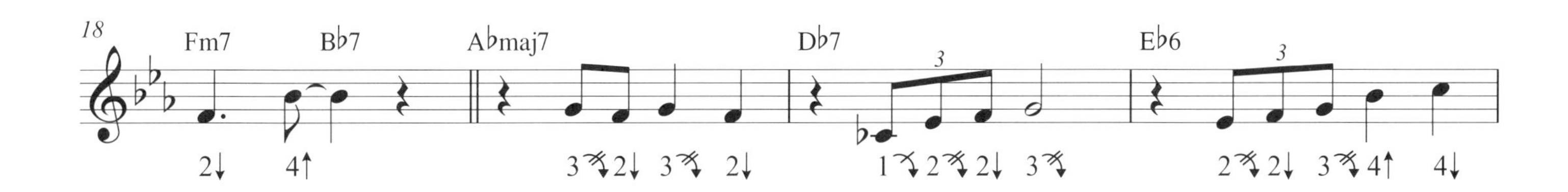

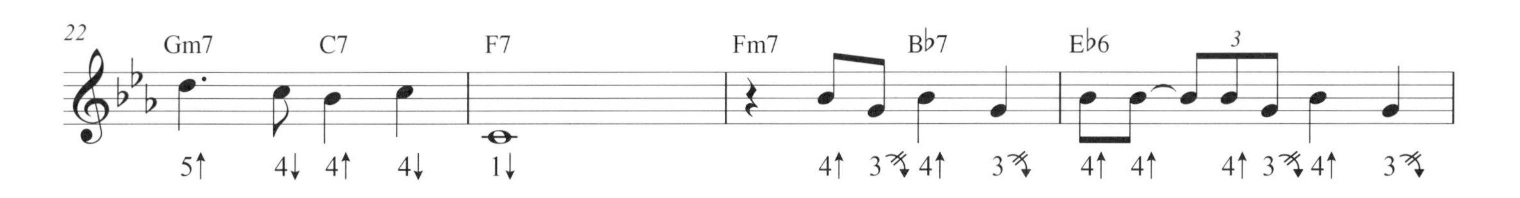

"Broadway" is a 1940 jazz standard popularized and long associated with the Count Basie Orchestra. PT Gazell recorded a great up-tempo version of the song on his album *Back to Back* with Brendan Power. The song features a clear emphasis of the upbeats both in the melody and the accompaniment. The melody is very playful and can be interpreted in various levels of bluesiness through different shades of the 3-hole-draw half-step bend. There is a challenging melodic phrase in bars 13 and 14, which features the descending 6th between F and A♭.

BROADWAY

Words and Music by Billy Byrd, Teddy McRae and Henri Woode

E♭ Harmonica

"What a Wonderful World" is a beautiful ballad in 2nd position that will help you become more comfortable using the 2-hole-draw half-step bend. Clear articulation of the 3-hole-draw bend is crucial for playing the B section. On the B♭ harmonica, it is preferable to use the middle part of your tongue to touch your palate. This song was first recorded by Louis Armstrong and released in 1967 as a single. It topped the pop chart in the United Kingdom, and the recording was later inducted into the Grammy Hall of Fame.

WHAT A WONDERFUL WORLD

Words and Music by George David Weiss and Bob Thiele

B♭ Harmonica

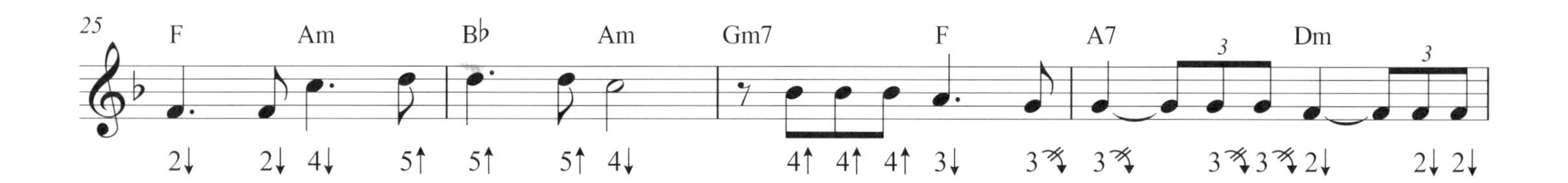

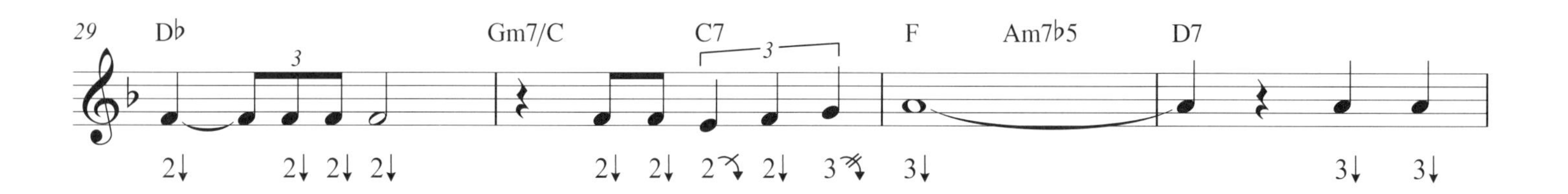

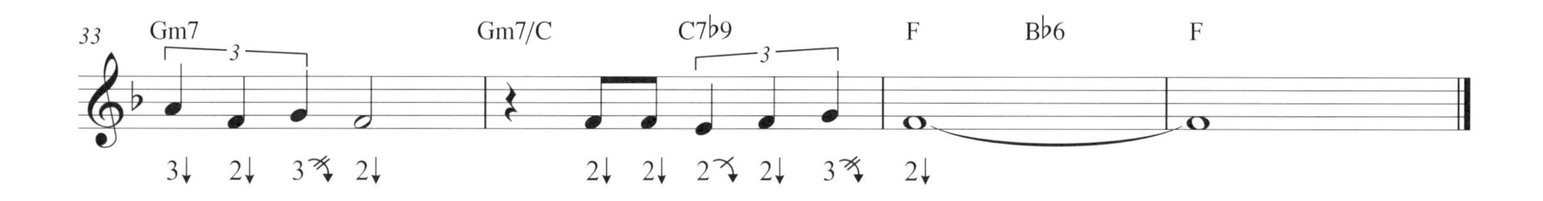

TOOLBOX

The Blues Scale

The *blues scale* is the point of departure for many harmonica players who want to start improvising. Usually, the blues scale is constructed by adding an out-of-key *blue note* to an existing scale, notably by adding the flat-fifth (♭5) to the minor pentatonic scale. It is a scale that can help you evoke the sound of the blues even more. Both in blues and jazz, the scale is commonly based on the key of the song and is used over all changes in a 12-bar blues progression. The blues scale can also be used to improvise over a minor chord.

Blues Scale in G

Regular Tempo

Slow Tempo

"Miss You" is a song by the English rock band the Rolling Stones, and it features the great American blues harmonica player Sugar Blue.

MISS YOU

Words and Music by Mick Jagger and Keith Richards

D Harmonica

♩ = 109

Am Dm 1. 2.

"Cantaloupe Island" is a jazz standard composed and recorded by Herbie Hancock for his 1964 album *Empyrean Isles*. Check out Freddie Hubbard's wonderful solo on the original recording. The three chords and scales to work with are Fm11 (2nd-position minor), D♭7♯11 (10th-position Mixolydian ♯11), and Dm11 (5th-position minor).

CANTALOUPE ISLAND

By Herbie Hancock

B♭ Harmonica

"St. Louis Blues," published in 1914, is a popular American song composed by W.C. Handy in the blues style. As one of the first tunes to succeed as a commercial pop song, it remains a fundamental part of the jazz musician's repertoire. The form is unusual and includes a 16-bar bridge written in the *habanera* rhythm. This tango-like rhythm is notated as a dotted quarter note followed by an eighth note and two quarter notes. While the 12-bar blues in bars 11–34 is in the key of G major, bars 1–10 are in G minor (both 2nd position), creating a nice contrast between the two sections. The melodic motif at the end of the piece follows the chord progression by using the 3-hole draw on the I chord (major 3rd), the 3-hole-draw half-step bend on the IV chord (minor 7th), and the 3-hole-draw whole-step bend on the V chord (perfect 5th).

ST. LOUIS BLUES

from BIRTH OF THE BLUES

Words and Music by W.C. Handy

C Harmonica

Generally speaking, a "work song" is a piece of music closely connected to a form of work. Most of the time, it was sung while conducting a task that required you to coordinate timing. It could also be a song linked to a task (a narrative, protest song, or description). Nat Adderley called his 1960 album *Work Song*, and the title track has become a standard in both vocal and instrumental forms.

WORK SONG

By Nat Adderley

B♭ Harmonica

"Blues by Five" is a catchy blues melody composed by Miles Davis. The original recording on *Cooking with the Miles Davis Quintet* features John Coltrane on saxophone. The key of B♭ requires you to play an E♭ harmonica in 2nd position. A regular E♭ harmonica is comparably high-pitched, and bends have to be intonated more carefully. However, harmonica manufacturers also produce low-E♭ instruments nowadays. If you want to play a lot of melodies written for horns, this could be a clever investment.

> The overblow in bar 12 can be neglected and is usually just played by the rhythm section.

BLUES BY FIVE

By Red Garland

E♭ Harmonica

"Slow Blues in G" is an advanced composition of mine that emphasizes the contrast between playing very bluesy lines and more major-sounding phrases. It follows the standard 12-bar blues form, and its main motif is introduced in bar 1. I usually play the main motif using the tongue-blocking technique with additional tongue slaps right in front of the notes—and even a rolled "r" in front of the E in bar 1. In this song, I tend to use the throat vibrato technique on longer notes (like the D played over the G7 chord). You can also find a *trill* using the 2-hole blow and 3-hole blow in bar 2.

> **TOOLBOX**
>
> **Trills**
>
> A *trill* (tr~~~~~~) is a musical ornament consisting of a rapid alternation between two adjacent notes.

After a partial ascending arpeggio, a bent tongue split leads into bar 5. The lower gradations of the 3-hole-draw bend clarify the chord change before leading back to the main motif, which conclusively adapts from the V to the IV chord in bars 9 and 10, and concludes in bars 11 and 12. I teach the song in even more detail on my YouTube channel.

SLOW BLUES IN G

By Konstantin Reinfeld

C Harmonica

"Melodic Jazz Blues" is an advanced song that I composed for my students. The goal was to include as many bends as possible while avoiding overbends. The first motif is basically just an ascending G major pentatonic scale that skips one note only. However, to give the phrase a bluesier feel, you could *scoop* the B note in bar 1, quickly approaching it from a bend below. The melodic content in bar 2 is a great exercise to isolate and loop. Then, you can move on to the 4-hole-draw half-step bend being used as a chromatic approach note in bars 3 and 4. In the two bars that follow, the melody basically outlines the chords before approaching the turnaround. The chromatically descending passage in bar 10 contains another great pattern to zoom in on. You can find a more detailed explanation of the song on my YouTube channel.

MELODIC JAZZ BLUES

By Konstantin Reinfeld

C Harmonica

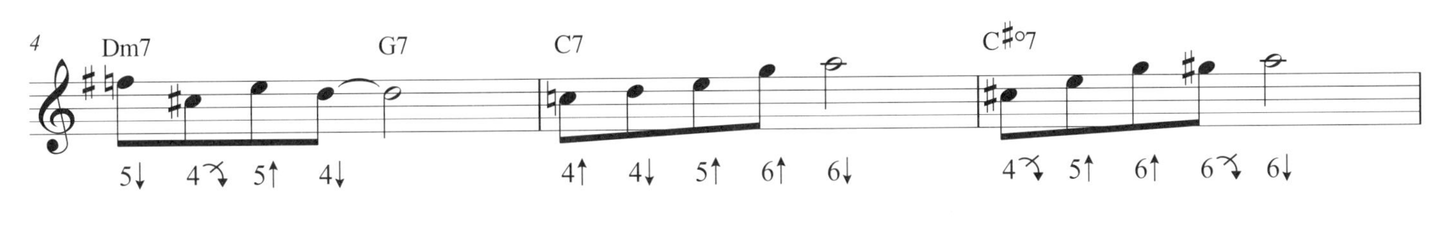

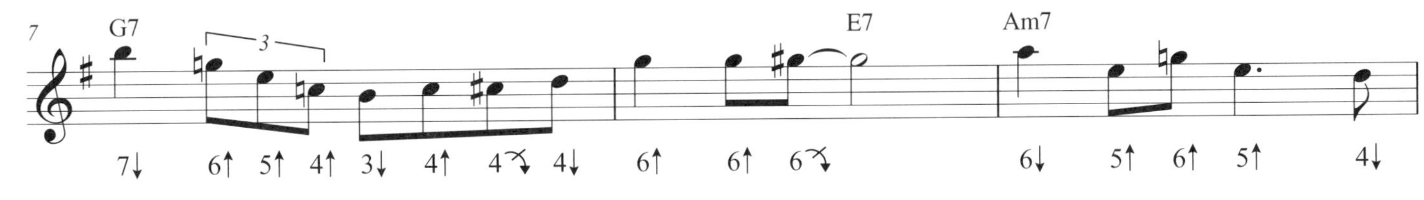

"Get Up Again" is one of my deep house productions that puts a spotlight on the harmonica. It features a blistering solo built on the major pentatonic scale. Check out the transcription below for reference. (**Note:** In the second-to-last measure, you will see the symbol ʌ. This indicates a strong accent, or emphasis.) To make the solo section more expressive, use vibrato on the long notes. I included this song to give you an idea of what a fully transcribed solo can look like.

GET UP AGAIN

By Konstantin Reinfeld

E♭ Harmonica

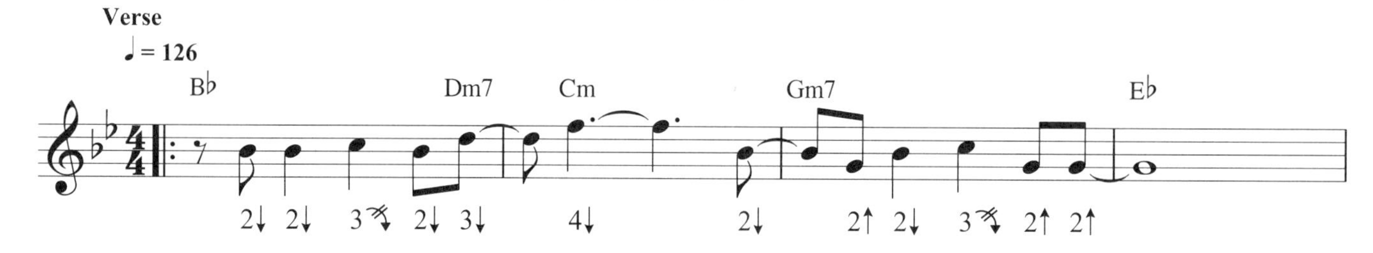

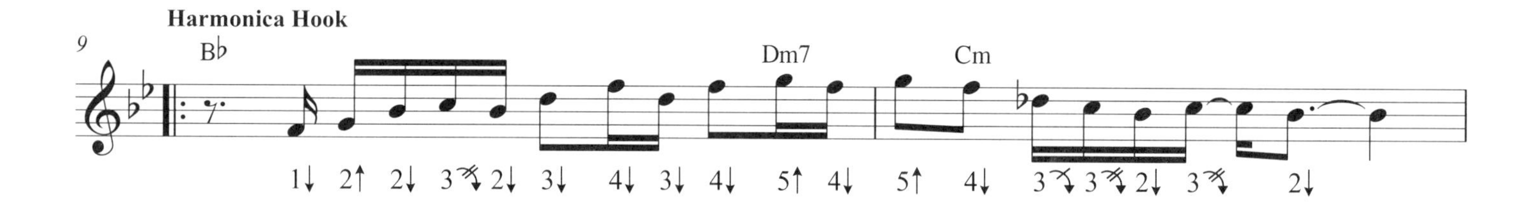

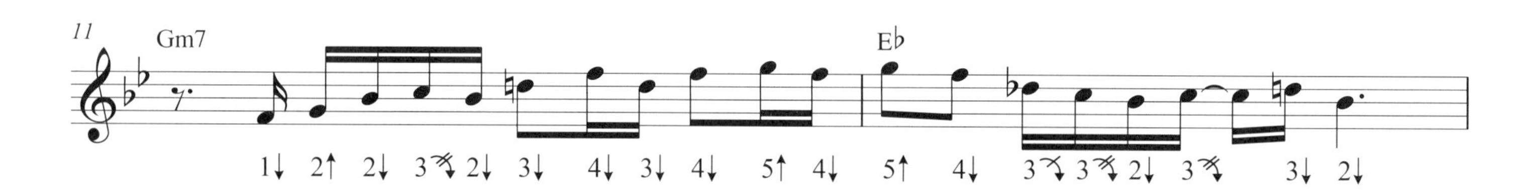

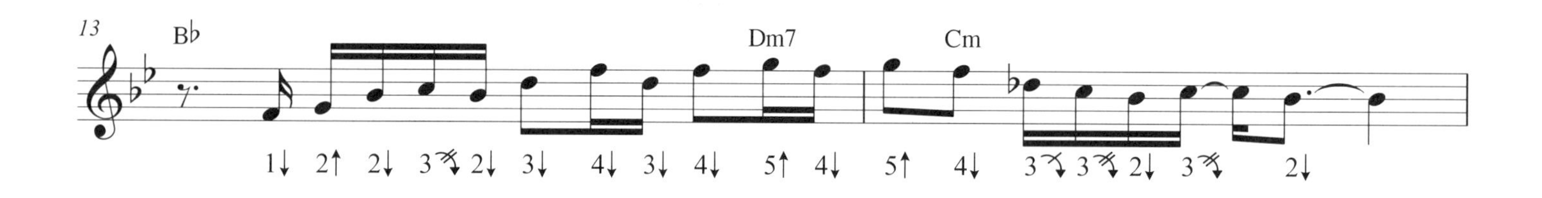

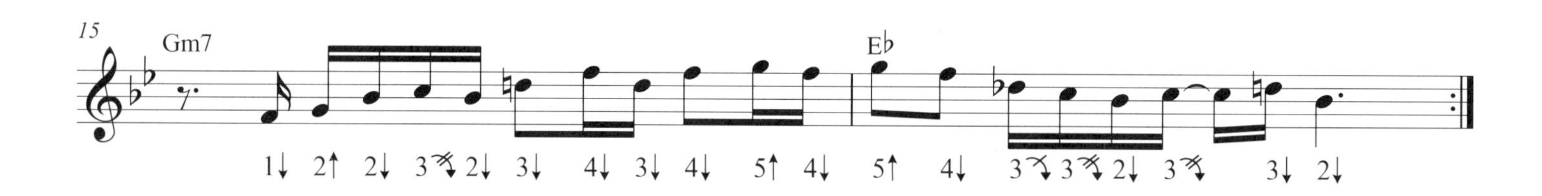

Harmonica Solo

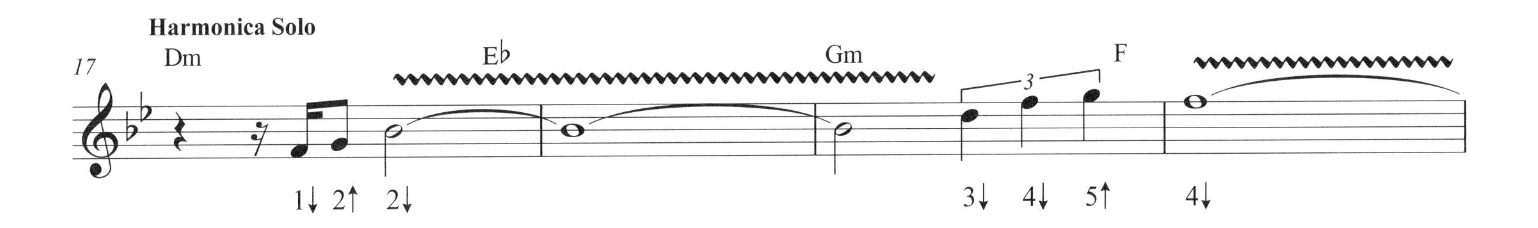

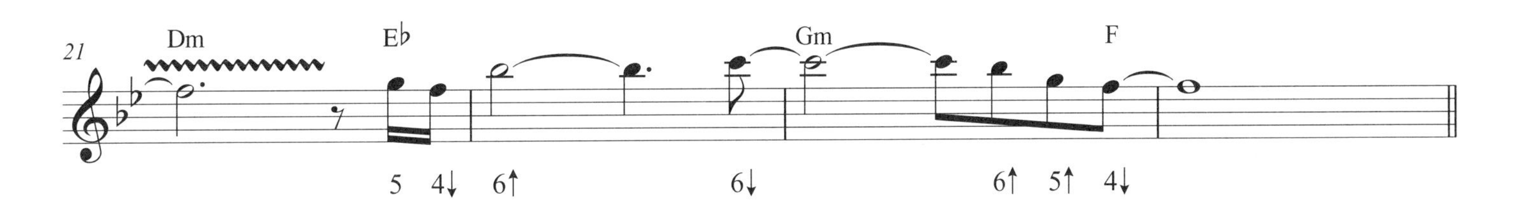

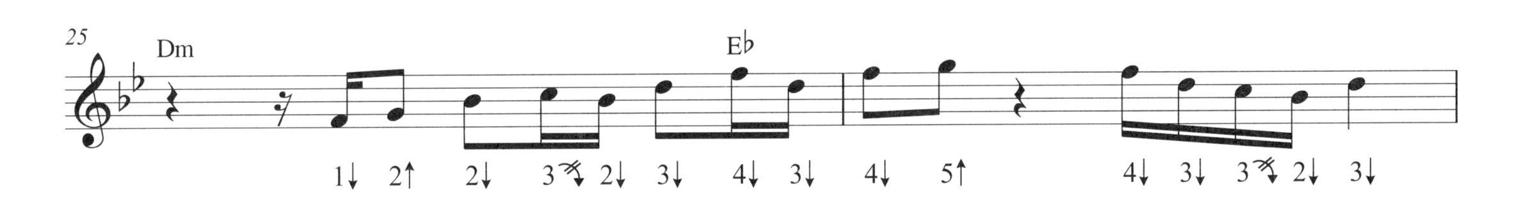

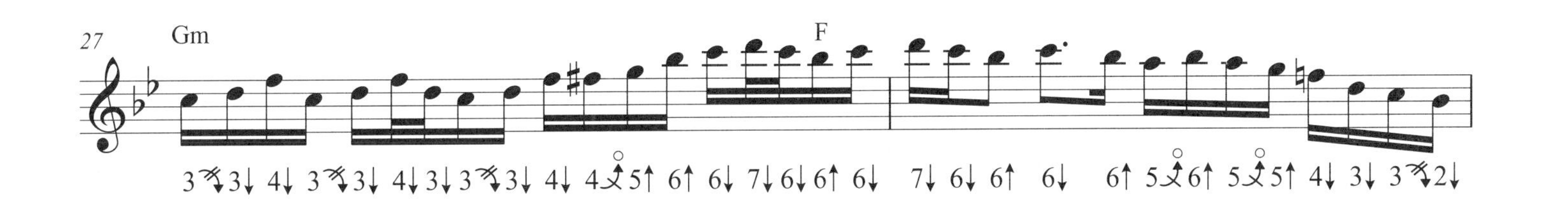

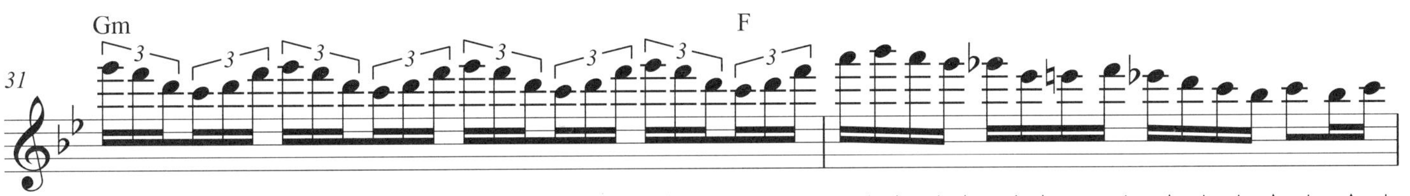

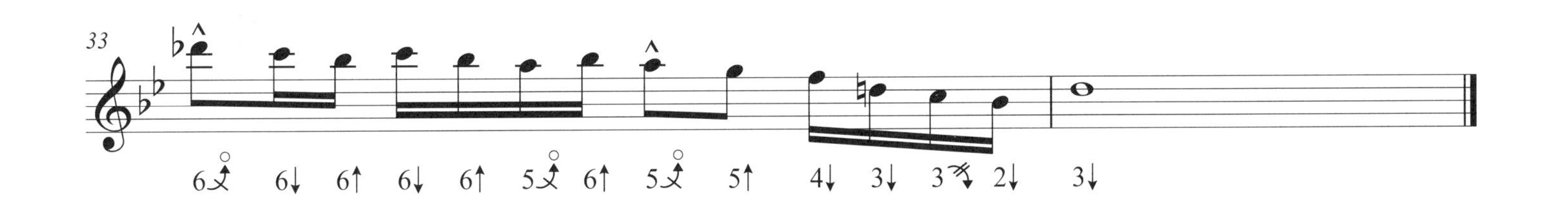

LESSON 24:

Songs in 3rd Position

"Comin' Home Baby" was originally written as an instrumental by Ben Tucker. The song has been covered numerous times, but the vocal version by American jazz singer Mel Tormé became a U.S. Top 40 hit in 1962. Michael Bublé released another well-known recording of the song in 2008. The chord progression is based on a minor 12-bar blues. The alternate subdominant sound in bar 5 and the chromatically descending turnaround give the song its unique character. Try to play the last note of every phrase staccato to leave space and support the groove.

TOOLBOX

Staccato

To play notes *staccato* means to play them in a sharp, detached way. Staccato is indicated with a dot above or below a note or chord. An example of this can be heard in the recording of the next tune, "Comin' Home Baby."

COMIN' HOME BABY

Words and Music by Robert Dorough and Benjamin Tucker

C Harmonica

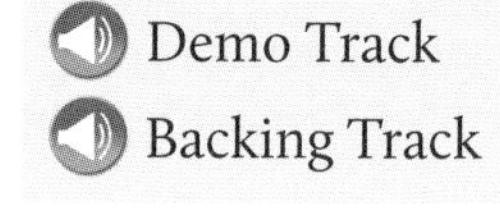

"Blue Drag" contains a comparably easy melody, and its short structure allows for extended improvisations. You can add scoops on the 6-hole draw. In bar 7, you can really lean into the 6-hole-draw half-step bend to intensify the blues feeling. The Argentinian harmonica player and teacher Mariano Massolo initiated a worldwide collaboration of harmonica players that recorded the song together. The result was published in October 2020 and features Federico Linari (Argentina), Howard Levy (USA), Indiara Sfair (Brazil), Carlos del Junco (Canada), Antonio Serrano (Spain), Cy Leo (Hong Kong), Billy Branch (USA), Rick Estrin (USA), Babak Safarnejad (Iran), Franco Luciani (Argentina), Rachelle Plas (France), and yours truly.

BLUE DRAG

By Josef Myrow

C Harmonica

"Equinox" is a minor blues jazz standard by American jazz saxophone player and composer John Coltrane. It is a great and easy introduction to playing a 12-bar minor blues in 3rd position. At the same time, it gets you used to the bluesy ♭VI–V–i turnaround.

EQUINOX

By John Coltrane

B Harmonica

"It Don't Mean a Thing (If It Ain't Got That Swing)" is a great exercise for improving your swing feel and articulation. It might be one of the fastest compositions in this book. Duke Ellington wrote the song in 1931, and in 2008 his own recording was inducted into the Grammy Hall of Fame. You can listen to a very energetic harmonica version of the composition on Mariano Massolo's album *Dark Eyes*. The melody sounds one octave higher than written.

IT DON'T MEAN A THING (IF IT AIN'T GOT THAT SWING)

Words and Music by Duke Ellington and Irving Mills

F Harmonica

"The House of the Rising Sun" is a traditional folk song. The most successful commercial version, recorded in 1964 by the British rock band the Animals, was a number-one hit on the UK Singles Chart and in the U.S. and Canada. The melody makes almost exclusive use of the minor pentatonic scale, except in the second-to-last bar where it outlines the E7 chord. You could practice the transition between the 4-hole-draw half-step bend and the 3-hole-draw whole-step bend using a drone in E or D♭.

THE HOUSE OF THE RISING SUN

Traditional English Ballad

G Harmonica

Ennio Morricone's soundtrack for the film *Once Upon a Time in the West* includes some of the most famous harmonica melodies ever. His main theme for *The Good, the Bad and the Ugly* also features a harmonica, but the fast-paced guitar melody—which includes reoccurring jumps between holes 6 and 8—is worth practicing, too. Try to stop the airstream during the jump by pressing your tongue against the roof of your mouth.

THE GOOD, THE BAD AND THE UGLY

from THE GOOD, THE BAD AND THE UGLY

By Ennio Morricone

C Harmonica

"Summertime" is an aria composed in 1934 by George Gershwin for the opera *Porgy and Bess*. It soon became a popular jazz standard, and even the late George "Harmonica" Smith recorded the melody on the chromatic harmonica. Make sure that you get the correct intonation of the 3-hole-draw whole-step bend.

SUMMERTIME

from PORGY AND BESS®

Music and Lyrics by George Gershwin, DuBose and Dorothy Heyward and Ira Gershwin

G Harmonica

"Song for My Father" is probably Horace Silver's best-known composition. The melody was inspired by Cape Verdean folk music, and it is layered on top of a bass *ostinato* (repeating accompaniment pattern). Playing the melody on the E♭ harmonica sounds very sweet and funky. It can feel a little unfamiliar to use a comparably high-pitched harmonica, so try to be careful about the intonation of your bends.

SONG FOR MY FATHER

Words and Music by Horace Silver

E♭ Harmonica

"Água de Beber" by Antônio Carlos Jobim is a bossa nova jazz standard with a bluesy flavor. This is most notable in the opening melody, which highlights the ♭5 beautifully. The title of the composition is inspired by water running close to Catetinho, the provisional palace of the former president of Brazil.

ÁGUA DE BEBER

English Words by Norman Gimbel
Portuguese Words by Vinicius De Moraes
Music by Antonio Carlos Jobim
G Harmonica

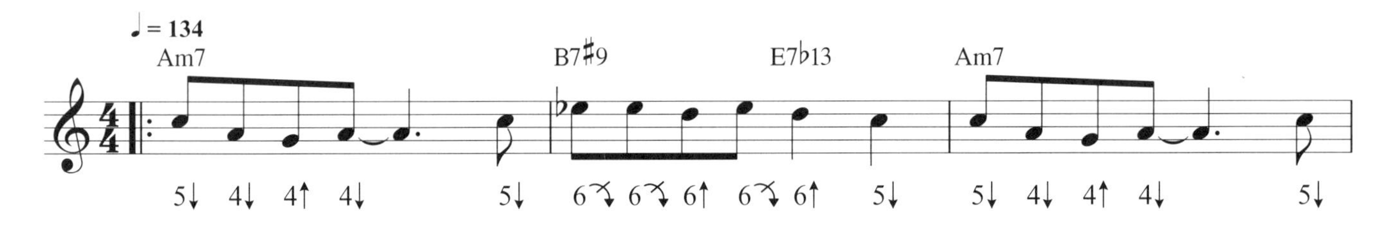

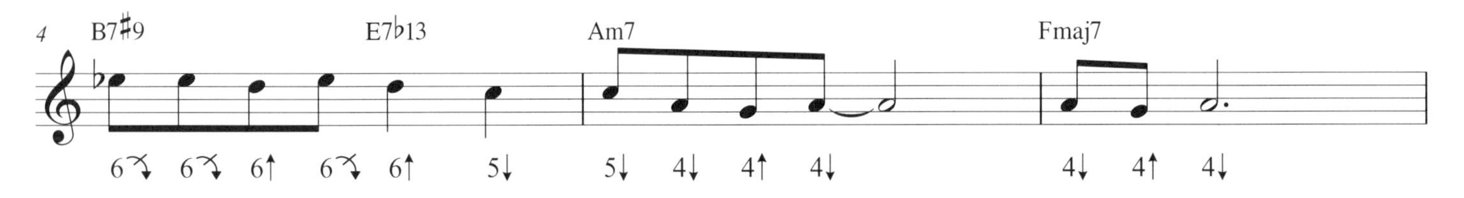

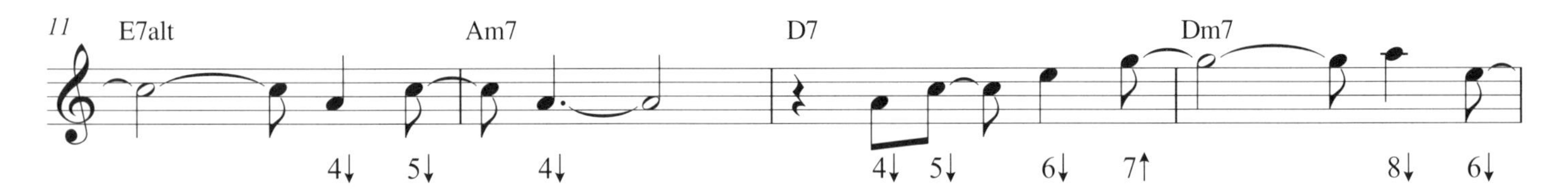

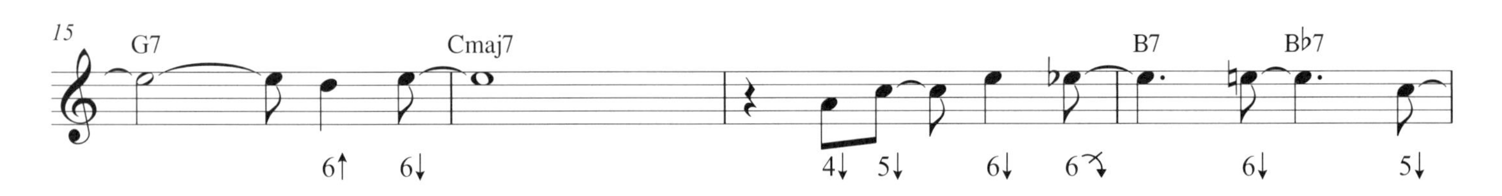

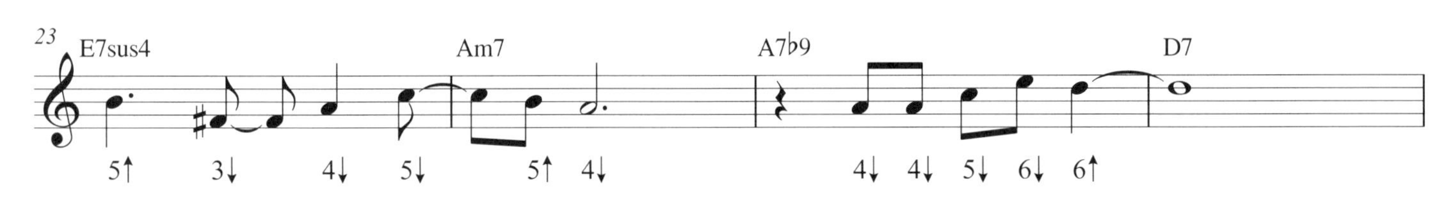

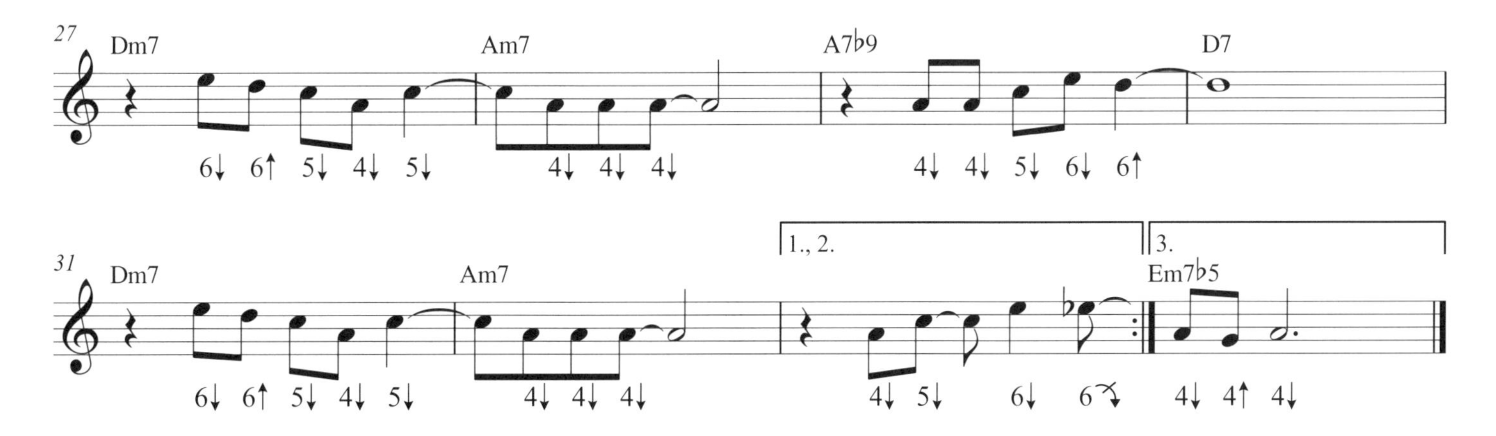

"Bei Mir Bist Du Schon" is a popular Yiddish song that became a worldwide hit when recorded by the Andrews Sisters in November 1937. You can find a truly captivating recording of it on YouTube played by Argentinian harmonica player Mariano Massolo. It really highlights the bluesy flavor of the melody.

BEI MIR BIST DU SCHON (MEANS THAT YOU'RE GRAND)

Original Words by Jacob Jacobs
Music by Sholom Secunda
English Version by Sammy Cahn and Saul Chaplin

B♭ Harmonica

"Afro Blue" is a jazz standard composed by Mongo Santamaría. The original recording is built on a typical African 3:2 cross-rhythm, or *hemiola*. While the bass plays six cross-beats per two main beats, the flute and the marimba emphasize the two primary beats (dotted quarter notes). You can listen to an eclectic version of "Afro Blue" on the album *Done with the Devil* by Jason Ricci and New Blood.

AFRO BLUE

By Mongo Santamaria

C Harmonica

You can find countless harmonica recordings of "Ain't No Sunshine" online, and most of them are being played in 3rd position. Listen closely to the rhythm of the melody, and be sure to hit those sixteenth notes. It is always a good idea to stick to the original phrasing of the melody first, knowing it by heart before taking any liberties. Bill Withers was inspired to write the song after watching the 1962 movie *Days of Wine and Roses*.

AIN'T NO SUNSHINE

Words and Music by Bill Withers

G Harmonica

"Lambada" is a wonderful pop song from France released by Kaoma in 1989. The melody was played by the famous Argentinian bandoneon player Juan José Mosalini, and it sounds very authentic on the harmonica. Be careful to produce the correct intonation on the 3-hole bends. In bars 3 and 6, the melody resolves to A, the 5th of the key. However, starting in bar 7, the 3-hole half-step bend takes over, representing the minor 3rd of the G minor chord.

LAMBADA

Words and Music by Jose Ari, Marcia Ferreira, Alberto Maravi,
Ulises Hermosa and Gonzalo Hermosa

C Harmonica

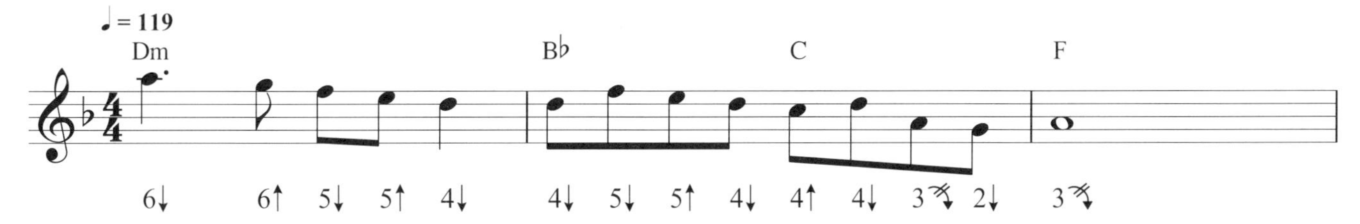

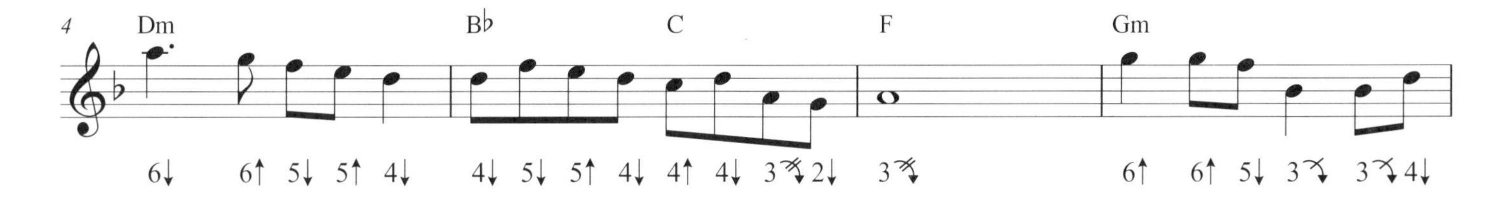

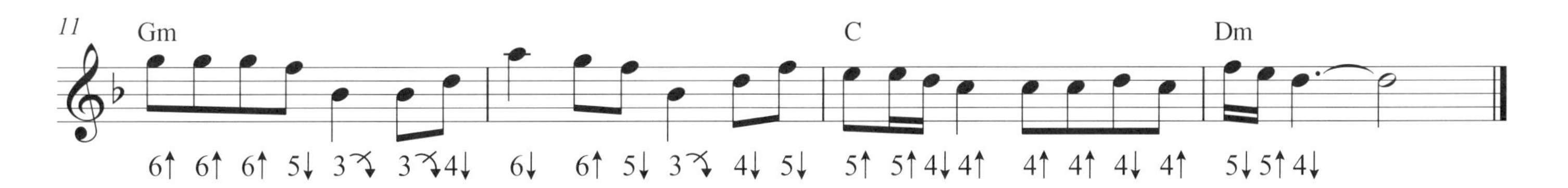

"My Favorite Things" is a fast waltz written by Richard Rodgers for the musical *The Sound of Music*. It was sung by Mary Martin on Broadway and later by Julie Andrews in the film version. The main motif of the melody is supported by an E minor harmony, which then switches to G major. Brad Mehldau's interpretation of the piece on the album *Live in Marciac* is a noteworthy recording. The melody even found its way into recent pop culture with Ariana Grande's release of "7 Rings" in 2019.

MY FAVORITE THINGS

from THE SOUND OF MUSIC

Lyrics by Oscar Hammerstein II

Music by Richard Rodgers

D Harmonica

"Toxic" by Britney Spears is an example of a melodically and harmonically more interesting pop song that is a real challenge for every harmonica player. The bluesy and Eastern European flavors induced by the high-pitched Bollywood strings are recreated by the 6-hole bend. Only later does the minor color turn a little brighter with the use of the Aeolian and Dorian modes.

TOXIC

Words and Music by Cathy Dennis, Henrick Nils Jonback, Christian Lars Karlsson and Pontus Winnberg

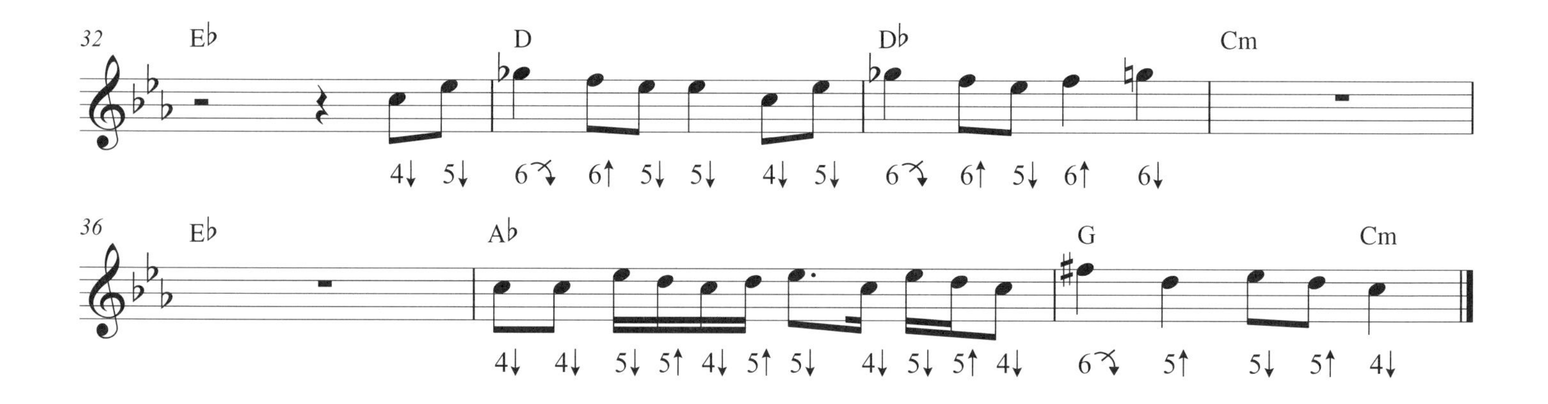

"Badinerie" is part of *Suite No. 2 in B minor* by Johann Sebastian Bach, and it has become a showpiece for solo flautists because of its quick pace and difficulty. Playing the melody on the diatonic harmonica requires a lot of precision and clear articulation. Even though the recorded guitar accompaniment presents a Latin version of the piece, you still have to think like a classical musician. Try to highlight the downbeats by using a little more air while practicing the melody slowly. You can really exaggerate by turning the melodic material on the upbeats into ghost notes. Listen closely to the recording to hear which notes to articulate and which phrases to play legato. Also on the recording, some of the eighth notes are embellished to give you a sense of how this can sound when mastered. For now, however, you can play the regular eighth notes as written.

BADINERIE

By Johann Sebastian Bach

A Harmonica

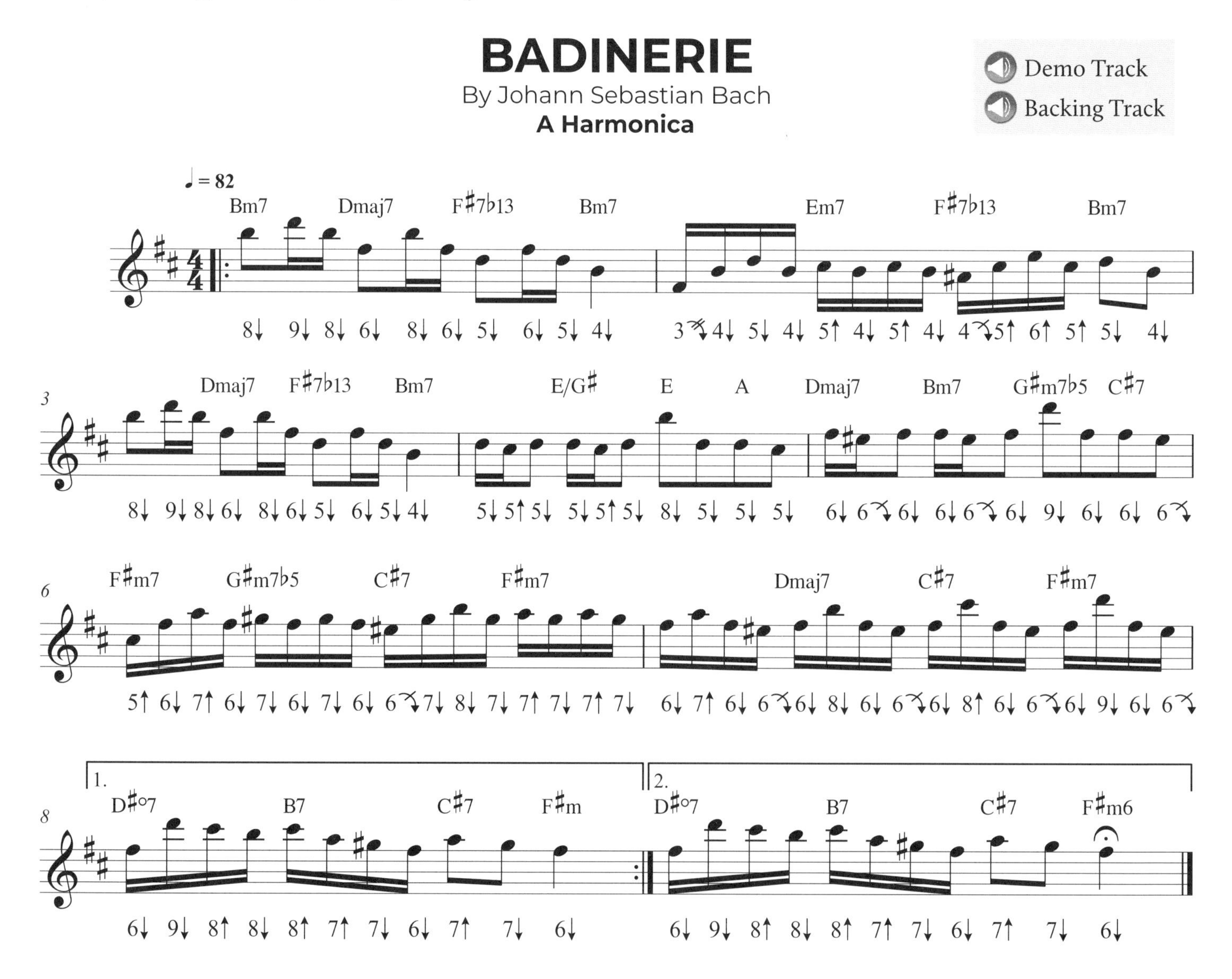

"Mr. P.C." is a 12-bar jazz piece. It offers you a great opportunity to dive into an up-tempo minor blues while practicing your articulation and syncopation. The composition by John Coltrane is named in tribute to the bass player Paul Chambers. Say "hah-dah" through the instrument while playing the ascending scalar passages in bars 1 and 5. The chord progression features a bluesy turnaround with a ♭VI7 chord in bar 9.

MR. P.C.

By John Coltrane

B♭ Harmonica

"Seven Orange" is one of my very first compositions, and it came to life in 2012. It features a nice *montuno* pattern that enables the harmonica to lay out the complete harmonic structure of the piece. The term *montuno* refers to a piano *guajeo*, which is an ostinato figure accompanying the montuno section of a song in Cuban music. It describes a repeated, syncopated piano vamp. In this case, the chords follow the Andalusian cadence, which is often categorized as a flamenco guitar chord progression, though it is used in many musical genres. You can listen to the recording on my album *Mr. Quilento*.

SEVEN ORANGE

By Konstantin Reinfeld

LESSON 25:
Songs in 4th Position

Playing in 4th position can be a great choice if the melody of a song is based on the natural minor or the *harmonic minor scale* (natural minor scale with a ♮7). It feels very natural to play in this key, since it is the relative minor key of the 1st-position major. "Manhã de Carnaval" ("A Day in the Life of a Fool") is a song by Brazilian composer Luiz Bonfá, and it appeared as a principal theme in the 1959 Portuguese-language film *Orfeu Negro* ("Black Orpheus"). Many diatonic harmonica players like to use a C harmonica to interpret the melody. However, another special version of the song can be found on the album *The Brasil Project* by chromatic harmonica old hand Toots Thielemans.

MANHÃ DE CARNAVAL

By Luiz Bonfa

C Harmonica

> **TOOLBOX**
>
> **Relative Keys**
> *Relative keys* are major and minor keys that have the same key signature. They share all the same notes, but the scales are arranged in a different order of whole steps and half steps. For example, the keys of C major and A minor are relative keys.

"O Morro Não Tem Vez" (also known as "Favela") is a bossa nova jazz standard composed by Antônio Carlos Jobim. The phrase has been used in opposition of economic injustice in Brazil. The melody makes almost exclusive use of the minor pentatonic scale in A (A section) and D (B section) and is easy to play on a C harmonica.

O MORRO NÃO TEM VEZ

Words and Music by Antonio Carlos Jobim and Vinicius De Moraes

C Harmonica

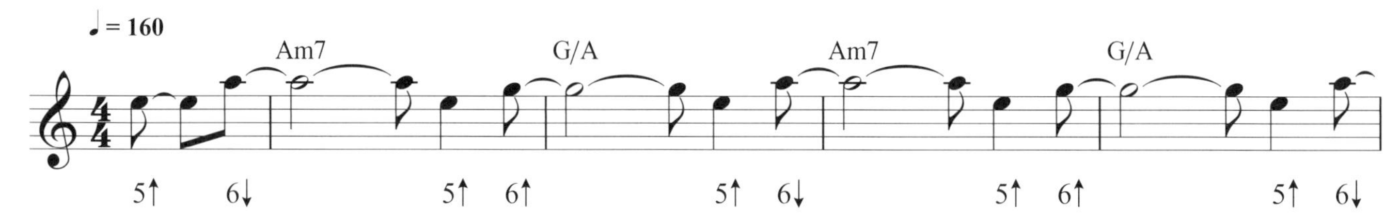

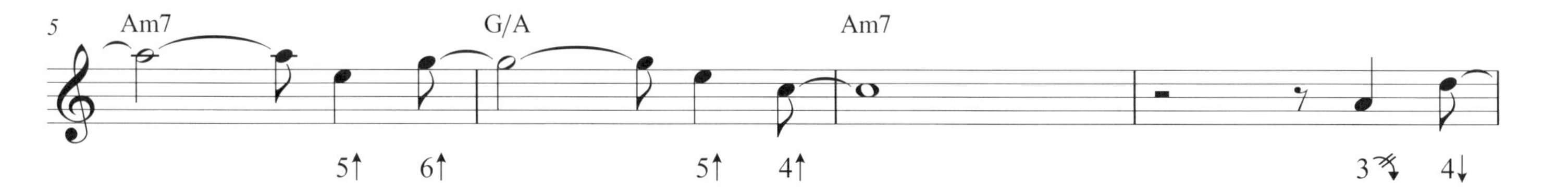

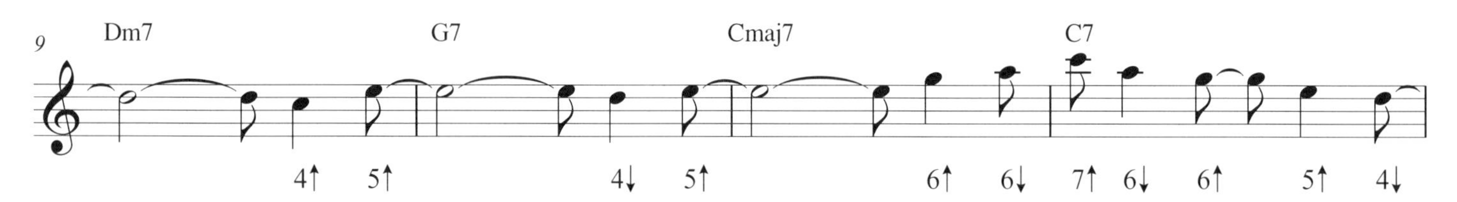

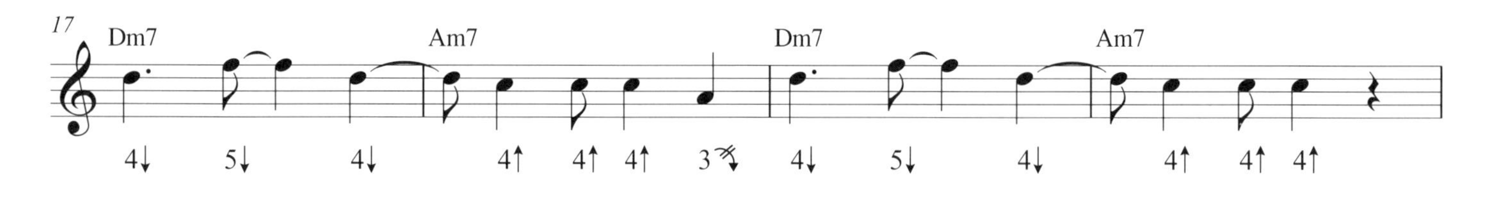

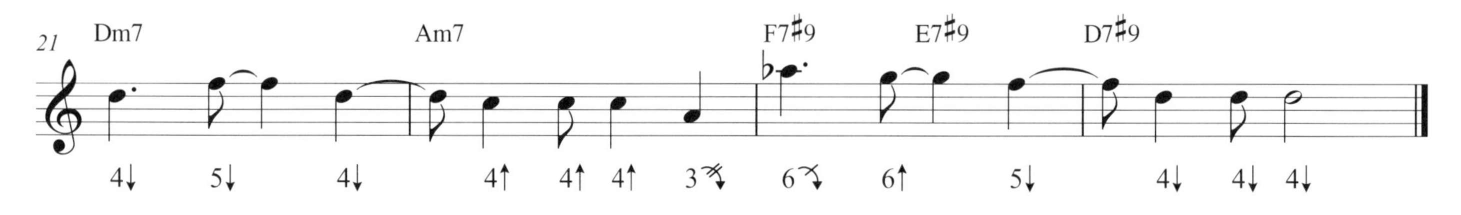

"Autumn Leaves" is probably one of the most popular jazz standards in the world. An instrumental version by pianist Roger Williams was a number-one hit in the U.S. Billboard charts in 1955. Playing it in 4th position on the G harmonica works well and enables you to improvise diatonically using the natural notes of the instrument. It is a great way to become acquainted with jazz harmony. The song's chord progressions (ii–V–I–IV in G to ii°–V–i in Em) follow the circle of 5ths, which is typical for jazz. You can listen to a rather unorthodox harmonica recording of this tune on Reinberg's album *Old Friend*.

Replace the note A♯ (4-hole overblow) in bar 24 by playing A (4-hole draw) for now.

AUTUMN LEAVES

English lyric by Johnny Mercer
French lyric by Jacques Prevert
Music by Joseph Kosma

G Harmonica

"Popcorn" is a melody that can be played comparably staccato by using a lot of articulation. The first bars outline the Am7 chord very nicely, while the second half of the melody relies on descending scalar motion. Written by Gershon Kingsley, the song was released in 1969 and many famous cover versions followed.

POPCORN

Music by Gershon Kingsley

C Harmonica

Playing the *Game of Thrones* theme almost feels like a scale exercise. The first bar outlines the C minor chord using the 1st, 3rd, 4th, and 5th degrees of the scale. The second bar outlines the C major chord, raising the 3rd degree of the scale by a half step. Make sure to articulate the 4-hole draw here.

GAME OF THRONES

Theme from the HBO Series GAME OF THRONES

By Ramin Djawadi

The melody of Britney Spears's debut single "...Baby One More Time" is a great example of using the harmonic minor scale, which lays out exceptionally well in 4th position. The transition from the characteristic notes on the 5-hole draw and 6-hole half-step bend feels very fluid. Another big advantage of playing a minor key in 4th position is having the option to bend down the tonic note to the major 7th.

...BABY ONE MORE TIME

Words and Music by Max Martin

LESSON 26:

Song in 5th Position

5th position is a useful option for minor-key tunes. It enables you to play the natural minor scale with bends, providing the opportunity for more expressiveness than in 4th position. It almost feels like playing in 2nd-position major, which is the relative major key.

"Saint James Infirmary" is an American blues song of uncertain origin and is a popular melody to play on the harmonica. Louis Armstrong made the song famous in his 1928 recording. You can encounter many different interpretations of the song online. Most of them are being played in 3rd position though. In order to avoid the 6-hole overblow, the following example gives the tablature for 5th position.

SAINT JAMES INFIRMARY

Words and Music by Joe Primrose

C Harmonica

LESSON 27:
Songs in 12th Position

Playing in 12th position (the key of the 5-hole draw) is a useful option when coming face to face with major melodies that still need to be a little more expressive and/or bluesy. Especially, the middle octave is easy to navigate and more lively compared to 1st-position major.

"Ain't That a Kick in the Head" is a perfect example of chromatic approach notes being used in a melody. Both the major 3rd and the perfect 5th of the F major and G minor chords are approached from a half step below.

F Major Chromatic Approach

Regular Tempo

Slow Tempo

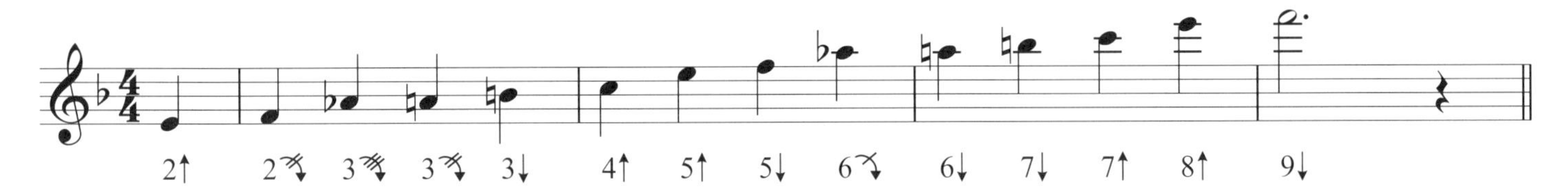

Replace the note E♭ (1-hole overblow) in bar 12 by playing D (1-hole draw) for now.

AIN'T THAT A KICK IN THE HEAD

Words by Sammy Cahn
Music by James Van Heusen
C Harmonica

"Georgia on My Mind" is a popular song among diatonic harmonica players. Written in 1930 by Hoagy Carmichael, it has often been associated with Ray Charles. The B section of the song modulates to the relative minor key.

You can listen to a harmonica recording of the song on my album *Mr. Quilento*. That recording feels comparably edgy and bluesy because it was played in 11th position, while the example below is in 12th position. Without waiving the blues feeling, it could sound a little less heavy this way. Mariano Massolo, one of the most influential harmonica players in South America, recorded a soulful version of the song on his album *Dark Eyes*. Willie Nelson released the song featuring country harmonica legend Mickey Raphael, who interprets the melody in 2nd position. Another notable recording from 1992 showcases Charlie McCoy's expressive harmonica playing.

GEORGIA ON MY MIND

Words by Stuart Gorrell
Music by Hoagy Carmichael
C Harmonica

"Pure Imagination" is a song from the 1971 film *Willy Wonka & the Chocolate Factory* and was sung by Gene Wilder. The song has been covered hundreds of times by a wide variety of artists. One of many mentionable arrangements of the piece is Jacob Collier's a capella recording, which features a wonderful melodica solo.

PURE IMAGINATION

from WILLY WONKA AND THE CHOCOLATE FACTORY

Words and Music by Leslie Bricusse and Anthony Newley

A♭ Harmonica

Henry Mancini composed the Grammy-winning song “Days of Wine and Roses” for the eponymous movie in 1962. Pay close attention to the descending jump from A to D♭ in bar 7. Practice the jump slowly by itself. It is necessary to anticipate the 1-draw half-step bend in advance for good intonation. Even though the melody is tabbed out here in the lower octave of the harmonica, it lays out well in the middle octave, too.

DAYS OF WINE AND ROSES

from DAYS OF WINE AND ROSES

Lyrics by Johnny Mercer
Music by Henry Mancini

C Harmonica

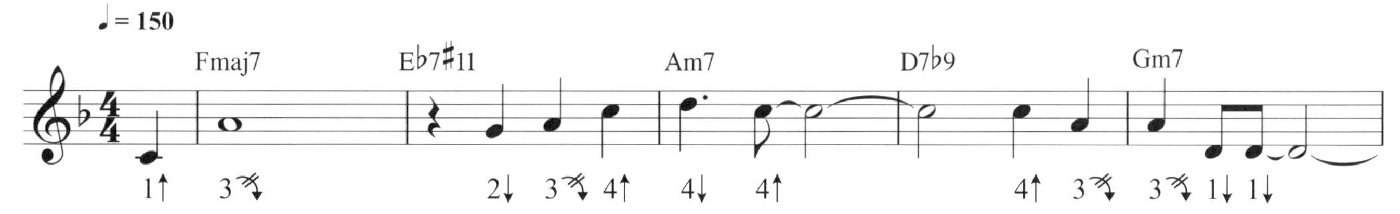

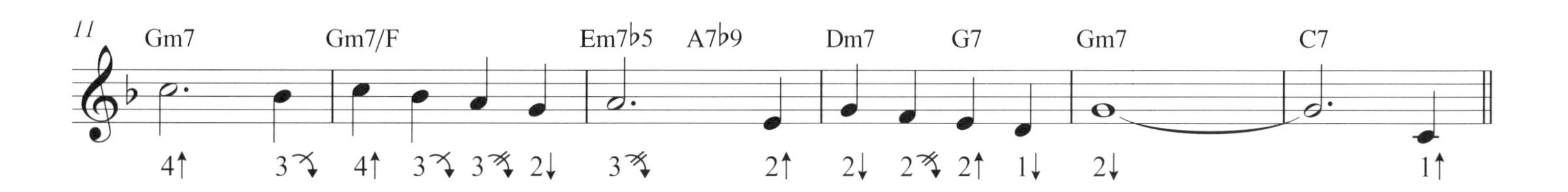

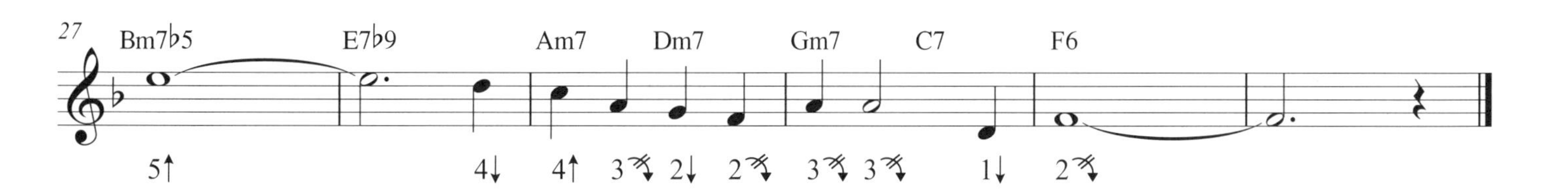

"In Walked Bud" was composed by Thelonious Monk in honor of his friend, fellow pianist Bud Powell. The live album *Misterioso* features a memorable saxophone solo by Johnny Griffin. Playing the song on the harmonica is an incredible exercise for your bends on holes 3 and 4. The chromatically descending melody feels very bluesy at the same time. Playing this melody in 12th position gives a sweet feel to it, while the F minor passages can sound comparably dark. You can find a solo interpretation of the song on YouTube played by half-valved harmonica master PT Gazell. The melody sounds one octave higher than written.

IN WALKED BUD

By Thelonious Monk

E♭ Harmonica

"I Just Called to Say I Love You" by Stevie Wonder was a number-one hit in many countries. You can find a few harmonica recordings online played in 1st position, which is definitely the easiest option. However, the sound of playing the verse one octave lower on an A♭ harmonica gives the song a very intimate feel. The challenge here is to differentiate between the 2-draw whole-step bend and the 2-draw half-step bend.

I JUST CALLED TO SAY I LOVE YOU

from THE WOMAN IN RED

Words and Music by Stevie Wonder

"They Can't Take That Away from Me" is another absolute evergreen from the Great American Songbook. Playing it in the lower octave of the harmonica is quite a challenge and requires you to articulate the tonic note (2-draw whole-step bend) several times in a row using the front part of your throat. The song modulates to 4th-position minor in bar 17 and lays out pretty well on the B♭ harmonica.

THEY CAN'T TAKE THAT AWAY FROM ME

Music and Lyrics by George Gershwin and Ira Gershwin

B♭ Harmonica

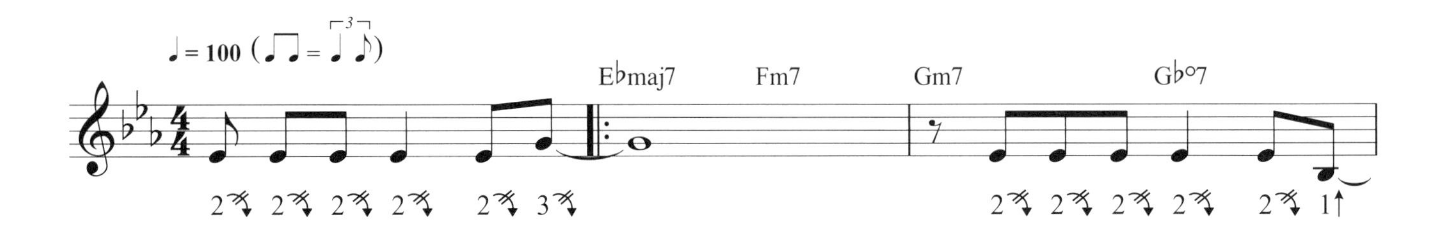

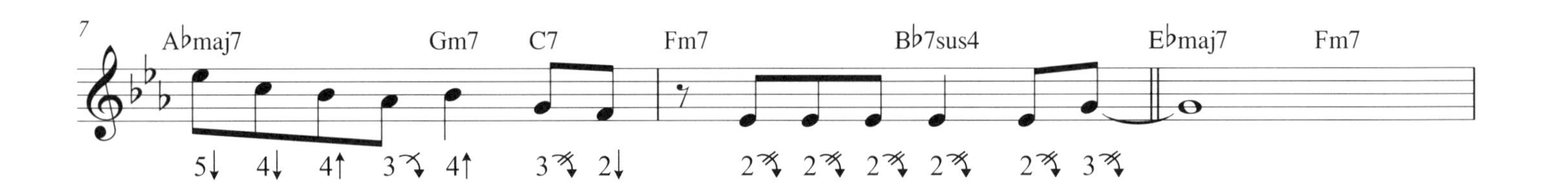

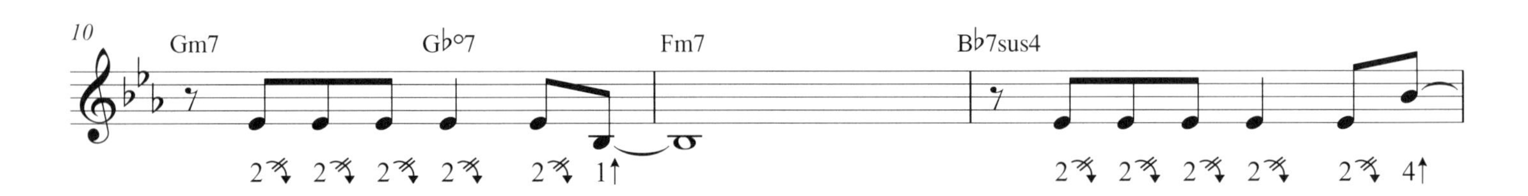

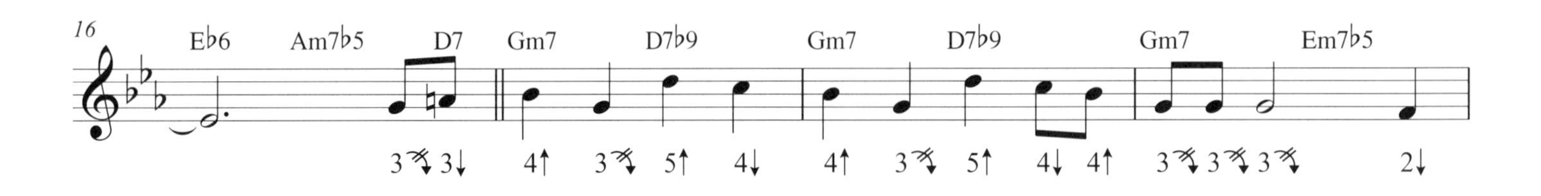

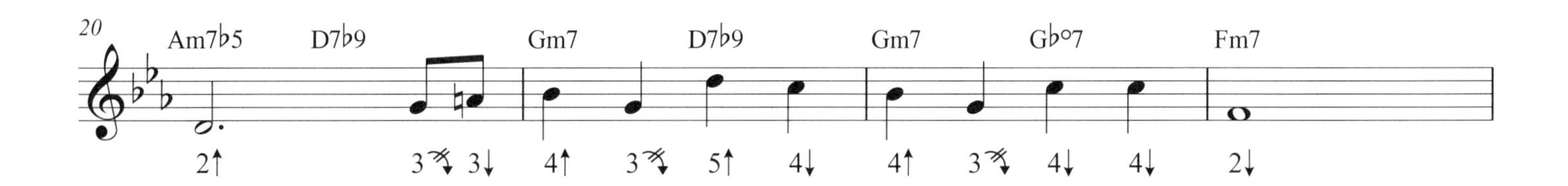
20
Am7♭5
D7♭9
Gm7
D7♭9
Gm7
G♭°7
Fm7

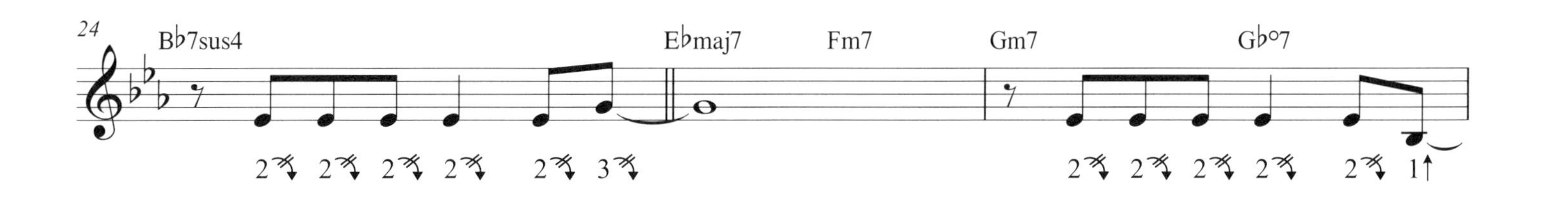
24
B♭7sus4
E♭maj7
Fm7
Gm7
G♭°7

27
Fm7
B♭7sus4
B♭m7
E♭7

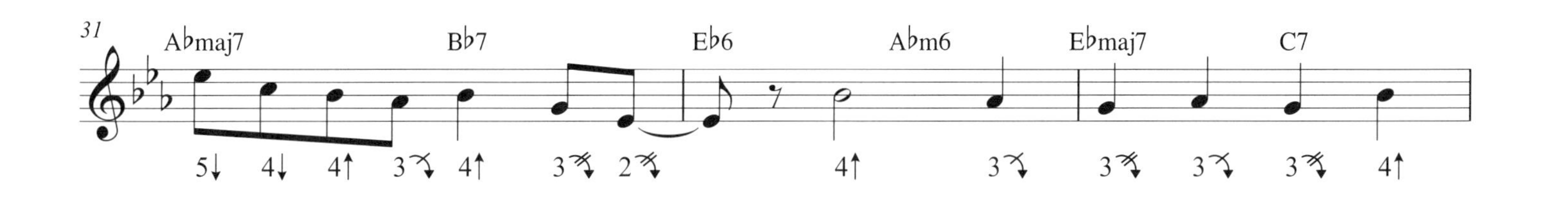
31
A♭maj7
B♭7
E♭6
A♭m6
E♭maj7
C7

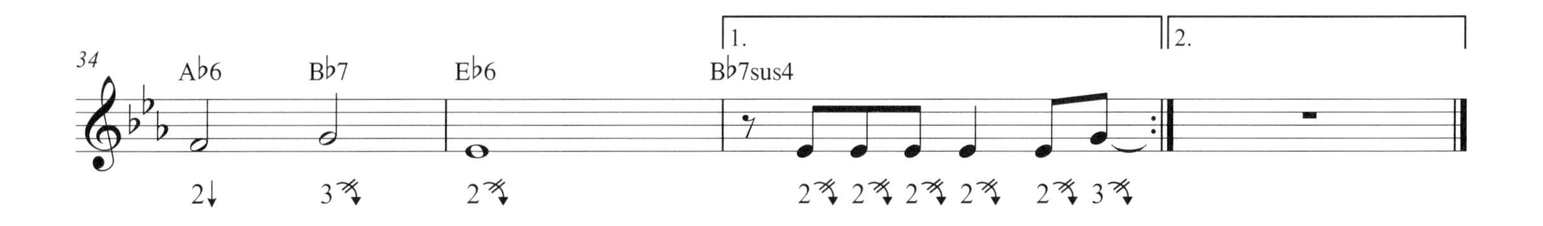
34
A♭6
B♭7
E♭6
1.
B♭7sus4
2.

HARMONICA TALK

Harmonica Care and Maintenance

When you play the harmonica, it slowly builds up moisture. Tap it (holes down) against the palm of your hands several times so that too much saliva does not remain inside the instrument after playing.

To minimize this effect even more, make sure your harmonica is warmed up before you start playing. Just place the instrument between your hands or in your pocket. Then you can start to softly blow and draw some air through the instrument.

However, don't worry about this too much. From my point of view, a hint of dried moisture helps to make the harmonica more airtight. This effect is even greater when playing wooden comb instruments.

It is still important to store your harmonica in a pouch, box, or case to stop other foreign substances like hair and lint from entering the instrument. Also, make sure that your mouth is clean before picking up your harmonica.

Playing your harmonica with clean hands is recommended, since germs are transferred to your harp by your hands and then to your lips. Just wash your hands to avoid getting ill.

You can clean the cover plates of your harmonica with a wet, lint-free cloth, and get rid of too much dried saliva in the opening part of the holes with a very soft toothbrush. More persistent residues can carefully be removed by using a toothpick or similar tools.

Connect with the Harmonica World

The harmonica world is comparably small but very active and generous. Enthusiasm for the tiny little instrument can be felt all over the world. Nowadays it is easier than ever to connect with like-minded people.

Lessons

It is possible to get in touch with top professionals and take lessons. Many of the best teachers also upload free video tutorials. However, sometimes you can learn a lot more in a single one-on-one lesson than practicing on your own. Especially, corrective feedback can be very helpful in the beginning. There are many physical nuances of technique and many different tastes. It is good to taste some different flavors to see what you like best. Harmonica teachers are increasingly using applications like Skype or Zoom to teach online. Getting harmonica lessons from your favorite player has never been this easy.

Concerts

Seek out musical events that maybe even feature a harmonica player. You will most likely meet other enthusiasts. There are many harmonica groups on Facebook that include gig postings. At the same time, you can check listings in your area for blues, jazz, and maybe even classical concerts. Even if there is no harmonica player on stage, harp players do not stay far away from blues concerts.

Jam Sessions

You can also seek out jam sessions that focus on other genres you like. Even if you don't meet other harmonica players, it's extremely valuable to play with other musicians. The atmosphere is usually very collegial and there is no pressure involved at all. Another option would be to join an open mic night to get in front of a crowd.

Online Interaction

The online harmonica community has great potential and really connects the world. Forums and other online discussion groups are a great way to exchange information or just read posts and search for information.

Harp-L is the oldest harmonica discussion group, founded in 1992. Everybody is welcome. Some of the best players contribute to Harp-L, along with customizers and builders of microphones, harmonicas, and amplifiers. All posts are archived and can still be found.

Modern Blues Harmonica is a site hosted by Adam Gussow, who is likely the most important figure of online harmonica teaching. No other harmonica player has reached and influenced as many students with YouTube tutorials as he has. His website is dedicated to all aspects of blues harmonica and also includes a forum.

Discord is a platform that emerged from the gaming world and basically enables you to create your own forum, or server; two big ones are **Harmonicats** and **Harmonica Hangout**. These can be joined by using an invite link. Both groups hold fun challenges and competitions on a regular basis. Discord offers the ability to communicate with members from a wide variety of servers.

Of course, many players also share their music and knowledge on social media. Facebook and Instagram can be great places to connect, learn, and share. If you are specifically looking for video tutorials, you can find some great teachers on YouTube. Noteworthy players include Jason Ricci, Tomlin Leckie, Liam Ward, Adam Gussow, Ronnie Shellist, and Filip Jers.

Lately, quite a few harmonica podcasts and interview series have evolved. **Tomlin's Harmonica Podcast** and **The Harpslinger Podcast by Jamey Garner** offer great conversations. The **Hohner Live x Konstantin Reinfeld** interview series is another bi-weekly livestream that enables you to ask your own questions during the broadcast.

Online Information

At the same time, you can find many informational websites online. Some of them are even for free.

Pat Missin's harmonica website is an incredible resource for learning about the history of the harmonica. At the same time, it provides valuable information about alternate tunings, fine-tuning harmonicas, and the physics of the instrument.

Tinus Koorn's harmonica website is a great place to learn about harmonica customization. It also includes a powerful scale tool that enables you to visualize any possible scale or arpeggio on differently tuned harmonicas. Tinus Koorn studied music at Koninklijk Conservatorium Den Haag.

Additionally, several great teachers host paid teaching sites that offer the advantage of getting direct feedback and more structured learning materials.

The Online Harmonica School with Howard Levy offers personal feedback by video exchange, and the catalog of instruction videos ranges from holding the instrument to playing the most complex jazz standards on the diatonic harmonica.

BluesHarmonica.com is a website by David Barrett, who might be one of the best harmonica educators in the world. You get access to a big catalog of artist interviews, a discussion forum hosted by other professionals, and of course very well-structured multilevel lesson plans.

Harmonica123.com is hosted by Ronnie Shellist, who has a strong online presence. He hosts online webinars regularly.

Harmonica Clubs

Sometimes it's nice to get together in real life to talk shop, play, and learn from one another. Here are some harmonica clubs that offer you these opportunities:

SPAH: The Society for the Preservation and Advancement of the Harmonica is a national-level harmonica club in the United States and Canada. The annual summer convention is a big highlight for every harmonica player.

HarmonicaUK (f.k.a. National Harmonica League): HarmonicaUK is the national-level harmonica club in the United Kingdom. The NHL magazine *Harmonica World* can keep you informed about the harmonica players and the harmonica scene in the UK. HarmonicaUK also hosts an annual harmonica festival.

Harmonica Festivals

Visiting a harmonica festival can be a fascinating experience. Sharing your enthusiasm and excitement with hundreds of others is a rare occasion. The festivals usually include concerts, jam sessions, workshops, and sometimes even competitions. Here are some of the most popular festivals worldwide:

The **World Harmonica Festival** takes place every four years and is organized by the Fédération Internationale de l'Harmonica. The historic town Trossingen is located in Germany's Black Forest where Hohner has produced harmonicas since 1857. In addition to workshops, concerts, factory tours, and jams, there are hotly contested competitions for prizes in several categories.

The **SPAH convention** is held every summer by the Society for the Preservation and Advancement of the Harmonica. The weeklong convention stages in different U.S. cities and features professional performing acts, workshops by top-level teachers, and demonstrations by manufacturers.

The first **Seoul International Harmonica Festival** took place in 2013. Since then the festival attracts more and more harmonica fans to the capital of South Korea. The line-up features world-class harmonica acts performing in prominent concert locations. Additional competitions and workshops offer the chance to really get to know the Asian harmonica scene.

The **Asia Pacific Harmonica Festival** is staged in even-numbered years in an Asian host country and attracts several thousand attendees to competitions, concerts, and workshops.

Harmonica Seminars

Harmonica seminars and workshops solely focus on teaching and learning. While learning from great players in a variety of settings, you can connect with other harmonica players at your level. Here are a few seminars that have been around for a while now:

- **The Harmonica Collective**
- **Hill Country Harmonica**
- **Kerrville Folk Festival**
- **Harmonica Jam Camp**
- **Chromatic Seminar for Diatonic Players**
- **Harmonica Masters Workshops**

You also might be able to find harmonica workshops at an education institute in your area.

Harmonica Albums You Should Hear

Listening to music consciously and discovering new sounds is almost as important as practicing your instrument. There might be a few essential harmonica records that every fan of the instrument should listen to. However, you would most likely receive different recommendations from different people.

In this list, I would just like to suggest some albums that influenced me and my playing, showcasing the wide variety of musical styles in which the harmonica is present.

The harmonica is the perfect blues instrument, and players you should hear include Sonny Terry, Sonny Boy Williamson, Little Walter, George "Harmonica" Smith, Kim Wilson, Jimmy Reed, Sugar Blue, John Németh, Charlie Musselwhite, Mark Hummel, Walter Horton, James Cotton, Junior Wells, Mitch Kashmar, and Paul Oscher.

William Clarke: *Blowing Like Hell, Groove Time*
To me, William Clarke is the undefeated master of playing in 3rd position using the tongue-blocking technique. "Blowin' the Family Jewels" is a song that really stuck in my mind with its strong melodies, lower-octave melodies with great intonation, and big tone using the octaves in the upper part of the instrument.

Rick Estrin: ***Twisted***
Rick Estrin is one of the greatest living entertainers out there. It is great fun to see him perform, and you can always sense a lot of humor in his playing. His vocal phrasing really influences his harmonica playing, and the videos of Rick Estrin playing free-handed are just iconic.

Joe Filisko & Eric Noden: ***I.C. Special***
The harmonica scene can't be imagined without Joe Filisko and Eric Noden. The blues roots duo from Chicago is keeping the traditions alive, while sounding fresh every single time they play. On this album, you can hear beautiful two-part singing, bluesy ballads, high-energy chugging rhythms, and everything in between.

Rod Piazza & the Mighty Flyers Blues Quartet: ***ThrillVille***
Rod Piazza is another big entertainer in the harmonica world. He has been playing with his band the Mighty Flyers, which he formed with his pianist wife Honey Piazza, since 1980. Their boogie sound combines the styles of jump blues, West Coast blues, and Chicago blues.

Jason Ricci and New Blood: ***Done with the Devil***
As soon as you start to look for harmonica videos online, there is a strong probability of discovering Jason Ricci. He is a living harmonica legend and virtuoso who plays fast-paced runs with precision and intensity. Besides presenting the harmonica in a rock context, this album also includes beautiful melodies in 12th position like "Sweet Loving."

Brendan Power & PT Gazell: ***Back to Back***
This might be one of the most interesting albums featuring two harmonica players. Both Brendan Power and PT Gazell are pioneers in many ways. Brendan Power is an inventor and innovator of different harmonica types and tunings, and PT Gazell is a master of the half-valved diatonic harmonica. The sound of the two players blends very nicely and allows for some wonderful two-part melodies.

Howard Levy, Bela Fleck & the Flecktones: ***Rocket Science***
Howard Levy revolutionized the diatonic harmonica world by using the overbend technique to play chromatically on the diatonic harmonica. Over the years, it has taken him on dozens of musical journeys, and this reunion album with the Flecktones really left an everlasting impression. It also features his Grammy-winning composition "Life in Eleven."

Carlos del Junco: ***Big Boy***
Seeing Carlos del Junco perform for the first time really left me in awe. His tone and phrasing—connecting jazz and blues styles on the diatonic harmonica—is unmatched. He is one of the few players that really stands out due to his memorability. His album *Big Boy* features some of the most beautiful ballads, quirky funk songs, and laid-back jazz-blues compositions ever recorded on harmonica. Carlos del Junco is also a great singer with a very recognizable voice.

Mariano Massolo: ***Dark Eyes***
Mariano Massolo is the leading harmonica player in the world of jazz manouche. His album includes some of the most popular jazz compositions brought to life by his incredibly energetic and bluesy playing and his wonderful band. You can find recordings of quite a few songs from this book on his records. He is also the founder and director of the Instituto Internacional de Armónica in Argentina.

Bonus Videos

The Wah-Wah Effect

Blues Demonstrations
Rhythmic Blues Accompaniment 0:00–0:32
Farewell: Melodic Jazz Blues 0:33–1:25

ABOUT THE AUTHOR

Konstantin Reinfeld is one of the world's most sought-after harmonica virtuosos, renowned for his profound musicality and mastery transcending genre boundaries. His accolades include the prestigious Opus Klassik, Germany's classical music Grammy, awarded in 2019, underscoring his exceptional artistry. From Bach to Bartôk to Chick Corea, his repertoire spans classical, jazz, film, and world music.

A pivotal moment in Konstantin's life came at age 13 when he was moved by the harmonica's soulful sound on a televised music show. This deep connection with the harmonica, akin to that of the human voice, inspired him to explore its depths. With boundless zeal, he honed his skills, mastering all semitones on a diatonic harmonica through self-guided exploration and online forums, where he continues to innovate creatively with tenacity.

His prowess garnered attention, leading to invitations to headline major international harmonica festivals, solidifying his status as a preeminent virtuoso. Significantly, he became the youngest ambassador for Hohner, the world's leading harmonica manufacturer. This marked the onset of a lasting partnership.

Konstantin Reinfeld is not only a virtuoso player but also a pioneer in academic study of the instrument, being among the few to pursue formal education in harmonica at the university level. Under the mentorship of harmonica maestro Howard Levy during his master's studies, he elevated his craft to new heights.

Beyond his solo endeavors, Konstantin's musicality extends to the realms of blues and jazz, showcased in his acclaimed debut album *Mr. Quilento*, which he recorded during his high school years. The follow-up album, *Algiedi*, delves into jazz fusion rock, demonstrating his adaptability and creativity.

Looking ahead, Konstantin is poised to contribute significantly to the classical harmonica repertoire with the upcoming release of two brand-new compositions for harmonica, piano, and orchestra. His worldwide collaborations as a producer and mixing engineer further highlight his versatility, cementing his reputation as a trailblazer in the world of harmonica playing.

photo by Steven Haberland